*f*P

Hope Endures

Leaving Mother Teresa, Losing Faith, and Searching for Meaning

Colette Livermore

FREE PRESS

NEW YORK   LONDON   TORONTO   SYDNEY

FREE PRESS
A Division of Simon & Schuster, Inc.
1230 Avenue of the Americas
New York, NY 10020

First Free Press hardcover edition December 2008

FREE PRESS and colophon are trademarks of Simon & Schuster, Inc.

For information about special discounts for bulk purchases,
please contact Simon & Schuster Special Sales at
1-800-456-6798 or business@simonandschuster.com.

Designed by Kyoko Watanabe

Manufactured in the United States of America

1 3 5 7 9 10 8 6 4 2

Library of Congress Cataloging-in-Publication Data

Livermore, Colette.
Hope endures : leaving Mother Teresa, losing faith, and searching for meaning /
Colette Livermore.
p. cm.
Includes bibliographical references
1. Livermore, Colette. 2. Spiritual biography. 3. Missionaries of Charity—Biography.
4. Ex-nuns—Biography. I. Title.
BL73.L58A3 2008
204.092—dc22
[B]
2008027881

ISBN-13: 978-1-4165-9361-4
ISBN-10:   1-4165-9361-6

The author thanks Visva-Bharati for the quotation from Tagore's *Gitanjali X*.

TO MUM

Your life ebbs away,
The links of memory falter,
A shared lifetime ephemeral,
We say our long farewells,
As you drift into the night.

—PAT LIVERMORE (JUNE 12, 1928–JULY 13, 2008),
"LOVE NEVER ENDS."

Sister Tobit in Calcutta, 1980.
(Photographer: unknown French volunteer)

Hope Endures

AUTHOR'S NOTE

The title of the BBC documentary written and presented by Richard Dawkins, *The Root of All Evil?*, asks whether religious belief, which has inspired much that is great in human culture, is the primary source of evil in the world. Such a title is hardly scientific or dispassionate. If we could eliminate all religious belief, would the world be enhanced or diminished?

The fault lines dividing the believer and the nonbeliever, the wealthy and the destitute, crisscross our world. I belong to a generation of transition. Though I was born into belief, I will die a nonbeliever. Many others are losing their faith and confronting nonexistence. Those with faith in God continue to be comforted by the consolations of religion—life after death and ultimate justice—while others retreat behind the bastions of fundamentalism and rigidly adhere to unquestionable dogmas.

My quest for meaning has led me from faith to agnosticism. It has also brought me face to face with the anguish of those born into extreme poverty.

This is an account of my time in Mother Teresa's order, the Society of the Missionaries of Charity (MC), and my subsequent struggle to work through the paradoxes I encountered there. The writing of this book was slow; over many years I put it aside and then returned to it. I have based my account on diary entries and the letters I sent to my mother while I was an MC. Some of the events occurred more than thirty years ago, but I have recounted them as faithfully as I can within the constraints of memory and personal perspective. The passages of dialogue are necessarily reconstructed and are not verbatim accounts. On some occasions I have deliberately not made clear who the sister was who wrote, said, or did a particular thing. I have changed or omitted the names of most of the sisters, and of some of the people I worked with to protect their privacy. My recollections and reconstructions of Mother Teresa's talks and her conversations with me are based on contemporaneous notes. Within the manuscript I have referred to letters I received from Mother Teresa and also to correspondence sent by other sisters. I have paraphrased the content of those letters and quoted only key expressions and phrases. I have also quoted only briefly from Mother's letters to her spiritual guides which were first referred to in articles in *The Review for Religious*, September–October 2001 and then published in full in *Come Be My Light* (Kolodiejchuk, B. Doubleday, 2007).

I am grateful to the many people who have encouraged me to persevere with my writing, especially Kathryn Anderson and the Entrance Writer's Group which she led, for their comments and suggestions. Catherine Hammond from the New South Wales Writers' Center also gave me valuable advice. Many friends have encouraged me to continue despite setbacks.

I feel that my story is relevant to all people of faith today as they will encounter the same questions and dilemmas that I did. It is my hope that this account will help others struggling with the demands of blind faith and obedience. May they not surrender their inner self, but discover a new way to live a truthful life.

COLETTE LIVERMORE, 2008

PROLOGUE

When I was seventeen I watched a TV documentary about Mother Teresa of Calcutta, who was shown to respond to the needs of the poor and dying with a strong, practical love. The documentary was called *Something Beautiful for God* and it changed my life. I became determined to work with Mother Teresa.

Thirty years later, tears of confusion welled up from within me as I stood at the back of St. Peter's Square in Rome amid the throng of flag-waving, hymn-singing pilgrims, who had traveled there to witness the beatification of Mother Teresa. Some distance away, at the front of the crowd, a sea of blue-and-white habits swirled as the sisters of the Missionaries of Charity (MCs) gathered together to celebrate the holiness of their founder. I had been one of them for eleven years and wondered what had gone wrong.

The assembly cheered as a giant, gold-bordered tapestry depicting the "Saint of the Gutters" smiling, wrinkled, and clothed in her iconic sari was unfurled from above the entrance to the Basilica. Swept along by the crowd and the music, I was happy for Mother Teresa. All her life she strove to become a saint, and now, in 2003, six years after her death, she was on the verge of becoming one.

I had given all I had to live Mother Teresa's ideal of "serving Christ in the distressing disguise of the poor," but had left her order in 1984 disillusioned and far short of wholeness. My youthful beliefs and ideals had not withstood the realities of that life.

The square in front of the papal altar was a sea of festive color. A multitude of flags fluttered above the three hundred thousand people gathered to celebrate Mother Teresa's life: the Indian tricolor of saffron, green, and white; the black double-headed eagle of Albania flying in crimson skies; and the austere red and white flag of Poland were the most common. India and Kolkata (known as Calcutta until the Bengali pronunciation was reintroduced in 2001) had been Mother's home for sixty years, Albania the land of her birth, and Poland the country of her pope, who, now frail and inarticulate, struggled to beatify his friend before death also claimed him.

Chants, songs, and prayers rose in many languages—Latin, Bengali, Arabic, Albanian, English, French . . .

"I thirst not for water, I thirst for love."

"It is Jesus who feels in himself the hunger of the poor, their thirst and their tears."

Mother Teresa's teachings have been seared into my spirit, and they cast both light and shadow over my life. In that square I decided to write my story. To have remained silent would have been dishonest.

CHAPTER ONE

Path to Mother Teresa

(Left to right) Rodney, Tony, Colette, and Judy, Mittagong, 1962.
(Photographer: Pat Livermore)

*M*um's first child, Gabrielle, died at birth on Christmas day, 1950. Four years later I was born. Baptized as an infant, I was named Colette as the priest splashed water over my head. From then on, I was imbued with the stories and values of the Catholic tribe. As a child, I believed them all to be trustworthy.

I grew up with my two younger brothers, Tony and Rodney, in Leeton, a rural town in the Murrumbidgee Irrigation Area of New South Wales. The flat arid country around our town had been made fertile by a series of dams, weirs, and irrigation channels built by the government at the beginning of the twentieth century. Our district produced grapes, citrus, and stone fruit as well as rice. The rice mill and Letona cannery, where Mum worked for a while grading fruit, were local landmarks. My father, a tall, lean man, spent most of his time at the Leeton Bowling Club, where he was the manager.

Just before I started school we moved from our rented house at the back of the Hydro Majestic Hotel in the center of Leeton to an orchard on the edge of town. Dad had arranged for Mum to cook and clean for Bill, a bachelor carpenter, and in return we stayed rent-free in a partitioned section of his large brick house.

Our new home was surrounded by a garden of perfumed roses in the front and an orchard of apricots and citrus that filled several acres at the back. Behind the house grapevines with sweet white and purple fruit trailed over a rectangular frame to make a large outside room and fernery. It made a cool, shady place in summer and a tapestry of colorful leaves in autumn. Bill tended his fruit trees and garden on the weekends.

"Do you want to steer the tractor for me?" he called as he pulled on his gumboots near the shed. Once the irrigation pump spluttered to life, water frothed like liquid chocolate along the channels that we had furrowed. I loved to ride in the back of his pickup truck when we went for a swim or to fish for perch or catfish in the eucalyptus-lined Murrumbidgee River. I liked the feeling of the wind in my hair. Sometimes I caught a fish, but mostly I snagged my line on submerged branches.

Across the road from our house was the Common, where the Jackson boys kicked their football high into the air. There we had bonfires each year on Cracker Night, June 12, which coincided with Mum's birthday. The flames roared upward, throwing showers of sparks into the night sky. Roman candles, bungers, tom-thumbs, rockets, and sparklers banged, swirled, crackled, and swooshed heavenward.

In the bush to the side of the cleared area, beautiful birds with iridescent pink plumage shimmered in the sun. Boys from up the road hunted them with rocks and sling-shots or shanghais as we called them. I wondered why they wanted to harm such beautiful creatures. I loved to watch the wedgetail eagles soar overhead and was devastated to see them strung out on fences, killed by the ignorant for sport or by farmers who feared them.

I walked a long way to school in my broad-brimmed, straw school hat, carrying my schoolbag along a narrow path that led through the vineyards, across the irrigation canal, past the rice mill and Bill's workshop into town. St. Joseph's Primary School was on the other side of the railway line, a few streets down from the overpass. Dad had the car, and there were no bus routes going out to our area.

My father was largely absent, and I was a bit apprehensive when he did come home. He returned from the Bowling Club late at night and dumped the club's takings at the end of my sleeping mother's bed. She always woke up to count it and did the bookkeeping so that it was ready for the morning. Dad slept in until about 10, then screeched off to work in a cloud of dust, leaving skid marks on the dirt road. Even on weekends we rarely saw him.

At times I would huddle outside with my brothers when Mum and Dad argued inside the house. Mum wanted him to spend less of his wages at the club. I tried to keep the boys quiet and out of trouble. Mum was a kind, chatty sort of person who took ages to do the shopping because she'd talk to everyone she met down the street. She was fiercely protective of her children, but otherwise, was the one to give in to keep the peace. Dad had fought in Burma and New Guinea during the war and this probably changed him. I never liked ANZAC Day, when the veterans march and remember the wars Australia has fought, because on that day Dad drank more than usual.

When Mum was in labor with her fifth child Dad just dropped her off on the steps outside Leeton Hospital with her bags. He seemed happy enough, jumping up on the table to celebrate, when we heard the news of Judy's birth, but one night a few weeks later I heard him and another man shouting in the front room. The angry visitor accused Dad of having an affair with his wife. Soon after that, Dad left us.

I cried when Mum said that we had to leave Leeton and stay with her parents in Nowra, a town on the banks of Shoalhaven River on the New South Wales South Coast. I didn't understand why we had to go, but Mum said it wasn't right for us to stay at Bill's after Dad had gone. I lay on the top bunk of the sleeper carriage staring at the shadows on the frosted window as the train hurtled through the darkness. I wondered what living with my grandparents was going to be like, but finally I fell asleep, unable to resist the lulling rhythm of the train.

The next morning we pulled into Moss Vale Railway Station, where Mum's brother, John, waited for us. We squeezed into the car with our luggage—two adults and four children for the hour-long trip to Nowra—and drove through the cleared pastureland around Moss Vale. Close to Fitzroy Falls, a beautiful waterfall over 250 feet high, the landscape changed as we entered Morton National Park, where the Yarrunga Creek crashes down the escarpment to the eucalypt valley below. We descended slowly in low gear, down Barrengarry Pass around densely wooded hairpin bends, into the cloud-shrouded Kangaroo Valley, where Friesian cows chewed lazily in the shade of willow-lined creeks. This lush beautiful countryside was very different from the flat, hot plains around Leeton. We passed through the arches of the stately Hampden Bridge, hewn from local sandstone, and then ascended Camberwarra Pass, where Uncle John's car radiator boiled over. We admired the view for a while to let the car cool down, but Mum was on edge.

"I want you to be very good at your grandparents' house. No fighting! No shouting! No tearing around everywhere! Do you understand?"

We all nodded glumly.

John tooted the horn to signal our arrival at 6 Worrigee Street and Gran rushed out onto the veranda and down the stairs. Grandfather Bertie followed at a more sedate pace. There were hugs and kisses all around.

Gran's eyes fixed on Judy, the new addition. "She's beautiful!" she said as she looked at Mum. "Definitely worth all the struggle." She hugged Mum and, after smothering Judy with kisses, carried her off through the front door with Mum at her side. Bertie smiled at the rest of us and ruffled our hair as we followed him into the house, which smelled of a baked dinner and furniture polish.

After my sudden uprooting from Leeton, I found it hard to settle into my new school at St. Michael's in Nowra in the middle of term. Mum hadn't had the time or the money to buy me a new uniform, and

I felt awkward wearing the one from St. Joseph's Leeton. It was September when I joined the class, and they were celebrating the feast of the birthday of Our Lady. Sister had told all the students to bring a bouquet of flowers to place in front of Mary's statue, but since we had only just arrived I hadn't received the message. Sister paraded me in front of the class. "You're the only girl who didn't bring flowers for Our Lady's birthday," she said accusingly, poking me in the chest. "Don't you love your mother? Or do you have such a barren house that there are no flowers in the garden?"

I had no idea that she was talking about Mary as our mother and stood there determined not to cry, wondering what she could mean, and what it had to do with Mum, whom I loved very much. If I were only still in Leeton, I could've brought in bunches of roses from Bill's garden. I wanted to run out of that schoolroom, back home to Bill, the orchard, and the tree-lined Murrumbidgee River.

In contrast to my difficulties at school, I got on well with Bertie and sometimes watched him work in his accountancy office as he ran his finger down columns of four-digit figures, adding them up faster than any machine. Short, with thin gray hair that he combed back with Brylcreem, he wore his glasses halfway down his nose and always seemed to peer over them. He loved gardening, so I often escaped from the confines of the house to help him in the yard, just as I had helped Bill in the orchard in Leeton.

Mum told us that Bertie had been furious when, some years before, his youngest son, Toby, had left a career in economics to become a Franciscan priest. "He's throwing his life away," my grandfather said. "It's not natural, all those men living together."

"He thinks it's what God wants him to do," Gran defended.

"If he wants to cut himself off from us, I'll have nothing more to do with him," Bertie fumed.

The Catholic Church had given my grandfather, a Methodist, grudging permission to marry Gran in the Church provided all their children were raised as Catholics. Mum said her parents were not married at the altar during Mass, as was usual, but had to make do with a short ceremony in the side room, or sacristy, usually used as the priest's dressing room, as if their mixed marriage of Catholic and Protestant were shameful and dangerous.

Bertie had kept his part of the bargain and sent all his children to Catholic schools, but when Toby left to become a priest, it was too much for him. Christianity, the belief that both men professed in different forms, couldn't overcome this rift. Bertie died without ever speaking to Toby again.

While we were growing up, Mum sometimes drove Gran to visit Toby at the fog-shrouded friary, St. Anthony's in Robertson, where he was training to become a Franciscan. A giant of a friar, over six feet tall, opened the door to us and ushered us into the chapel where we waited a long time for Toby to finish his prayers. The clock ticked, the Rosary beads rattled, and Mum glared at us if we dared breathe. Later, as Toby ate the ice cream Gran had brought him, he imitated some of the brothers in charge and made us laugh. He told us ridiculous stories about how he had to ask repeatedly for simple things like a toothbrush and couldn't get a new one till nearly all the bristles were gone.

At the beginning of 1963 Gran and Bertie helped Mum buy a house on a large block about three miles out of Mittagong, the gateway to the frosty Southern Highlands, about an hour and a half from Nowra. A wood-burning stove heated the house, but the green linoleum floors were always cold. At the back was an untidy collection of sheds, a chook yard (chicken coop), and vegetable garden. We had a milking goat that we tethered on a long rope tied to a metal stake so that it wouldn't break through the fences. Once Mum was nearly hit by lightning trying to move the goat to shelter during a thunderstorm.

Mum tried to spruce up the dilapidated house. Tony and I splattered paint on the lower part of the outside walls, while Mum went up onto the corrugated iron roof to paint it red. She had never liked heights and became stuck trying to get back down onto the ladder. As a skinny nine-year-old, I reassured her, "Don't worry, Mum, I'll catch you."

"Just steady the ladder!" she yelled.

My brothers and I played together in the gullies around our house, which had wombat burrows large enough for a small person to crawl into. Mostly the wombats hid from us in their burrows during the day, but we'd sometimes catch a glimpse of the sturdy marsupial's rear end amid a hail of dirt and rocks as it tunneled out a new home. During spring the crimson waratahs' rounded flower-heads swayed above us as we made our way to our favorite swimming hole, which was rimmed by sandstone boulders. Judy was still too young to join us on our bush explorations, so we pushed her in a swing in the backyard or ran behind her tricycle up and down a cement path at the side of the house.

Mum received no money from Dad and found it hard to support us, especially when Judy was still a toddler. She tried running a secretarial and typing service from home, but it wasn't much of a success. Occasionally Bill drove up from Leeton in his red Chrysler pickup truck and I gave him my room. He'd take us to the beach just south of Nowra, and photographed us, just as he had done in Leeton. Since we didn't have a camera or a car, it was like being on holidays when Bill came. During Christmas vacation, Bill invited Tony and me back to his orchard, where he taught us to drive the tractor and furrow the irrigation channels and we helped him pick apricots, even though the canvas bags were nearly as big as we were.

Sometimes I wondered if Bill would become our new father, but the Church said Mum was still married to Dad even though he'd left us. She never remarried, because the Church didn't allow it. Bertie convinced Mum to get a civil divorce in an attempt to force Dad to pay child support, but it didn't work. Dad had disappeared and made no contribution to our upbringing.

On Sundays we walked into town for Mass, Mum struggling up the hills of the Hume Highway, pushing Judy in the pram, while the rest of us slipped in the gravel at the edge of the road.

We were Catholics without the trimmings. The certainties of faith had been passed down through the generations: Live a good life and you will be raised up on the last day and live forever. Our beliefs gave us rituals, the "fish on Friday" identity, and a framework of meaning on which to hang our lives. "What you do is more important than what you say you believe," Mum told us. For some reason our family felt a bit embarrassed to talk about religion, even though Mum said she'd named me after a saint.

When my sister Gabrielle died at birth, Mum was devastated. Grieving and ill with mastitis, she hadn't been allowed to see the tiny body. "Was she malformed?" Mum asked the nurse. "Where have they put my baby?" No one answered her. Mum failed for some years to fall pregnant again and so asked the Poor Clare sisters to pray for her, as she desperately wanted another child, and when I was born four years later Mum named me Colette after the sisters' reformer saint, whom they said had been born in difficult circumstances.

In 1965 Mum became the head teacher at the Donkin Memorial Nursery School in Moss Vale, about five miles from Mittagong. Her doctor had given her a reference; at that time, a person didn't need special qualifications to care for preschoolers. She bought a secondhand, blue Morris Minor so she could get to work, where she cared for about thirty children with the help of an assistant. Judy, who was nearly three years old, was able to go to nursery school with Mum, while Rod, Tony, and I took the bus to and from our school in Mittagong.

Since Mum couldn't leave nursery school until all the children were collected, she was very late one day and I had started to make our tea. "I wasn't really worried, Mum," I told her when she returned. "But I didn't know how I would start the mower if you didn't come back for a while."

"Don't be silly," Mum replied. "Of course I was coming back. I waited for an hour for Mrs. Johnson to pick up Brian and in the end drove him home. Her car had broken down."

About a year later we all moved to a house in Moss Vale, just walking distance from Mum's work and our new primary school, St. Paul's. It was winter, and we spent our first night in the new house with no heat or electricity, wrapped up in gray blankets. We all screamed when a bat swooped out of the darkness as we entered the front bedroom holding candles. The following night we gathered in front of the blazing fireplace in the living room, the power was on, we were warm and secure.

We had a half-acre block with turpentine pines behind the house that were home to a family of magpies. In the morning they sang their warbling song back and forth to each other. In nesting season they swooped on people walking down our street so that everyone had to wave sticks or put buckets on their heads, but they never swooped on us. After a while the adults brought the young magpies down onto the lawn under the clothesline to visit us.

After school my brothers and I caught yabbies (crayfish) with string and bits of meat in a creek at the back of the house and built tree houses in the turpentine pines. Sometimes we rode our bikes as far as Fitzroy Falls, about five miles away. We tended a milking cow, did the mowing and gardening, and went searching for mushrooms and blackberries for Mum in the paddocks across the road.

We children raised several poddy (orphaned) calves, putting our fingers in buckets of milk and allowing them to suck on them. Our parish priest, Father Higgins, gave us a Jersey cow that we learned to milk. Mum used an old red separator she had bought at a garage sale to spin off the milk from the cream. She also made butter.

Bertie died. "Went to heaven," Gran said, though she still cried a lot. I was very sad, but at age eleven I wasn't allowed to go with Mum to his funeral down in Nowra. Then Gran came to live with us in a flat built onto the side of our house. She brought some of her furniture from Nowra, including a big wooden sideboard, which was the hiding place for her store of butterscotch. On her wall hung a painting by Albert Namatjira of ghostly desert gums and distant blue mountains. She taught us to play canasta and baked lemon meringue pies. Later, as she became frailer, Mum looked after her, taking in all her meals, usually with one or more of us kids with her. Mum was hurt when she overheard Gran telling her friends, "I'm alone in here all day. No one ever visits me!" She must have forgotten our frequent visits.

After Gran came to stay with us, my uncle Toby, who was teaching at Padua College in Kedron, came to visit us every Christmas. One year, just before his holidays, he had completed a one-week course in positive parenting and decided to give Mum some tips. "You can take over if you like!" she yelled at him. "You are such an expert!" They were having some disagreement over my mowing the lawn. Mum usually didn't get angry with Toby because he was a priest.

Once I reached high school, I attended the Dominican Convent school on Moss Vale's main street. The tree-lined driveway led to a two-story stone building in front of which was a turning circle around a statue of St. Dominic. My friend Liz was the only other girl in my class who lived in town. The other students were boarders or came by bus from different parts of the district. Because Mum couldn't afford the full fees, she helped catalogue books in the library, typed out some of the sisters' university assignments, and did other secretarial work to decrease the tuition, as she had done during our primary school years. She also continued working at the nursery school and doing the books at Beer's garage.

In 1969, when I was fifteen and in third form—equivalent to a junior in high school in America—astronauts landed on the moon. The sisters opened the concertina partitions dividing the classrooms of the junior secondary school and the whole school assembled to watch the fuzzy black-and-white television images of Neil Armstrong and Buzz Aldrin as they bounced around the moon like kangaroos.

Later that day, in religion class, a black-veiled sister dressed in white robes taught us about the Assumption of Our Lady. It seemed far-fetched to me, Mary just rising up into the sky, with no means of propulsion. I raised my hand. "Sister, if Our Lady was assumed into heaven, where physically did she go?"

Sister St. Matthew eyed me suspiciously. "What do you mean?"

"Well, if Mary rose up into the sky, where did she land? Where did her body go? Did she orbit like the astronauts?" The class gave a suppressed laugh.

Sister was irritated. "Sit down and stop asking such ridiculous questions."

Usually well behaved, I studied hard at school but did get into a bit of strife for arguing with my teachers. I was sent out of French for objecting when Sister taught us that Mauritius was a colony of France just as Australia was a colony of Great Britain. I reminded her that Australia was no longer an English colony and was sent out to stand in the corridor for the rest of the lesson. Fiercely republican, I was also in trouble for stubbornly remaining seated for "God Save the Queen," which was then the Australian National Anthem.

The Church called ours a broken family, and I had the usual insecurities of a fatherless child from a low-income family. I didn't have the clothes or the confidence to compete with some of the boarders, and so felt self-conscious at dances and on outings. Nevertheless, it was a small school and I did well. Along with Liz, my fellow "day-bug," I had lots of great friends among the boarders. They were always looking for ways to evade the strictures and regimentation of convent life. Every day the priest from Chevalier College in Bowral said early Mass for the nuns. While the nuns were occupied, the boarders concealed letters behind the hubcaps of the priest's car for secret delivery to the boys at his school. He drove home unaware he was Cupid's mailman. The boarders also asked me to smuggle in special food for their midnight feasts, because their visits into town were restricted. When they had day leave, they came to our house for meals, or sometimes we went to Bernie's café to eat his famous sundaes with ice cream, almonds, malted milk and caramel sauce. I went horse riding with Bren on her farm in Tumut and visited Denise, a diplomat's daughter, who lived in Canberra. Her mother cooked wonderful spicy food and Chinese roast pork, a change from my mundane "meat and two veg" diet. Our family never ate out except for fish and chips on Fridays. I didn't have much contact with boys, as I went to an all-girls school dominated by boarders and students from out of town, which isolated me from the other teenagers in town.

I loved music and worked at a cocker spaniel kennel to earn pocket money to buy a record player and pay my swimming club fees. I fed the dogs and cleaned their kennels, which were made of old tramcars. In the cold Southern Highland winters I cracked the ice that covered their water bowls so that they could have a morning drink. The owner, Miss Harper, gave me Peggy, a blue cocker spaniel who followed me everywhere and was a great friend, even though she sometimes rolled in cow manure or hid our shoes, causing panic in the morning.

My brothers began high school at Chevalier in Bowral, at the time an all-boys Catholic school, and Judy continued primary school at St. Paul's, Moss Vale. Tony was good at fixing things and could always beat me at chess; Rod scavenged old TVs and speakers from the dump and got them to work. He would be up on the roof moving the aerial in different directions while little Judy yelled up at him from the window to let him know if the TV was receiving a picture or not.

Our young religion teacher, Sister Frederick, encouraged us to discuss the war in Vietnam, the plight of the poor, and other social issues. "Imagine if you were born in another country, where your family struggled just to survive," she said.

"But we can't help where we are born, Sister," I said, feeling guilty to have grown up in the lucky country.

"No, but you can use the opportunity, make the most of the talents you have received, and give something back," she replied. Her compassion touched me and motivated me to think of how I could contribute.

My school friends, Evelyn from Laos and Peggy and Agnes from New Guinea, told us stories of their homelands, where people suffered through poverty and war. Groups of us sat around listening to songs by Leonard Cohen and Bob Dylan and had animated discussions of what we would do after high school. My wall was full of peace posters. I read about a doctor, Tom Dooley, who had worked with injured and orphaned children in Vietnam and died from cancer as a young man. I admired him and wanted to do similar work.

When we studied Hitler and the Holocaust with Sister Frederick we learned about the gas chambers and saw graphic pictures of mass graves. I was most appalled by a story about Nazis making lampshades out of human skin. "Sister, how does God allow people to do such cruel things?" I asked.

"God gave us free will, and some people decide to do evil."

"But how is it we're taught to turn the other cheek? Surely we have to fight evil like that. And what about the kids burnt with napalm in Vietnam, and the famine in Africa. Is God on strike?"

"Evil entered the world with the first sin and with it came violence and disorder. We do what we can. Our faith gives us hope that all will be well in the end; good will prevail. In God's kingdom, everything will be made right; suffering will pass, but love will endure forever."

Although I thought a lot about the suffering that was in the world, I was not very religious. My report card chided, "Colette seems to consider secular subjects more important than Christian Doctrine." This was a fair comment. I enjoyed school and played a lot of sports. I was the center in the school netball team, and we competed with other schools on weekends. Our school had three sports teams, or houses, and I was vice captain of the Sienese team.

When I was seventeen, Mum went into Bowral Hospital for a simple gynecological operation and had an unexpected, severe hemorrhage. Gran and the four of us children were waiting for her to come out of the operating room when the doctors called me alone into a white, sanitized room to tell me that her heart had stopped beating during the operation, and she was still in some danger. Since Mum had named me her next of kin, they told me they didn't know how she'd be when she woke up, because her brain had been without oxygen for some time. I emerged from the room crying.

"Don't worry, she'll be all right," Gran said. But I felt angry and walked away because I thought her reassurance was false.

When we were finally allowed into her room, Mum's face was ashen and her lips dry. Even though she was attached to many machines and lines, she was able to whisper, "Water."

She could speak! We were very relieved.

The next day our little black-and-white, hand-raised calf died from diarrhea. Tony and I dug its grave, all the while hoping that Mum wouldn't die as well. It was holiday time, but I wandered around the school, hoping to see one of the sisters I was close to. I wanted to talk to them about Mum and my fears that there was no God and no afterlife. I thought that Mum might die and be gone forever, leaving us alone. But even though the nuns still lived in the convent during the students' vacations, no one answered the doorbell. My friend Liz was out of town, and all the boarders had gone home. I didn't want to worry the rest of the family with my fears that Mum might die. I felt I had no one to talk to and was very alone. I was not at all sure there was a God.

Gran couldn't drive, but one of our neighbors took us to visit Mum every day. Slowly she became better and began to eat and drink. She told us that during the surgery she had been up in the corner of the operating room looking down on herself and had heard the doctor say, "Turn her up! Turn her up!" The doctor dismissed her experience, saying she must have overheard the nurses talking, but Mum could describe the scene and relate what everyone said. It made me wonder what happens when we die.

Sometimes my family watched TV at night while we ate our dinner. Pictures of starving children in Biafra, Nigeria, confronted me. I didn't need a church to tell me it was wrong for me to be full while they were so empty. I kept wondering why some people were born to a life of poverty and others to plenty. I tried to understand suffering, and wandered around at night looking up at the stars, wondering if there was a God. There needed to be one, I thought, to make sense of the world.

In my bedroom at home glass crystals hanging near my window fractured light into colorful rainbows that danced on the wall. Perhaps Mum's out-of-body experience in the hospital indicated that life had a hidden dimension. I thought that just as the colors in light are made visible by crystals and the sounds all around us are made audible by a transistor radio, so there may be a way to perceive God.

Camping out with friends at a music festival in a cold wooded valley in the Galston Gorge, where a cleared area at the base of the slope acted as a natural amphitheater, my body resonated with the music, which told of a life-song ready to be sung.

At that time I was not in the least interested in becoming a nun, although a friend of mine, Jenny, intended to join the Dominicans. I admired many of the nuns at school, but to me they were part of the establishment.

"Don't you think the Church has lost the fire of the Gospels?" I asked Jenny. "What happened to 'Sell what you have and give the money to the poor and follow me' (Luke 18:22). All the orders have a lot of land and money. They're richer than the people who support them."

"You have to be practical, Colette. The sisters couldn't teach you from the side of the road!"

Then, toward the end of my last year of high school, as I prepared to take my final exams, I saw the film that told the story of Mother Teresa, *Something Beautiful for God,* produced by Malcolm Muggeridge, an agnostic British journalist. Muggeridge had first met Mother Teresa when he interviewed her for British television, which had been difficult to do because of her brief replies and her refusal to answer personal questions.

Yet the interview precipitated an unexpected public response, and in 1969 Muggeridge took up Mother Teresa's invitation to see and film her work in Calcutta. This resulted in his conversion to Christianity and the production of the film, which prompted me to embark on a religious vocation.

As the film relates, in 1948, when the states of Pakistan and Bangladesh were partitioned off from India, West Bengal was in turmoil. Mother Teresa walked out the gates of the leafy establishment school of St. Mary's in Calcutta, where she taught geography, onto the teeming streets to respond to the destitute who were dying unattended on the sidewalks. She felt she had received a "call within a call" to attend to Christ in his "distressing disguise of the poor."

The idea of compassionate, practical service to the poor captivated me. From the time I saw that film, the whole direction of my life changed. I had been striving since junior high school to be accepted into medicine at a Sydney university. But on the eve of my looming exams, I decided that I didn't need to waste time becoming a doctor. It seemed very simple: people needed food more than complex medical care. Mother Teresa lived with the poor and served them, so I decided to join her. Having made that decision, I took my exams anyway. I was more relaxed about them as it didn't matter what marks I achieved, and I did quite well.

Although I had attended a convent school, I knew little about the inner workings and constraints of religious life. I wanted to join Mother Teresa's group because I thought they were trying to redress injustice. I was on the verge of becoming an accidental nun.

After watching the documentary I saw an article in the *Catholic Weekly* about a branch of Mother Teresa's order, the Missionaries of Charity, which was working in Bourke, a remote town in outback New South Wales. Surprised that they had a convent in a rich country like Australia, I wrote to Sister Felicity, a Bengali who was featured in the newspaper article. She replied full of encouragement and put me in contact with Sister Regina, the novice mistress in Melbourne. We wrote letters back and forth and Sister Regina asked me to meet her in Mona Vale, where she was staying overnight with relatives on her way from Bourke to Melbourne.

Short, bespectacled, and energetic, Sister Regina greeted Mum and me warmly and told stories of her own journey from Malta to Calcutta to join the order in the early days of the Society, when there were only about a hundred sisters. "There are nearly a thousand sisters in the order, now," she said. "We have many houses in India, but also some overseas in countries such as Venezuela, Jordan, England, and Italy." Her enthusiasm was contagious.

When she first joined, Regina had worked in the Home for the Dying in Calcutta, nursing people who were brought in off the streets. She explained how the MCs were trained. "Training is in three stages. Postulancy lasts for six months. It serves as a sort of introduction to the order. During that time, you'll wear ordinary clothes and work with one of the sisters. In Melbourne we visit the elderly in their homes and boardinghouses, work with immigrant families from the high-rise flats, and care for the alcoholics and street people. In India and in other centers where English is not the first language, we have a more basic six months of training called aspirancy. It's a time for girls to come and see what living in the Society is like and to learn English, our common language. We don't have that stage of training in Australia.

"Then, following postulancy, there's the first-year novitiate, a time of intense training. At that time, your hair will be cut off." At this I started to laugh and looked nervously at Mum. I didn't fancy myself bald, but Sister Regina didn't seem to notice. "You'll be dressed in a white habit and sari," she continued. "In the first year, the novices don't do much outside work. It's a time of religious study and reflection. In the second year, half the day is dedicated to work and the other half to study. After that, you'll make your first vows for a year and renew them yearly for five years, according to Church law. But in our own minds, the commitment is for life. Five years after first vows there is a further training year called tertianship, and then you'll make your final vows, probably in Calcutta."

"If she lasts that long!" Mum chimed in.

"I think she's got what it takes to be faithful to God's call. You know what it says in the Gospel: 'Once the hand is laid on the plough, no one who looks back is fit for the kingdom of God' (Luke 9:62). It doesn't matter what stage you're at. If He calls you, you're His for life."

Sister Regina set the date for me to go to Melbourne to join the order: January 6, 1973.

My mother was bewildered by my decision and, as we drove home from the meeting, she tried to reason with me: "You'll be more useful if you're trained as a doctor or nurse first, and then if you leave you'll have something to fall back on." I refused to listen. I had to join as soon as possible. This was what I wanted to do.

My friends were dumbfounded that I planned to throw away the chance to study medicine. We had all planned to go together to university in Sydney if we were lucky enough to get scholarships.

My teachers and the rest of my family thought my decision was foolish. They felt that Mother Teresa's sisters were poorly educated and did menial work. "You're throwing your life away," my uncle John remonstrated.

"You don't say that about Toby," I replied.

"That's different. He's a priest in a proper order. You'll end up everyone's dog's body."

All the opposition made me even more determined.

As usual at Christmastime Uncle Toby came to stay with us and brought some of his students with him for the holidays, one of whom, Paul, who was my age, had become a friend of the family. We went walking in the bush together and I told him I wanted to join Mother Teresa. He didn't say much, nor did he tell me that he intended to join the Franciscans, which he did a few months later. Maybe he hadn't decided then.

Sister Regina had given me a list of things I needed to join the order: three collared shirts, white or blue, with short sleeves; two blue cardigans; one pair of sandals; one pair of winter shoes; three skirts; three sets of underwear and socks. In addition, I needed two books: the Bible and *The Imitation of Christ* by Thomas à Kempis, a fourteenth-century monk. This latter volume had catchy chapter titles such as "Having a Humble Opinion of Oneself" and "Obedience and Subjection." Toby said it represented an old-fashioned form of spirituality. "Why don't you wait a while, Colette? Go to university. Experience life a bit, and then decide." I was disappointed. "I thought at least you'd understand, Toby. I'm sure this is what God is calling me to do. My heart's not in medicine anymore."

CHAPTER TWO

The Novitiate

Missionaries of Charity Convent, George Street, Fitzroy, Victoria, 1983.
(Photographer: Pat Livermore)

Never turn your face from the poor and God will
never turn his from you (Tobit 4:7).

I hugged Mum, Judy, Tony, and Rod on the platform at Moss Vale
Station. The whistle sounded and the guard lowered his flag as
I scrambled onto the Spirit of Progress with my small bag. I could see
Mum crying as I waved through the window. She kept pace with the
train for a short distance and then was out of sight. Young and naïve, I

had had little experience of life, cocooned as I was by the constraints of Catholicism and the values of a conservative country town.

The train was late into the Spencer Street Station in Melbourne. I hadn't slept much because an air force officer sitting next to me kept falling onto me as he slept. Two sisters were there to meet me, unmistakable in their white saris with blue borders. Sister Regina recognized me at once. "Welcome, Colette. This is Sister Augustine, our superior in Melbourne."

We drove to the single-story white house that served as the training center, or novitiate, for the Missionaries of Charity in Australia. Nestled among the terraces of George Street, Fitzroy, a working-class suburb of inner Melbourne, it was next door to the Federal Trolley and Truck Company. Across the road another factory made cardboard and paper products. I followed Sister Regina through the gate into the front yard which had a small garden bordered by a hedge. Unlike the convents of other orders, which often had impressive stonework, landscaped gardens, and high walls, this house was distinguished only by a statue of Our Lady set on a stand in the corner of the veranda.

The convent had a hall down its center, with rooms on either side. As we entered the front door, a chapel was on the left, with mats on the floor and no chairs. A crucifix, with the words I THIRST written above it, hung on the wall behind the altar. The sisters genuflected in the doorway as they passed the chapel, so I did the same. Nervously, I glanced around at my new surroundings to try to take it all in. On the other side of the hallway was the parlor, a room for receiving guests. A curtain marked off the quarters for eleven sisters: three dormitory-like bedrooms with metal beds and small cupboards squeezed into them. Taut blue bedspreads covered thin mattresses. There were no other furnishings or decorations of any kind.

Multistory housing commission tenements rose above the house at the back, throwing a long shadow over the convent. The backyard had been cemented over, but enough sunshine still came through to allow a fruiting grapevine to flourish. It grew over a wire frame, shading half the yard, and reminded me of the cool vine room we had enjoyed at Bill's place in Leeton.

· · ·

The laundry contained a large copper tub set in bricks with a fireplace under it. Sister Regina explained that the fire was lit every morning to provide hot water for our showers. We had a copper tub at home but mainly used it for washing clothes. About once a month the sisters also used it to boil their habits and saris and then rinse them in bluing to stop them from going gray. They didn't have a washing machine, not even an old wringer like the one we had at home. One of the rooms, which Sister Regina called a bathing room, was a cubicle with a cement floor and a drainage hole in the center. There was no showerhead or other plumbing in the strange room. Sister Regina explained that, to bathe, we put some hot water from the copper tub into our own metal bucket, mixed it with cold water from the tap, and threw the water over ourselves with a powdered milk tin. There was a conventional shower in one of the bathrooms, but we were not to use it. I supposed we did this to conserve water or because that's how it was done in India, but I already knew not to ask why.

Along the back wall of the house was a line of buckets, each with a number topped with a cross painted in black. Sister said that we used them for everything: washing, bathing, and housework. My bucket was sitting there waiting for me, the number 4 painted on it, complete with a matching soap tin also marked with a 4.

At the back of the house was the novices' refectory and study room, a long, oblong room with large tables. There was no fridge, TV, radio, or electrical appliances in the spartan house. Everything was neat and regimented, unlike my untidy room at home. Pious pictures of the Blessed Virgin Mary and the Sacred Heart, an effeminate Jesus with his externalized heart encircled by thorns, decorated the otherwise bare walls.

As I waited for my three companions I had a breakfast of funny-looking round, flat pancakes called *chapattis*. Betty, a fun-filled, smart-looking girl about my age, was the first to arrive, with her parents. I suddenly felt a bit self-conscious because I was sporting a black eye and a graze on my face, having fallen off a hand-throttled trail bike while trying it out with my cousins the weekend before I joined.

"Hi," I said to Betty.

She smiled back. "Where are you from?"

"Moss Vale in the Southern Highlands of New South Wales. What about you?"

"I've lived in Melbourne all my life."

Betty's clothes were well fitted and fashionable and only vaguely complied with Sister Regina's specifications for our wardrobe. I wore a daggy (unfashionable) gray, below-the-knee skirt and a blue shirt. I wished then that I had allowed myself a bit more latitude in the interpretation of the dress code.

"Put your bags up here on the table," Sister Regina instructed. I felt embarrassed as she inspected our belongings.

"Betty, only three sets of clothing are necessary. You can return these to your mother when she visits again." Betty rolled her eyes.

"Colette, you don't need this," Sister Regina said as she discarded my toiletry bag. "Soap, a comb, toothbrush, and paste are all that is necessary."

Eileen and Sophia, our other two companions, arrived then and gave us temporary respite from Sister's inspection. They were older and had been working for some time. Eileen was from Brisbane; Sophia, like Betty, was from Melbourne.

Sister Regina addressed us all. "It will be hard at first, but starting from today I want you to keep the silence."

Betty and I exchanged glances. We were not sure what that meant until later, when I was putting my things away neatly on my assigned shelf. Betty was lying on the bed munching an apple as she chatted to me. Sister Regina came in unexpectedly. "Sisters, this is not our way!"

Betty jumped up. We were the sisters she was addressing.

"Silence means not talking at all between meals. We don't come into the dormitory except at rest time and only eat at meal times. Is that clear?"

"Yes, Sister," we replied, chastened.

We also had to get used to the bell. One bell sounded for meals and for the evening recreation time, and five for prayer and Mass. Then there were the more complicated ring patterns for the prayers of Angelus at midday and 6 p.m. and the De Profundus, the prayer for the dead, at 7 p.m. The bell had to be obeyed immediately; even if we were in the middle of something, we must stop straight away. Sister told us it was like the call of God.

Later that first morning, Sister Regina introduced us to Sister Christine, who was to supervise and care for us during our postulancy. She had just returned from working at the MCs' shelter for homeless men at 101 Gore Street. A quiet woman from Bihar in northern India, Sister Christine seemed apprehensive about being responsible for such unruly charges.

Our community in George Street was made up of five novices, Sister Regina, the four of us postulants, and Sister Christine. Although we lived in the same house, we postulants had a different dining room and dormitory from the novices. The fully fledged members of the order, referred to as the professed, lived in another house farther down George Street. They had made their first or final vows and dressed in a sari with a blue par (border), unlike the novices, who wore plain white. The professed staffed the men's shelter at 101 Gore Street, visited the disadvantaged, and taught catechism to the Catholic students in the state schools during the period set aside for religious instruction. Besides this, the sisters fitted in about three hours of prayer a day and managed their own cleaning and cooking. They had Thursday off to allow for extra periods of prayer, rest, and domestic duties.

During a brief ceremony on the first evening, Sister Regina gave us each a small cross, which she herself pinned to our shirts. We sang hymns expressing our surrender to God, and Sister Annette, one of the novices, read a story from Luke's Gospel of the rich young man who refused to give up all he owned to follow Christ. Sister Regina gave us an instruction about this story, saying that, unlike the rich aristocrat, we had been prepared to give up all we were and all we had to follow Jesus. She reinforced Christ's promise that "there is no one who has left house, wife, brothers, parents or children for the sake of the kingdom of God who will not receive many times as much in this present age and in the world to come, eternal life" (Luke 18:29–30).

After the prayers, we had a meal together with the whole community.

After Sister Regina said, "Praise be Jesus Christ," the phrase that allowed us to speak, the five novices in their white saris clapped and called out, "Welcome." Later, during recreation, Sister Jasmin performed a traditional dance from the Kerala region of southern India that symbolized the offering of oneself to God. She moved gracefully and was accompanied by the singing of the other novices and the tinkling of bells strapped to her feet.

The community members of the Missionaries of Charity came from many countries and backgrounds. Even among the Indian sisters there were different languages, different writing scripts, and different cooking and dancing traditions. Sisters Patience and Karina were from Bihar, a state in northern India; Sisters Jocelyn and Jasmin were from Kerala, in the south. Only Sister Annette was Australian, from the Croatian community in Blacktown. All the other novices were from India and had been sent to Australia to form a nucleus for the training house. The novices were at different stages of training. Sister Patience and Sister Jasmin were senior second-years, due to make their first vows in May 1973; Sisters Karina, Annette, and Jocelyn had just started their second year and were to be professed in May 1974.

Our postulant community room was near the kitchen, but we usually ate and had recreation separately, except on Thursdays and Sundays, when we had meals and recreation together with the novices and Sister Regina. We learned to keep silence before lunch, dinner and recreation until after permission to speak was given.

Initially, Sister Christine was guarded and shy with us postulants, as we were rowdier and more opinionated than the Indian sisters and our accents were hard for her to understand. We adopted a singsong intonation and Indian expressions to make ourselves more clearly understood. "When I first joined it was very hard," Sister Christine explained. "I had to speak English in the community and Bengali when I went out to work around Calcutta. I didn't know either language."

"What language did you speak, Sister?" Betty asked.

"Hindi is my language. I found it hard to understand anyone in Calcutta. It was like being in kindergarten again. Even our writing is different."

"But weren't there other sisters from your state you could talk with?"

"Yes, but Mother Teresa didn't allow it. She wanted us all to speak English, not to split up into language groups."

"It must have been a struggle," Betty sympathized. We postulants were finding it difficult enough and we didn't have all the language problems.

"Yes, the life was hard and I felt very homesick, but I kept going. Once I had left home, there was no turning back."

As the order expanded, Indian sisters had had to adjust to serving in houses all over the world. Sister Christine had been very ill on several occasions while serving as an MC, and had nearly died of cholera. Her life had been very different from ours in Australia.

We slowly became accustomed to the rhythms of MC life. Back home the kookaburras in the turpentine pines waited courteously until the predawn to laugh me awake, but here the bell clanged at 4:40 a.m.

"Let us bless the Lord!" the caller intoned. We jumped out of bed and got immediately onto our knees.

"Thanks be to God" was the reply, even for those of us who were not morning people. We dressed in silence, under the cover of a sheet next to our beds, in the darkness of the dormitory.

Six months later, when we became novices, we wore wire chains with inward-pointing spikes on the skin around our waist and arm during the hour of Morning Prayer. Even these failed to keep me awake during meditation. I couldn't pray the way Sister Regina had taught us: "Read the passage, imagine you are there in the Gospel scene, and then listen to what Jesus is saying to you in your daily life." I don't consider myself imaginative, and this way of praying seemed artificial. I was unable to keep my mind on it, nor could I get into a comfortable position on the floor, and my stomach grumbled in the silence, impatient for breakfast. *If only I could have a cup of tea first,* I thought. *That would wake me up.*

The whole community walked to Mass saying the Rosary, which consists of five sets of ten Hail Marys, said as we contemplated the Joyful,

Sorrowful, and Glorious mysteries of Christ's birth, death, and resurrection. The bluestone parish church of All Saints Fitzroy was two decades of the Rosary away. When Mass was finished, we recited aloud prayers asking that we become worthy to serve the poor who lived and died in poverty and hunger. We also said the Peace Prayer of St. Francis: "May I not so much seek to be consoled as to console; to be understood, as to understand, to be loved as to love; for it is in giving that we receive, it is in pardoning that we are pardoned, and it is in dying that we are born to eternal life."

For breakfast we ate four *chapattis* in silence, while one of us read aloud from a spiritual book or Mother Teresa's letters. The rules did not allow us to decide for ourselves how much to eat.

I soon learned to wash my clothes in my metal bucket and take a shower using the same bucket and the milk tin. We did the housework on our knees and in a hurry, using our buckets and instead of a mop we used a rag.

The different household duties were rotated each month. Each sister cleaned her area in addition to doing the duties associated with that part of the house. For example, the kitchen mistress did all the cooking; the person in charge of the chapel prepared the vestments and altar for Mass and for the hour-long evening prayer before the Blessed Sacrament called Adoration. Other community duties also rotated each week. A roster made it clear who should ring the bell, read at meals, answer the door and phone, serve at table, and lead the prayer. The novices performed most of these tasks, but we postulants had our own reader and server.

Sister Christine was constantly putting her finger to her lips to remind us of "the silence"; however, once we knew the routine we had little need to speak. Life was predictable. The timetable governed our lives. The bell for lunch was at 1 p.m., and I had to be there; it was the will of God.

Four days each week I went out to work at 8:30 a.m. with Sister John, a professed sister from southern India. We visited the elderly living in rented rooms around the city. The other postulants visited other areas or worked in the shelter at 101. No MC ever went anywhere alone, and we were expected to recite the Rosary aloud, with our companion, as we walked together. Because I preferred to be quiet and didn't like being stared at, I felt awkward as we prayed aloud on crowded buses or at the traffic lights. Sister John sometimes relented and said we could walk in silence, but only if we had said all fifteen decades of the Rosary.

We visited privately owned boardinghouses with tiny, fetid rooms whose occupants slept on urine-soaked mattresses that were rotten and collapsing in the middle. Sister John and I visited Vince, a gaunt man with a beard of gray stubble, who lived in such a room overlooking the tramline. We knew him because he had sometimes eaten at the shelter in Gore Street before he found his own room. Vince seldom shaved and his clothes were stiffened from dirt. The air in his room was heavy with the smell of stale urine and roll-your-own cigarettes. Sister showed me where to empty his night bucket into the common downstairs toilet, and then we began cleaning his room. We had to scrub down through the encrusted dirt to reveal the flower pattern and green color of the underlying linoleum. Work like this—cleaning and rendering personal service—was called "the humble work of the Society" and was part of Mother Teresa's ideal, but also why my family worried I would become a menial laborer. As the weeks went by Vince became gruffly fond of us and waited for our visits. Later on he'd sometimes change his clothes so we could take them to the Laundromat, though he seldom seemed to bathe.

"Hello, Vince! How ya going?" I'd ask.

"Not bad, Sister. Not bad. Have you got a light?"

I lit his cigarette, taking the first draw to get it going. He had a lighter, but his hands shook and he couldn't raise a spark. "Here you go."

"Ta."

"Any luck on the horses this week?" Sister John asked.

"Nah. Maybe next week."

We got to know many of the residents in those rooms and helped them out in various ways. Some were too shaky to shave, some needed shopping done or their room cleaned. We also visited and got to know the many immigrant families from the high-rise tenements behind us who attended Mass at our parish of All Saints. The bonds of family life unraveled for some people who were trapped in these apartments in a new country, unable to speak the language. There were several suicides. The day before one of our visits, a woman had jumped from the sixteenth floor. People were agitated and had gathered outside in groups.

"I saw the lady pull herself up onto the other side of the railing. Then she just fell backwards," a teenage girl blurted out to us.

"There was a terrible thud," an older man said. "Then the sirens started: Police, ambulance. It was a while before the blood was finally washed away."

I didn't understand then how it was that someone could lose hope and want to die, but later realized that a person may love and not receive love, may give and not receive anything in return, may do good and be repaid with evil.

Once a week the trainee sisters took over at the shelter at 101 Gore Street so that the professed could have a day off. Every day the sisters served free meals for a hundred or so unemployed men and also provided beds for about thirty of them. Most of the regulars were heavy drinkers, whose use of the "white lady" (methylated spirits) sometimes bored holes in their stomachs. Some had psychiatric problems. The majority were old or sick. It was upsetting to see them sprawled out in the alleys and bluestone gutters around Fitzroy when they went on a bender; they weren't permitted into 101 for a meal if they were drunk. We cooked, cleaned, made beds, and talked to the regulars who had made the shelter their home. One man, Jimmy, had a wooden leg and was always in the kitchen peeling veggies and doing the dishes, except during his lapses. Other residents helped with carpentry and painting. Sometimes, however, they swore and got drunk. One man, angry because he had been locked out, punched me as I tried to get through the gate on my way to work, and I fell to the pavement.

I found it hard to adjust to city life, with its cement and confined spaces. I sometimes escaped, in my mind, to the rain forest trails around Fitzroy Falls and the vistas of Manning Lookout. I loved the bush, the cool silence interrupted only by the cracking call of the whip bird or the magpies' warble. I loved the beautiful clear streams lined with ferns and strewn with boulders. I loved the crashing waterfalls and the thrill of sighting a lyre bird or wallaby as it scurried through the undergrowth. I felt excited and uplifted when surrounded by such beauty. But I needed to get used to tarred roads, graffiti, and concrete.

After the morning's work we were scheduled to return to the convent by 12:30. Sister John and I were late a couple of times, so Sister Regina allowed me to wear a watch to improve our punctuality. We had midday prayers and examination of conscience, during which we reviewed the day so far to see how our thoughts, words, actions, and motives measured up to our morning resolutions. We wrote down any failures in our *examen* book for later confession.

In Catholic schools the nuns encouraged students to go to confession once or twice a year, but in the convent I was expected to think up enough sins for weekly confession, even though there seemed to be little opportunity for wayward activity. At first I didn't know what to say to the priest, but Sister Regina taught us to keep our thoughts, words, actions, and motives under constant scrutiny. She taught us that the Pharisees, who thought they were good because they performed outwardly virtuous deeds, were actually worse than anyone else because they were hypocrites: they did good things just to be admired. Up to this point in my life I had interacted with people in a carefree way, but now I started to question whether I was conceited, doing good acts just to impress people. My weekly sins included doing kind actions to impress others, being angry and upset following public correction, and being unfaithful to God's call by thinking about leaving the order and joining my friends at university.

After prayer we filed silently into the refectory, said the Grace before Meals, picked up our tin plates, took our place on the benches, and listened to a short religious reading. The server placed the midday meal, usually rice and curry, at the top of the table and then each sister served herself. The server then came to the shoulder of each sister and poured water into her cup. Once Sister Christine said "Praise be Jesus Christ" there was a lot of laughter and chattering while we had our meal and caught up on the morning's exploits.

"There was a man bleeding on the footpath outside the Champion's Pub," I recounted.

"What happened to him?" asked Betty.

"I don't know—maybe he was bashed [mugged]. He had large jelly-like lumps of blood coming from his ear and the back of his head, and he was unconscious. He was well dressed, not someone from the street. No one was attending to him, so Sister John and I went over to him and tried to stop the bleeding from the back of his head with a handkerchief. I asked the pub manager to call an ambulance, but I don't think he did because we waited for about twenty minutes and they didn't come. It was frustrating because the hospital and ambulance depot were only a few streets away."

"Meanwhile, he's bleeding, so what did you do?" asked Sister Christine.

"Well, it was on the corner just near the traffic lights and so many cars stopped there. We tried two taxis but both refused to take us. We were getting worried as he was bleeding a lot and his eyes rolled back. We knocked on the windows of some of the cars and asked them to take us just a few blocks to the hospital, but no one would."

"It's terrible that a man could just lie there bleeding," exclaimed Sophie.

"Yes. Well, finally, one of the Italian men we know from the back flats drove past with his daughter. At first he also refused to help, but eventually he agreed to take the man to Casualty. The orderlies helped us get him out of the backseat and onto a stretcher. We didn't know his name. The doctor said he had a fractured skull. We'll visit tomorrow and see if he's awake."

"Maybe you should have split up, Colette. One of you stay with the man, and the other go to ring for an ambulance yourself."

"Yes, maybe, Sister, but Sister John thought we should remain together. We kept thinking any moment the ambulance would come."

After half an hour for lunch we said Grace after Meals and returned to silence. We were to stay recollected and not let our minds wander to family, friends, or alternative ways of life. We washed our own plate and cutlery and took one of the serving dishes to clean. Instead of detergent we used ash from the fire under the copper tub to rub the plates clean.

After lunch we had half an hour's rest, during which we had to lie down and couldn't read or do anything else. After a while I got used to it and could take a short nap.

In the afternoon in the postulants' refectory, Sister Regina taught us two classes on scripture and the MC way of life. She was full of fun but also blunt and strict, with high standards and ideals, and could administer a devastating dressing-down about vanity, laziness, or disobedience.

From Sister Regina we learned that Mother Teresa had been a Loreto sister for the first twenty years of her life. First envisioned in 1609, the Loreto Institute was to be a new type of religious life for women inspired by Saint Ignatius. Mary Ward, an Englishwoman, attempted to create an order in which her sisters would be educators, free of the cloister and able to engage with the world. However, the ecclesiastical climate of the seventeenth century thwarted her vision, but her ideal was resurrected in 1821 in Dublin by an Irishwoman, Frances Ball, who was inspired by Ward's writings to found the Loretos as educators of women. Frances took the name Mother Teresa, and the archbishop of Dublin gave her Rathfarnham House as a novitiate, where 107 years later Mother Teresa of Calcutta trained as a novice.

In her late thirties Mother Teresa became increasingly distressed by the poverty surrounding the walled, middle-class high school where she taught in Calcutta. While on her way to Darjeeling for a retreat in September 1946, she felt strongly that God was calling her to live and work with the poorest of the poor on the streets of Calcutta. In administering to the destitute, she believed, she was serving Christ disguised as the poor, the hungry, the naked, and the homeless. As Christ had said: "I was hungry and you gave me food, I was thirsty and you gave me drink, I was a stranger and you made me welcome, lacking clothes and you clothed me, sick and you visited me, in prison and you came to see me. . . . In truth I tell you in so far as you did this to one of the least of these brothers of mine, you did it to me" Although Mother's main source of inspiration was from the Gospels, her great Indian contemporaries in the Hindu tradition, Tagore and Gandhi, shared a similar compassion for the poor and taught that God manifested Himself in the helpless poor. Rabindranath Tagore, the Nobel laureate of Indian literature who died in 1941, said that God was not adorned in finery, nor was He to be found in temples but He was dressed in tattered clothes and kept company with the destitute, the marginalized and the lost.

> Here is thy footstool and there rest thy feet where live the poorest, and lowliest and lost . . .
>
> My heart can never find its way to where thou keepest company with the companionless among the poorest, the lowliest and the lost (Gitanjali X).
>
> Leave this chanting and singing and telling of beads! . . .
>
> Our master himself has joyfully taken upon him the bonds of creation; he is bound with us all for ever . . .
>
> Meet him and stand by him in toil and in sweat of thy brow (Gitanjali XI).

The MCs often sang hymns based on English translations of Tagore's poems.

Mother waited while Church authorities tested her resoluteness and the genuineness of her mission. In 1948, nearly two years after she had received "the call," she was finally able to leave Loreto to join the dangerous ferment that was Calcutta at the time. She laid aside her Loreto habit and put on the simple blue-bordered Bengali sari that was to become emblematic of Mother Teresa and her Missionaries of Charity. In that same year when she became an Indian citizen, Hindu extremists assassinated Mahatma Gandhi. According to Sister Regina, the Loreto sisters had often described Mother Teresa as ordinary and sickly, but it struck me that, when she was able to live her dream, she became strong, charismatic, and resilient. Given freedom, her potential was unleashed.

After Rome granted her dispensation, Mother trained for six months with nursing sisters in Patna, which is on the banks of the Ganges two hundred miles northwest of Calcutta. Then she returned to Calcutta, where she opened a school in the slum. Father Henry, a Jesuit, introduced Mother to a Christian layperson, Michael Gomes, who offered her the free use of spare rooms in the upper story of his house, vacated because his brothers and their families had moved to Pakistan during the partition. After about six months on her own, she was joined by several young women from her former school of St. Mary's in Entally, a suburb of Calcutta. The first to join her was Subhasini Das, who was given Mother's baptismal name of Agnes.

Albanian by birth, Mother Teresa spoke Bengali and Hindi fluently. She started rescuing sick and dying people from the streets who had been gnawed by rats and struggled to find a place to care for them. Eventually she was given a disused pilgrims' hostel attached to the temple of the black Hindu goddess of death, Kali.

After classes we prayed for an hour. At evening Adoration Sister Regina placed the Blessed Sacrament (consecrated bread) in the monstrance, a golden stand shaped like the sun that was surrounded by oil lamps and flowers. Mother Teresa often pointed out that Jesus became bread for us, helpless and inanimate. We, in turn, were to imitate Him in His compliance. Incense filled the chapel as we knelt on mats and said the Rosary. The beads, handmade from grass seeds, clicked through our fingers. Then we prayed in silence for about twenty minutes. This was my favorite time.

In the second half of the hour, the superior, who watched the clock, knocked on the floor and we all stood to recite the Divine Office. Before the Blessed Sacrament was returned to the tabernacle, Sister held the monstrance aloft as we bent low, touching our heads to the floor. After the final hymn, we moved out in silence, placing our numbered prayer books neatly back on the shelf. At 7 p.m. a bell rang slowly. We knelt wherever we were and silently recited the Twenty-ninth Psalm for those who had died: "Out of the depths I cry to you O Lord. . . ."

Talking was allowed at the evening meal, after we had listened to a brief religious reading. More prayers followed dinner. At night, during recreation, we chatted as we mended our clothes or peeled vegetables for the next day. When we became novices, we would learn to make rosaries and the penitential chains using wire and pliers.

Five months after arriving at the house we became novices and were initiated into the practice of taking the discipline after the evening meal. This involved hitting ourselves on our bare thighs a prescribed number of times with a knotted rope in the privacy of the bathing cubicles. Sister Regina explained that this practice was meant to help us share in the suffering of Christ and the poor and to help us become better people. Some years later a Chapter, or worldwide meeting of the sisters, decided that corporal penance was to be optional, but Mother said this meant that we "choose to do it."

I thought this practice was strange, but Sister Regina explained that corporal penance was used by many of the saints to imitate the scourging of Christ, to obtain self-mastery and to make reparation for our sins. Among the Missionaries of Charity during my time in the order it was a routine practice with which we all mostly complied.

A few weeks after we joined Betty and I received news of our matriculation exams, which Sister Regina announced at recreation. We had both won Commonwealth Scholarships, which we deferred for a year. I had gained a place to study medicine at the University of New South Wales, but with a twinge of regret I declined the offer, even though it had been my goal since junior high school.

At the beginning and end of each day, before breakfast and after recreation at night, we filed past Sister Christine, or whoever our superior was at the time, with joined hands. She laid her right hand on our bowed heads in a gesture of blessing and authority. Evening prayer ended the day, and then we said ten Our Fathers with arms outstretched as we knelt beside our beds, asking God to grant us perseverance in this way of life.

This was the skeleton of my life for eleven years. Once a week we did no outside work and slept in until 5:45, and each month we spent a day in recollection and prayer; on this day we did not speak during meal times, had extra time for prayer and rest, listened to a talk from a visiting priest, and went to the usual weekly confession.

Mother Teresa came to Australia several times during the five years I was in Melbourne. Small, stooped, she had a wrinkled face, a radiant smile, and a will of steel. We hero-worshipped her, and her word was law. My first encounter with her was in 1973, a month after I had joined the order, when she was sixty-three and I was eighteen. Cardinal Knox had invited her to the Eucharistic Congress in Melbourne. Although based in Calcutta, she spent much of her time traveling the world, visiting the sisters in various countries, opening new houses, responding to various invitations to speak at meetings, and receiving awards.

Mother arrived at the novitiate late one night with Sister Augustine and some of the professed sisters who had picked her up from Tullamarine Airport. Excited, we welcomed her with garlands of flowers, singing, and clapping. She stayed with us for a short while and then started to walk with Sisters Regina and Augustine the hundred yards or so down George Street, toward the professed house. The sisters waited at their front door to welcome her. When they saw her emerge from our novitiate, they ran to her and had an emotional meeting with her in the middle of the empty, illuminated street. Some sisters were crying; others knelt on the asphalt as Mother laid her hands on each of them.

Mother stayed in Melbourne for two weeks, and our community swelled from eleven to twenty-five, as all the professed, including the sisters from Bourke, in the outer west of New South Wales, came to our house for meals and to listen to Mother's talks, or instructions, as they were called. The novices and we postulants gave up our beds for the visiting professed and rolled out our bedrolls on any spare floor or table space we could find. We had dinner in the backyard under the grapevine because none of the George Street rooms was big enough to hold us all.

For the first few days of her visit Mother spoke to us in a group about our way of life. I sat entranced. Her God was close, hidden in each of us, in the Eucharist, in the seemingly chance events of the day, and in the poor. I felt part of a privileged group. Life was to be lived in a simple, prayerful way. Nothing could go wrong, as all things, both good and bad, worked together for our good. Suffering and hardships were purifying and, if we were united with Christ, redemptive. For Mother, nothing in life was an accident; everything was under God's control. Her motto was "Your will be done," by which she meant that she accepted all that happened because God either willed it directly or allowed it. She took this expression from Jesus' words in the Garden of Gethsemane: "Father if you are willing, take this cup away from me. Nevertheless, let your will be done, not mine" (Luke 22:42).

Once people knew Mother had arrived, life at the novitiate became hectic as the doorbell and phone rang nonstop. Television and other media people went to 101 Gore Street to interview and film her. She kept a frenetic pace, rising with us at 4:40 for prayer, then embarking on a series of talks and appointments that often lasted until after midnight.

Mother had a special meeting with the coworkers, lay people who wanted to share in her work and spirit and who served as volunteers at the men's shelter and collected money and clothes to assist us in our work for the poor. She said that everyone could do something beautiful for God by reaching out to the poor and lonely within their own families and neighborhoods.

We took turns going to the Eucharistic Congress. Walking beside Mother on the way to one of the Masses, I carried her bag. People would silently press money into her hand, which she surreptitiously gave to me to put into the bag. As we left the showground where the Congress was being held, her hand went out for mine again, but just to steady herself in the crowd. I looked down and asked, "No money, Mother?" She laughed.

When we went to the ceremonies Mother asked us to encircle her to form a sort of shield. Then, she said, "Come sisters," and off we went like an express train. She thought she might escape notice if she was in the middle of a group; however, it was not an effective camouflage, as all the professed wore the blue-and-white sari, which shouted "Mother Teresa." As soon as people saw her they came up to speak to her and perhaps tell her their worries, as she had the reputation of being a living saint.

During the last Mass of the Congress Mother was up behind the main altar surrounded by Franciscans. My friend Paul, who had attended my uncle Toby's school, was among them. Once the ceremony was over, Sister Regina and I walked home. We were quicker on foot than Mother and the rest of the sisters, who were stuck in the gridlocked cars, and we started to prepare the evening meal. When I heard Mother arrive with Sister Augustine, I went out to the front of the house without being asked to do so. Still in civilian clothes, Paul stood among the brown-habited friars who had driven Mother home. We talked very briefly. "What's it like?" he asked.

"Pretty exciting at the moment. Toby wrote and said you'd joined."

"Yes, I thought I'd give it a go."

"Come, Sister!" Mother called as she walked back into the house.

"See you, Paul."

To celebrate Mother's visit, several carloads of us drove with her to Gordon, in rural Victoria, for a picnic. The Davidson family had donated a house for the order to use, and we later made our seven-day annual retreat there. In the car, after the obligatory Rosary, the sisters sang in many different languages. The old house had a fuel stove and Mrs. Davidson cooked up a feast of proper Australian tucker: lamb, baked potatoes, and scones with jam and cream. My life was usually so tightly regimented that I no longer had the freedom to get some space when I needed it, but on a picnic like this, I was allowed, after asking permission, to go on a short solitary walk. After lunch I escaped to a nearby forest, where red-and-white-topped toadstools emerged from the forest floor.

While Mother Teresa was in Australia she made many changes. She sent Sister Christine with three other sisters to Katherine in the Northern Territory to start a new house, working among the Aboriginal people. My visiting companion, Sister John, was transferred to Bourke. As well as moving sisters, Mother was fond of moving furniture around, both in the convent and at the Gore Street shelter. She had sisters running everywhere, moving cupboards and tables and changing the layout of rooms. Sometimes she found things that she didn't think conformed to the ideal of poverty, such as a tape recorder that the sisters used to learn new songs for catechism. It had to be given away. Her custom was to micromanage each house on her visits, to keep each community true to her original ideal. She also saw each of the professed and novices privately to encourage and counsel them.

After Mother's departure we postulants stayed in the same community as Sister Regina and the novices. Only Betty and I remained, because Sophia and Eileen decided not to continue as MCs. I no longer visited the old men in their tiny rooms, but worked at the men's shelter. The professed took over Sister John's work.

In April Sister Satya, one of the professed sisters, started making our habits in preparation for our reception as novices on May 14, 1973. I took about as long to attach the collar press-studs as Sister did to complete the whole garment. At the same time, Sisters Jasmin and Patience were making new habits for themselves, as they were to take their first vows at the end of May.

At a weeklong retreat in our Fitzroy house, a time of silence and reflection, we prepared to become novices, and Patience and Jasmin prepared for their profession. An Oblate father gave us talks every day about prayer, referencing a book called *The Cloud of Unknowing*, written by an anonymous fourteenth-century British monk who taught that the way to come close to God was not with thought and study, but with stillness, silence, and the repetition of a short prayer or word. I liked this way of prayer better than the Jesuit way of imagining a scene with a multiplicity of thoughts, words, and images. Instead, we were to pierce "the cloud of unknowing" surrounding God by repeating a single word. The unknown author advised his readers to use this word as a spear to penetrate the darkness and as a sword to smite all thought. He made his own the phrase "Be still and know that I am God" (Psalm 46:10). God, he felt, could be experienced in stillness but could not be known with the intellect.

At the time of our reception Sister Regina chopped at my hair tuft by tuft until my scalp resembled a bombed landscape. She gave us new names as a sign of our new life. Betty became Naomi and I became Tobit, after the biblical figure and my uncle Toby. Tobit was a good man who had come on hard times. He became blind, but later was cured and able to see again. He instructed his son, "Give your bread to those who are hungry and your clothes to those who lack clothing" (Tobit 4:16). I had trouble getting used to my new name. Once I had to read the first reading in All Saints Church, which started with the line "I Tobit, took a bath." The passage went on to tell how sparrows pooped in Tobit's eyes, blinding him.

I was also given the number 952, which I put as an identifier on all my clothes, my bucket, and my books. My feast day was October 4, the day the Church celebrates the life of St. Francis of Assisi. My identity as

Colette was being subsumed into my new identity as Tobit. Suppressing my individuality, preferences, and desires so that I could be molded into a true MC made me a bit uneasy, but I thought that the mold was true. I was the clay, Christ the potter. I was being fashioned according to His will, not mine. I thought I would be liberated and transformed in the process, not harmed.

With infinite patience my novice mentor, Sister Karina, taught me how to put on my new sari. Tie the rope around your waist and knot it firmly. Then tuck the sari into the rope on the left side, continue around the waist, double back again, then bring it up over the right shoulder, around the back to the shoulder again, and secure it with a safety pin and attached cross. Then pull the sari up over the knotted white head-piece and pin it on either side. Finally, she had me sari-bound. How, I wondered, was I to perform this feat in silence, in the dark, at 4:40 the next morning? My headpiece kept slipping around my smooth head, and it was always crooked. Naomi, on the other hand, always looked neat.

The ceremony for the reception to the novitiate was presided over by Father Ribiskini, who was our spiritual director and Cardinal Knox's secretary at the time. We had a celebratory meal at night, with *singaras* made from a spicy mince that was mixed with potato and peas, put into pastry, and fried. There was also a curry, rice, and ice cream. Later the novices performed an Indian village dance to celebrate our reception. The sisters sat cross-legged in a circle, dressed up and armed with the appropriate props—a fishing line, a plastic snake, and a net—and sang a story in Hindi, which they acted out in the center of the circle. At the appropriate time, one of them jumped up to express in dance what was being sung in the ballad. First there was a fish and a fisherman, a bird and a hunter, a snake and a snake charmer, then a girl and a boy! Everyone laughed as the boy grabbed the girl.

In the Missionaries of Charity first and final professions are in two groups, in May and December. Sisters don't make their final vows until six years after their first profession, when they commit themselves to the Society for life. However, we were taught that the yearly renewal of temporary vows was just a technicality of canon law; in our hearts our dedication was irreversible, and for life. God had called us, and the only answer possible was "Yes, Lord."

Just after our reception in May 1973 we celebrated as Sisters Jasmin and Patience made their first vows at All Saints Church. At the same time seventy sisters were professed in Calcutta. After the profession celebrations Patience and Jasmin went to Bourke to work.

Around the same time, a new postulant, Evelyn, from rural Victoria, joined us, together with Samantha, an Englishwoman who had been working with Aboriginal people in the Northern Territory. Later in the year Sister Laboni and Sister Elina, novices from our group in Calcutta, came out from India to join us. Like Sister Jasmin, Sister Laboni was a classical dancer in the southern Indian tradition. Elina came from Goa and like me, found the sari awkward, as she was Anglo-Indian and had not worn it as a young woman. Both still had long, black hair because the Mother House had stopped shaving novices' hair so that if they left the order in the first two years, before first vows, it was less shameful for them to return to their family. It was Mother's policy to send sisters from India out to novitiates in Rome and Melbourne to train with non-Indian novices in order to maintain uniformity of training and spirit throughout the order.

More comfortable in jeans, I kept tripping over my new ankle-length sari, which was white and flimsy and which soon turned gray and had to be darned. Naomi wore hers with more grace. We had two sets of clothes for daily use and one for emergencies and special occasions. It was a wear one–wash one arrangement, and we had to ask permission to use the third set. Mine was often in use as I had great trouble keeping my saris white and in one piece.

One day, while trying to climb down from the fig tree in the backyard after collecting fruit in a small bucket for the evening meal, I lost my balance and put my foot through the rusted roof of an old woodshed, leaving bits of me on the corrugated iron. Naomi saw what was happening from the refectory window. She quickly came to my rescue and pushed my foot up from inside the shed, laughing all the time.

Sister Regina was soon on the scene. "Sisters, a little more recollection, please. This is not a boarding school!" I was glad I couldn't see Naomi's face; otherwise, it would have been very difficult to stop laughing. I was scratched, but not badly injured. There was no thought of precautions such as a tetanus shot.

Sister Regina wanted us to have a guard dog at George Street and Mum volunteered to send Abby, a corgi-cross puppy she had adopted. Abby was duly dispatched on the train from Moss Vale, and Sister Naomi and I walked from Fitzroy to Spencer Street to pick her up. The train was an hour late, but eventually a guard found her in a special box cage attached to the side of the train. As we walked along the platform, everyone seemed to be looking at us, two MCs in their coats and saris with a puppy, which trotted along at our side, the puppy dressed in a coat with a matching carry-bag that Mum had made out of one of my brother Rod's old dressing gowns. The bag contained Abby's food and water bowl.

Sister Regina thought the dog was named Abbey, after a religious building. In fact, my brother Rodney had named her after Abigail, a star on a TV show who was far from being religiously inclined. Abby didn't know the rules and was in a lot of trouble at first. She caused chaos by scattering the sisters' sandals, which had been neatly lined up along the corridor outside the chapel while the sisters were at prayer. She chewed some of them, necessitating hasty repairs during recreation. Then she played with the patched saris blowing on the washing lines, growling and barking at them as if they were alive. One snap and the thin cotton shredded, leaving the hapless sister who owned it very busy that night as she tried to repair it for the next day.

We kept contact with other members of the Society throughout the world by sending out and receiving general letters at Christmas, Easter, and the Society's Feast Day, August 22. Mother also sent regular general letters to all the houses, mainly in the form of spiritual instruction, though she did include important news, such as the accidental death of a sister or the worsening instability in some part of the world where our sisters were working. But in general we were cut off from any source of local and world news. I had always been very interested in current affairs, and now I read other people's newspapers at any opportunity, on the bus or in the men's home, and I scrutinized the banner headlines posted at the front of paper shops as we walked down the street. Mother read the papers, but we weren't allowed to.

We were also cut off from our families, though we could have visitors on the first Sunday of the month, in the afternoon. I was excited when Mum and sometimes my sister, Judy, made the long trip down by train to see me, perhaps bringing with them a paper they had read on the way.

"You don't sound like you anymore," Mum complained. "You're talking in a singsong way."

"I have to talk like this, Mum, or the other sisters can't understand me."

"Well, try to stop it when you're talking to me!"

Sometimes Mum and I walked to the Fitzroy or Carlton Gardens in order to escape the parlor and confines of the convent. One day while we were walking Mum asked, "Why can't you ring me sometimes? I feel I've lost you."

"We're not allowed to, Mum."

"I don't see why you have to be so cut off from your family. We've been everything for you until now."

"I'm sorry. I miss you a lot. Sister Regina says it's like leaving home to get married."

"If you were married, I could still talk to you and visit you whenever I wanted."

I was permitted to write home once a month if Mum didn't visit, but was not allowed to send letters to any of my other friends and extended family, except at Christmas and Easter.

My friends were studying at Sydney University or at nursing or teachers colleges, and I was jealous of the exciting new life I imagined they were living. Once I received a parcel of rice and vitamin pills from my friends Rell and Bren. I was disappointed; a chocolate would have been nice. After a while they stopped writing because I usually couldn't reply, even if only to tell them that the last thing I needed was more rice!

In our first year at the novitiate we attended classes, studied and prayed, and went out to work only twice a week, on Sundays and Thursdays, to relieve the professed for their day off. We also walked to St. Patrick's Cathedral each day to make our hour of Adoration in a small alcove behind the main altar rather than in our chapel at home. The idea was to have other people join us and so make the cathedral a place of prayer rather than a massive monument used only intermittently for religious ceremonies.

One day it was my turn to light the charcoal in the censer, the brass vessel in which the priest burns incense and that he swings back and forth in front of the Blessed Sacrament during Benediction. Under the watchful gaze of the pious folk in the pews, I went up onto the sanctuary and tried to open the censer, but it was stuck. As I pulled harder, one of the chains came off and it collapsed in a heap of brass on the marble floor, the crash reverberating around the cathedral. I reattached the chain and tried to light the taper, but it went out twice. Once I got the charcoal alight, it started to spit and crackle. As I prepared the priest's vestments, longing to escape from the gaze of the congregation I was amusing, I smelled smoke. Fire! My sari had started smoldering, ignited by the sparks. I beat my chest, and glowing bits of sari flew everywhere. Blushing, I returned to kneel with the congregation, still under their silent scrutiny, my sari scorched and full of holes. I would have a lot of mending to do.

I had failed sewing at school after putting the sleeve of a dress in upside down, but I tried nonetheless to learn to use the convent's treadle sewing machine. Every time I used it I had trouble pedaling forward and ended up knotting the thread in the bobbin. Sister Karina, a natural on the confounded machine, helped me cut out and patch the burned parts of my sari, but my complete helplessness wasn't an excuse to Sister Regina. "You must learn to patch your sari yourself," she said, "especially as you tear it so often." Eventually I did learn to make and repair the basic clothing we wore.

After the Vatican Council, which ended in 1965, the wind of change blew through the Catholic Church and many religious orders strove to adapt to the modern world. The Missionaries of Charity did not change. As Easter approached, Sister Regina wanted us novices to learn to chant the Divine Office "like proper nuns." Being a poor singer, I was lukewarm to the idea. A Dominican priest who gave us lectures in spirituality asked one of the Dominican sisters to teach us the Gregorian chant. I was happy to learn that our teacher was Sister St. Vincent, who had been the prioress of my high school and subsequently transferred to Sienna College in Camberwell. The last time I'd seen her, I had imitated her in a skit during the senior class end-of-year celebrations. Sister St. Vincent had changed back to her own name, Patricia, and wore a modified habit, in line with Vatican II. She didn't recognize me at first—probably the hairstyle—but was amazed when she did and laughed and kissed me. Then she barraged me with questions, which I answered guardedly, surrounded as I was by all the other sisters.

After our lessons in the parlor at George Street we went to Patricia's convent to listen to the Dominican sisters chant the Office to get a better idea of how it should sound. The Dominican chapel was beautiful, with a courtyard and surrounding cloister, and the Dominicans very welcoming, inviting us to have tea there. Sister Regina politely declined. I thought there might have been a chance of a nice meal as they were also religious, but the rules that forbade meals outside our own convent held firm.

After the Office Patricia took me aside. "Are you still happy there, Colette?"

"Yes, I'm fine."

"You've lost weight."

"That must be why Rell and Bren sent me rice and vitamins," I joked.

I did not allow myself to think then that I was unhappy and brushed off her kind inquiries, but I was probably under some strain as I had lost about ten kilos (twenty-two pounds) and my period had stopped for nearly a year. At Easter we chanted the Office in our chapel, and afterward continued to chant on big feast days. The psalms that make up the Office were written as songs, not just as prayers to be recited, and despite my initial reservations I found the chants more rhythmic and peaceful than just reciting the words.

On the Easter Vigil we celebrated the Christian promise that, in the end, life will conquer death and good defeat evil. With the rest of the congregation we crowded onto the steps outside St. Patrick's Cathedral for the lighting of the Easter fire, symbolic of the light of Christ that had been extinguished on Calvary but rekindled with the Resurrection. Cardinal Knox lit the Paschal candle, engraved with the Greek letters A and Ω, alpha and omega, the beginning and the end of the Greek alphabet. We followed the lit candle, held aloft, into the internal darkness of the cathedral cave. Its flickering flame threw eerie shadows up the balustrades as the priest lifted it three times and chanted, "The light of Christ," to which the congregation responded, "Thanks be to God." At the end of each pew, parishioners lit their candles from the Paschal candle and the light was passed along the rows so that soon the whole interior of the cathedral was awash with candlelight. The organ thundered as the choir sang stirring hymns of Resurrection and life.

This belief, that resurrection follows death, was crucial to our way of life; otherwise, we would have been living a life which had no future promise and was just a barren negation of self. I had no reason at this stage to doubt the "true and certain hope of the Resurrection."

Our community of novices celebrated with an Easter picnic at a national park near Melbourne. I was excited because it reminded me so much of home. It was cool and heavily wooded with gullies of tree ferns; Tarzan vines hung down from the sun-seeking giant trees and the undergrowth was alive with birdsong. Thinking we were alone, we ran along the bush tracks singing and calling "Cooee" to each other, until we came upon a startled couple in a secluded place. At least they had had ample warning of the arrival of these strangely dressed people, who behaved as if they had been let out of prison for the day.

After Easter we returned to our studies and the drabness of the inner city. This was the reality of my life, and I accepted it. How could I think of gratifying my love of nature when people were dying of hunger on the street in many places around the world? I did not talk to my fellow novices about my feelings, longings, frustrations, or preferences, as it was not allowed. All conversation was public; we interacted as a group during meals and recreation, not as friends or individuals. We were like people traveling on parallel trains that were close but never met. We passed each other in the convent without greeting or exchanging glances in our quest to remain recollected.

Our regular schedule of classes was interrupted when Sister Regina and Sister Felicity from Bourke were chosen by a vote of the professed sisters in Australia to go as representatives to the General Chapter, the meeting in Calcutta that advised Mother about the running of the order. They were away for about a month. In the meantime some of the other professed and some visiting priests taught our classes, and we worked on essay assignments, such as writing out the story of our vocation or calling. We did these in private and gave them to Sister Regina when she returned. We didn't share them with each other.

Our year followed the Church's cycle of fasting, ordinary time, and feasts: Advent, Christmas, Lent, Easter, and Pentecost. We also celebrated days important to the order, such as the Society's Feast Day, Inspiration Day on September 10, which commemorated the day Mother felt called to start the Society, and Mother's Feast Day on October 1, the feast of St. Thérèse of Lisieux. Feast days played a big part in the life of the MC. Typically there was Mass in the chapel; toast and sometimes eggs for breakfast, instead of *chapattis*; talking was allowed at breakfast; and, often in the evening, there were dances, songs, or plays.

On Sister Augustine's feast day, for example, some of the sisters performed an Indian dance of lights. They entered the darkened refectory accompanied by singing and the beat of anklet bells. The sisters moved gracefully with lighted candles in both hands. The next item was a play I had written about the biblical character Job. People and animals died as God allowed Job's faith to be tested in what amounted to a wager between God and the devil. As in my high school classes, I was one of the questioners left unsatisfied with God's poetic explanation that we had no right to question Him.

Where were you when I laid the earth's foundation?
Is Yahweh's opponent going to give way?
Has God's critic thought up an answer? (Job 38:4; 40:2)

The archetypal Missionary of Charity was not a questioner. She was submissive, obedient, and trusting. She maintained a veneer of cheerfulness and surrendered her life without reserve.

I had a long way to go.

CHAPTER THREE

Becoming a Missionary of Charity

Outside the Fitzroy house with school friends Rell and Bren, 1974.
(Photographer: Kim Powell)

*W*e novices had much to learn about the Society. In two years'
time we were to make four vows, of poverty, chastity, obedience, and wholehearted and free service to the poor.

When Mother Teresa started the order in 1948 she wrote out a Constitution that listed the aim and rules governing the Society and also wrote a detailed commentary on these rules. The Constitution was sent to Rome for ratification, and the Vatican approved her institution as a new religious order on October 7, 1950, the foundation day of the Society.

We copied out the rules and their explanations into notebooks and learned passages by heart. Later, Mother and a group of senior sisters rewrote the Constitution to comply more closely with the spirit of the second Vatican Council; these changes were accepted by the sisters' delegates at a Chapter, or general meeting of the sisters. The document was longer and more fleshed out, but the life it described and regulated remained the same.

Several themes recurred throughout Mother's teachings. She often said that the aim of her congregation was "to quench the infinite thirst of Jesus on the Cross for love of souls." I had supposed that the Society's aim was more pragmatic: to relieve suffering, feed the hungry, and give water to the thirsty, and so I rationalized that this *is* what it really meant, and that Mother only expressed her aim for us sisters in more religious and figurative terms.

A hymn that we learned, "I Thirst," developed Mother's more mystical theme: "My chalice will be filled with love, sacrifices made all for Thee. Evermore I will quench Thy thirst, Lord." The sentiments were not natural to me, but I believed then that I shared an ideal with Mother Teresa.

Missionaries of Charity were to be contemplatives in the heart of the world. Sister Regina instructed us that the spirit of the Society was one of "total surrender, loving trust, and cheerfulness." We were to give up "our free will, our reason, [and] our whole life in pure faith." Mother often instructed us to "give whatever He takes, and take whatever He gives, with a smile."

Mother Teresa was strongly influenced by St. Ignatius of Loyola, who had been a soldier before he founded the Jesuits. The Loreto sisters had adopted the Ignatian ideas of unquestioning military obedience and a codified, regimented system of religious practices. Mother's Jesuit confessors and spiritual directors had guided her spiritual formation and consequently she considered obedience to be the paramount virtue and litmus test of true humility and holiness.

Mother had grown up in the time following the Church's suppression of what was termed the Modernist Heresy, which scrutinized Church teaching in a rational and scientific way. Modersnists taught that truth was not static or immutable but could evolve as our understanding changed. It challenged the teaching authority of the Church, and especially that of the pope, and the concepts of Divine revelation and papal infallibility. In 1907, three years before Mother was born, Pope Pius X counteracted this rationalist, secular movement by teaching that Catholics must submit their intellect and will to the teaching authority of the Church. Debate and scientific enquiry had clear limits. Pride, he wrote, was the root of all evil, and the only way to combat it was by humble obedience. It seems apparent that as a young woman Mother Teresa took this teaching to heart and felt that the best way to be guided by God was to obey Church authorities. "God could use people who were obedient," she said, but those who choose their own way are doomed to fail. She taught that "even God cannot fill what is already full." Our task as nuns was to empty ourselves in order to become conduits of the Divine power. Our inner selves had to die, as do grains of wheat, in order to yield a harvest.

We were to follow Mother Teresa's blueprint: to love and serve the poor and to live like them. However, submission was emphasized much more than cooperative love and equality. In Mother's words, "If we could obey promptly, simply, blindly and cheerfully we should at once reach the highest perfection."

I knew this wasn't true. *What if the command were wrong? What if we obeyed only out of fear or to ingratiate ourselves to those in power? Wasn't submission, in some circumstances, a sign of weakness, not strength?* To my mind, even then, obedience and goodness were not the same. Conflict situations churned me up, and I had always been sensitive to the way people spoke to each other, for instance, as a child, when I huddled outside with my brothers while Mum and Dad shouted at each other inside the house. I knew that a coward obeys out of fear, so obedience in itself couldn't be a sign of holiness. It was sometimes harder for me to speak my mind than to keep quiet; this caused inner conflict because what I was told was good and holy felt wrong and subservient. Sister Regina taught us to accept as God's will whatever our superiors asked of us. Compassionate service to the poor had been the bait that lured me into the order, but before I knew it I was hooked on the doctrine of obedience and blind submission. Humiliation and verbal dressings down were to be expected in the order and were considered a way to make us better people.

I was to learn what MC obedience meant. Early in the morning on the day after Pentecost Sunday in 1973, while Sister Regina was in Calcutta for the Chapter, Sister Annette and I were sent to work at 101 Gore Street. We were to relieve the professed sisters for a few hours because they had influenza and had been unable to rest. We rang the doorbell near the solid iron gate at the men's shelter, which had a grill at eye level. Sister Satya, when she answered the bell, looked unwell and fumbled to find the right key. She smiled wearily. "Ah, these men! You'll have your hands full this morning. They're acting up."

Sister Benedict, who was a little over four feet tall, was in the cement forecourt taking on a giant of a man who had smuggled in some grog. "The sisters try to help you and look what you do. You should be ashamed," she scolded, wagging her finger at the man. She rattled off her admonitions at a rapid-fire pace. This, along with her short stature, had earned her the name "Spitfire." The men knew not to mess with her.

The professed left to rest. The Gore Street home was chaotic, so we set about getting it in order. We marshaled the sober, able-bodied men into the kitchen. "Let's help the sisters out a bit. You know they're crook [sick]. We need to get this place back to normal," Sister Annette said as forcefully as she could.

Jimmy, with the wooden leg, agreed. "C'mon you blokes! No more silly-buggers. Who's going to help me with the washing up and the veggies?" A couple of men agreed to help.

"Yeh, all right, under starters' orders [ready to race or work]," said Bevan, a painter by trade. "What do you want me to do?"

"Count me in, Jim," replied Fred, moving toward the sink.

With the kitchen staffed, Sister Annette went upstairs, and I stayed on the lower floor making beds, emptying urinals, helping the frail ones to shower and shave, and generally cleaning up. A couple of men who were having a smoke outside were "volunteered" to mop. We were determined to have all the heavy work finished by the time we were due to leave. Our efforts paid off; the place was shipshape when Sisters Satya and Benedict returned a few hours later.

As we started to walk home, feeling happy with ourselves, a distraught, white-bearded man came running down from the top of Gore Street. "Sisters! Come quickly! It's Archie. I think he's dead in a shed up on Victoria Parade."

We turned back to the gate and rang the bell, and when Sister Satya appeared we asked her to call the police. But she wanted the details confirmed first. "Go up and see what's happened," she ordered.

We rushed up Gore Street and found a young pale man sprawled on the cement floor of an open garage attached to an empty house. He was surrounded by metho bottles, his eyes fixed and staring. I had not seen a dead body before, and my own heart started beating fast as I briefly attempted resuscitation, which I had learned in the swimming club at home. As soon as I started CPR I knew that it was futile. He was cold and stiff and his breastbone creaked as I pushed down on it.

We went around to a nearby doctor's surgery to see if the doctor would certify the body, but the secretary said he couldn't and she called the police for us. We stayed with Archie's friend until they arrived and then returned to 101 to report to Sister Satya. "It's Archie, Sister. He might have died overnight. He was pretty cold."

She shook her head. "He was here only last week. I wanted to take him to hospital. He didn't look well, but he refused to go. What to do?"

We arrived home late. Our superior at the time was in the front parlor with Jean, the head of the coworkers. "Where have you two been?" she demanded.

"A man died at the top of Gore Street," Sister Annette began.

"And what has that got to do with you?" she interjected.

"We were on our way home and his friend came to call us," I tried to explain.

"As if you were the only ones who could go with him. You're only novices. Why didn't you ask the professed to go up there?"

"Because . . . ," I began.

Sister cut me off. "You should have been home on time. Your duty is to do what you are told. No more, no less. You seem intent on doing what you like, when you like—always so indispensable and important." My face burned; I felt embarrassed to be corrected in front of Jean.

"Yes, Sister. Thank you, Sister," we said in turn.

As I tried to join in the prayers I could see Archie's sallow face and staring eyes. My mind was distracted as I mumbled words that had no meaning for me.

Hail, mistress of earth,
Hail, heavenly Queen,
Hail, virgin of virgins, all chaste and serene.

My thoughts raced. *For a while at least, a dead body looks much the same as a living one, but the invisible essence of life has gone. I wonder why he hit the metho so hard? We were taught to respond to a person in distress, and to show compassion. We had been asked by the professed to go up there.* I couldn't see that we had done anything wrong.

I made mistakes in the recitation of the prayer as it alternated verse by verse, from one side of the chapel to the other. Regardless of my inner turmoil, during lunch I acted as if nothing had happened, as was expected of me. Later that day, as I reflected on the incident, I copied excerpts from the *Constitution of the Missionaries of Charity* into my notebook: "Let each sister see Jesus Christ in the person of the poor." It was a paradox that we were being taught to respond with compassion to the distressed, but, when we did so, we were rebuked because such an action clashed with observing the timetable. Rigid obedience allowed no discretion in our dealings with people.

In the pursuit of a religious ideal I had taken on the full package and chosen to surrender my freedom to decide the most basic things: what I did, where I went, what I ate, when I went to sleep and woke, and what I read. I was becoming God's perfect *selfless* instrument, ready for any work, anywhere, under anyone. The MCs' easy smiles and laughter concealed many heartaches and struggles.

• • •

Poverty was another value cherished in the Society. According to the Gospels, the world order is inverted. Mother reasoned that, although Christ was God, He emptied Himself to become a poor man and a friend of the weak and despised, so we should do the same, sharing in what she called the "poverty of the Cross." Hence we were to live a simple life, free of the clutter of material possessions. We darned our clothes, mended our sandals, wasted nothing. We cleaned dishes and even our teeth with ash. We walked whenever possible. There was no television or radio. A sister could not receive personal gifts; she handed over anything she received to the superior, who judged if it was suitable for common use.

Total dependence on the superior was also considered part of the vow of poverty. The stories my uncle Toby had told us when he was a Franciscan novice were not an exaggeration; having almost to beg for a new toothbrush, he imitated the response of the brother in charge: "Look, there are still five bristles on this perfectly good toothbrush. Ask me next month." I had ended up in an even more dependent state.

If a sister needed anything, she wrote her requests in the Garment Book, a small notebook attached with string to a nail in the refectory that the superior reviewed weekly. For example, "Please, may I have a patch for my sari?" The superior would peruse the requests and, after admonishing the sister to try not to tear her sari so frequently, would sign the book, allowing the garment mistress to issue the items.

In part to fulfill our vow of poverty, we went begging for food every week at the Victoria Markets, a collection of long, covered sheds where vendors sold every form of fresh produce and other foods. Immigrant matrons in black headscarves and denim aprons looked quizzically at us as we approached, pulling our carts behind us and asking each stall owner in turn, "Can you spare something for the sisters?"

Some people liked to give us something. Others pretended not to see or hear us. I heard one young Australian laborer mutter "Bludgers" as we passed. My Indian companion didn't understand the term, which means "parasites," but it stung me. I wanted to leave quickly once I sensed hostility, but my companion was senior and made the decisions, so we stood waiting there, almost shaming the person into giving us something. One week we were given a large number of overripe bananas, another time there was a glut of cabbages. As we toiled back up the hill toward Fitzroy, I thought of the menu for the next week: cabbage soup, stir-fried cabbage, cabbage and beans. Naomi in particular disliked bananas, which made her feel ill, but she had to eat them.

Another aspect of poverty was that, each month, we renewed what was termed General Permissions, the permission to exist in the house and use its facilities. This formality demanded that the sister recognize her spiritual poverty, weakness, and unworthiness. So each sister knelt before her superior, touched her head to the floor, and "spoke her faults" for things such as losing her temper, gossiping, or breaking silence. She then was asked to be seated, and the superior had a talk with her about her spiritual development or corrected her for any bad habits the superior had noticed. Every time Mother came to a house, each sister also needed to give an account of herself in this way.

Mother stretched poverty further still, saying that we should "grab the chance" to be falsely accused, blamed, or despised, just as Christ was. We were to remain silent and not defend ourselves, just as He did. We were to seek out the lowest and most menial jobs and do them cheerfully. We were also to be detached from any work we did: no matter how much we had put into an effort or a place, we should be prepared to move on without reason or notice. Poverty meant that we had no rights and nothing belonged to us.

The vow of chastity meant more than just remaining celibate. A sister was not to seek emotional comfort or have friends within or outside the order. Friendship was considered suspect and a barrier to union with God. Close relationships were labeled "particular friendships" and were forbidden. No private conversations were permitted except with the superior or a priest in the weekly confession. It was a lonely way to live. I had trouble controlling daydreams of alternative life scenarios, such as going to university, having a normal social life, and taking up medicine, but I didn't speak of these thoughts to anyone.

I thought of leaving the Missionaries of Charity quite often. A sense of inadequacy and self-doubt was instilled in me and grew. The order taught that our motives and thought processes were so suspect that only submission could assure us of following God's will. Self-will led us away from God. We were encouraged to disclose our doubts to our novice mistress but forbidden to speak of them to our fellow novices lest we do "the work of the devil" and cause another sister to waver. So we struggled alone with our uncertainties and dealt with them in our own ways. That's why we had no warning when someone left; she just disappeared without explanation.

Because the Constitution did not permit us to eat or drink outside our convent refectory, we often offended people by turning them down when they invited us to join them. Even when members of our family visited us, we usually couldn't eat or drink with them. Many of the old ladies we helped who lived alone wanted us to have a cup of tea with them and couldn't understand why we refused.

Most religious orders have the same three vows of poverty, chastity, and obedience, but interpret them in different ways. Mother Teresa added a fourth vow of wholehearted and free service to the poorest of the poor, ministering to Christ in all His distressing disguises. The more repulsive or repugnant the work or the person, Mother instructed us, the more cheerful and devoted we should be. We were never to accept any payment for our service.

Criticized by people outside the order for not addressing the social problems that made people poor, Mother Teresa wanted to respond to the immediate need of each person whom she encountered. "Our people will die waiting for the world to change," she said, but "each of us can make a small difference." When she was blamed for giving a person a fish rather than teaching him to fish, she retorted, "The dying cannot fish." Nevertheless, Mother did help some of the people she served to acquire skills, such as typing or weaving, which ultimately made them more self-sufficient.

In Australia, however, the men we helped received a pension but they didn't contribute to their board and lodging. Some saved their pension money for a bond, so they could rent a place of their own, but others used the money to go on an even heavier alcoholic bender each payday, because they could return to us for food and lodging when the money was finished. I didn't think this did them any service, but I was not able to discuss it. If we had required that they pay some money for board, we could have saved it for them to buy something worthwhile later. But this was not how the MCs operated.

Spiritual life was paramount in the Society. Prayer took up several hours each day: morning prayer and meditation, Mass, spiritual reading of a religious book for half an hour each day, the hour's Adoration, and Divine Office in the evening or afternoon, midday, evening, and night prayers, examination of conscience, and Rosary. Mother believed that we needed to "pray the work," that even routine tasks were a holy activity. We were to live in the present moment and do everything we did carefully and well. She taught us to keep our thoughts and tongues in check in the hope that both interior and exterior silence would lead us to deeper prayer.

For me, the many prayers that we rattled off daily were a barrier to what I felt was true prayer or inner silence. I read *The Way of a Pilgrim*, which I had chosen from the spiritual texts in the novitiate library. It is the story of an unknown Russian peasant who wanted to learn how to pray continuously. I liked his way of repeating a short phrase to reach inner quiet. It was similar to what the priest had taught us from *The Cloud of Unknowing* during the retreat before our reception as novices.

The spirituality of the Cross was central to Mother's worldview. She made St. Paul's words her own: "I have been crucified with Christ . . . it is no longer I but Christ who is living in me" (Galatians 2:20). We were to accept joyfully any humiliations or difficulties as a way of being "nailed with Christ to the Cross" and of quenching His infinite thirst. We were, as St. Paul said, to make up in our own bodies what was lacking in the sufferings of Christ. Mother spoke of mortification—voluntarily giving up something to make up for sin—as central to her way of thinking. If you complained to Mother about a perceived injustice or a grievance, her response was that you should just accept it: offer it up, grab the chance to humble yourself, and don't complain.

Penances, a form of self-punishment for sin, were enshrined in the order's Constitution, and involved several practices, such as hitting one-self on the thighs (referred to as the discipline), wearing wire chains with spikes around the waist and upper arm during morning prayer, and praying with arms outstretched at the bedside at night. In addition, on the first Friday every month the community fasted and did public penances, such as begging for a meal, eating meals while kneeling, and kissing the feet of other sisters. Other practices involved admitting faults and apologizing to the community for getting angry, breaking something, and the like. These practices were part of many religious orders prior to the Vatican Council of the Church in the 1960s, but had mostly been discarded. Mother felt these practices were important, however, and often wrote to us prescribing extra penances.

I didn't realize then that by revealing my thoughts, desires, and motives in confession and in talks with Sister Regina I was increasing my vulnerability to criticism and self-doubt. There was no place to hide. Some of the spiritual practices we were taught seemed counterproductive, and increased our self-focus. We were required to scrutinize our thoughts, motives, words, and actions. Socrates said, "An unexamined life is not worth living," but I learned that you can overdo it. St. Ignatius himself, who had laid down this pattern of self-examination, was, at one stage in his life, so plagued by scruples that it nearly drove him to despair. The self-scrutiny caused an anxiety about motivation that otherwise would not have been present.

Isolated from family and friends, subject to acerbic public and private correction, my reading matter strictly censored, I was being locked into the impenetrable vault of conservative Catholicism. No other way of life seemed possible. I was attracted to the order's compassionate service to the poor, but for me to perform this service the Society demanded the total surrender of my life to obedience. I was slow to realize there was a conflict between my perception of a compassionate life and that of the order and this led to recurrent inner turmoil. I had understood early in my life that the world was conflicted, that there were shades of gray. Often questions had no clear answers, but in the Missionaries of Charity there was a veneer of false simplicity that was considered virtuous and childlike. Struggling with the rights and wrongs of a problem or situation was not necessary. I was just to obey.

For a while we studied one day a week at the Assumption Institute in Melbourne with the novices from other religious orders, who clearly had a more liberal way of life. We MCs remained separate, eating together as a group and then going to the chapel for midday prayer, while the other novices relaxed and chatted among themselves.

As I studied the Bible and moral theology, I had many questions. The God of the Old Testament was portrayed as violent and murderous, bearing little resemblance to the God I believed in. I questioned our lecturer, "Father, why does the Bible depict God as the killer of the firstborn of every Egyptian family? He is also described as fighting with the Israelites against the Egyptians, so that their bodies littered the shoreline of the Red Sea."

"That was how the Jewish people understood the events."

"But surely it was a mistaken understanding," I continued. "'God is love' and gave the command not to kill, yet He is depicted as causing the deaths of Israel's enemies."

"You can't speak for God. God is not limited by our understanding."

"But if the Bible describes God as a killer, doesn't that give us the wrong idea of who He is?"

"God is unknowable. You can't presume to understand His nature. I hope your understanding of the Scriptures is better than your theology." With that, I was silenced. But if God were so unknowable, why we were studying Him at all?

I asked several teachers what it meant, in practice, to love one's enemies. How could we do good to those who hated us or not ask for our property back, as the Gospel instructed, if someone robbed us? Did this mean we shouldn't defend ourselves? Did it mean we should just put up with cruelty and injustice to become the spiritual equivalent of a doormat? I didn't receive a satisfying answer.

The existence of hell was another sticking point with me. Those who cut themselves off from God's love might cease to exist, but I couldn't believe that they'd suffer eternally, because if people continued to suffer then the world would never be perfect. As at school, my teachers were irritated with my questions, and finally I stopped asking them.

At the end of 1973, Evelyn became a novice but kept her hair, in line with the decision made in Calcutta. Naomi and I were the last ones to have our hair cut early. Samantha, the other postulant, decided that this life was not for her and returned to Port Keats. A new group of trainees arrived: Lara from the south coast, Anthea from Sydney, Deidre from rural Victoria, and Leanne from Melbourne. Two novices also came out from India to be with Sister Evelyn.

The sisters were starting a new project on the outskirts of Melbourne. Sister Augustine, the professed sisters' superior and one of Mother's former students, was supervising the building of a new center called Corpus Christi, or Body of Christ, a place for men to retreat from the inner-city environment to help them become sober. It also housed men from the street who were too old and frail to continue roughing it in parks and alleyways. MC sisters were to staff the center. At Corpus Christi, the road to the right led to the sisters' two-story brick convent, which had living quarters upstairs and a chapel downstairs. Once it was completed, some of the sisters lived there, even before the men's center was completed, to supervise construction. On the left-hand side of the driveway was the men's building. From the beginning, Jesuit priests such as Fathers Phil Kurts and Brian Stoney worked with the sisters on the project, serving as chaplains and mentors for the men and living in the quarters with them.

Sister Augustine had tried to keep the building simple and functional, in line with the MC spirit, but she also had to comply with Australian building codes and regulations. The men's center had a large commercial kitchen, dining room, bathroom, and laundry facilities, and each man had his own room. Many of the men recovered there. They did their own cooking, as well as carpentry, gardening, and woodwork. One man, a pastry cook, had nearly died on a bender when he stayed at 101 Gore Street, but had recovered to supervise all the cooking in the new center.

In May 1974 it was getting close to the time of first profession for our senior novices, Sisters Annette, Karina, and Jocelyn. We other novices were to make our yearly, seven-day silent retreat with them. Fourteen of us drove in three cars to the house in Gordon, a small country town to the west of Melbourne near Ballarat, where a priest was to join us. In the afternoon before the silence of the seven-day retreat began, we went out to visit a farm that was the family home of one of our fellow novices. It was a picnic day before the retreat, so the strictures of daily life were more relaxed. There was a lady's pushbike on the side of the barn, so I tried to teach Sister Karina to ride it. We were a funny sight in our saris, as I ran behind her holding her seat and yelling at her to pedal while she kept squealing, frightened that I'd let her go.

The retreat began Thursday night without the priest, who was delayed a day due to flooding of some of the roads leaving Melbourne. Sister Regina did all the cooking for us so that we wouldn't be distracted. It was cold, so I chopped wood and looked after the fuel stove, the fire in the lounge room, and the chip-heater for hot water in the bathroom because I was familiar with them from home. It also helped me to think more clearly; I became stale just sitting inside.

The following Friday, when our time of prayer and reflection was over, we returned to Melbourne, decorated the refectory with leaves and branches brought with us from the country, and started cooking for the profession, which was the next day. We made congratulatory cards for the soon-to-be-professed. Carloads of Sister Annette's relatives came down for the ceremony from Sydney.

The sisters to be professed dressed in their new, blue-bordered saris and we all walked down to All Saints for the 8 a.m. Mass. The ceremony began with the Entrance Hymn to the Holy Spirit as the altar servers with lighted candles, the three sisters to be professed, Sisters Regina and Augustine, eight concelebrating priests, and Bishop Kelly processed up the aisle. The church was packed with family members, parishioners, and coworkers, there to witness the dedication of young lives to an ancient ideal.

After the sisters knelt together to make their vows in front of Sisters Augustine and Regina, they sang the hymn "All to Jesus I Surrender."

Then many of Sister Annette's relatives joined in a rousing Croatian offertory hymn, while at communion, Sister Karina and Sister Laboni sang a Hindi and then a Malayalam hymn with the aid of a microphone. Thus all the languages of the professed were represented during the Mass.

The parishioners, family members, and men from Gore Street came to celebrate with us and have a piece of cake. Later, after the community had a special lunch together, Sister Annette was allowed to go out with her family, while Sister Regina and one of the coworkers took Karina and Jocelyn out to the docks for a treat, to look over a Russian ship that was in port at the time. In the evening we put on a play that Sister Naomi had written for the newly professed, based on the biblical character Ruth, who left her family to marry and become part of God's chosen people. We had practiced the play in secret in one of the dormitories. It was difficult in such a small house to do anything without the senior novices knowing. After the profession, Sister Jocelyn was assigned to Bourke and Sisters Annette and Karina to the new men's center at Corpus Christi, in the suburb of Greenvale. Only the first wing had been completed, and ten men had moved in at the official opening.

At this point, Naomi, Elina, Laboni, and I became senior novices, keenly awaiting the day that we would finish our training and receive our own assignments. As second-years, we went out in the morning, visiting, teaching catechism in the state schools, or working at the Gore Street shelter. In the afternoon Sister Regina continued to give us classes on the Constitution, scripture, theology, and Church history. On Wednesdays and Sundays we went to Corpus Christi to replace the professed on their rest day and help with the cleaning, cooking, and serving.

Sisters Lara, Anthea, Deidre, and Leanne became first-year novices with the usual celebrations, and two junior professed sisters entered a period of tertianship, preparing for their final vows in Melbourne rather than returning to Calcutta. They lived a life similar to ours, with a half-day of work and the rest of the day filled with study and prayer. Sisters Regina and Monica and some Jesuit fathers taught them, but they lived separate from us in the professed house.

Around this time Rell, Bren, and Kim, my friends from high school, came to visit me. They looked me up and down. "Nice threads, Clot!"

Bren said, using my old nickname. We talked about our old school, university, nursing, and my visit to Sister St. Vincent for singing lessons, which they thought was hysterical as they knew I couldn't hold a note.

Liz, my friend from Moss Vale, also came to visit. She was horrified when she learned I had been begging at Victoria Markets, but she was polite as always. I later learned that she was angry with me and with the Church because she felt that I had betrayed my real self speaking with an Indian accent, dressing in Indian clothes, and throwing away, as she saw it, the chance to study and use my brain.

Sister Dolores became our superior, although Sister Regina was still in charge of the novitiate. We often didn't meet Sister Dolores's high standards and she stung us with a barrage of criticisms, often flipping her yellow woolen shawl over her shoulder as she spoke, eyes narrowing as she glared at us through her spectacles. Her lips were pursed together permanently, her resting expression a puzzled half-frown.

Sister Dolores loved to cook, or rather, to supervise others as they cooked, and we rarely measured up. The whole house would come to a standstill and all work cease if she decided to make particular curries or pastries for a feast day. If the dough wasn't rolled properly or the vegetables were cut the wrong way, she would sometimes knock the offending sisters on the head with her flexed index finger. "Cheh! I don't know how I put up with you people. Can't you do anything properly? Who made this rubbish?" She generated anxiety and confusion. I thought no meal was worth all the angst.

On the eve of one feast day Sister Dolores announced that we couldn't go out as planned for our usual visiting. "You'll be needed to help in the kitchen with the *singaras* and *paratas*," she commanded. This involved a lot of work: rolling dough, then filling and frying the pastries. I had promised a woman who lived alone in a house on Gertrude Street that I would go with her to a government office. "Sister, I've promised a lady that I'd go with her for an appointment with the Housing Commission. She doesn't understand English very well. Could we just go for a short time?"

"The world will survive, Tobit, if you don't go out for a day. Anyway, how are you going to help her? You can't speak Slovakian."

"We can explain her situation, and the problems she is having with the stairs."

"No, Tobit, you're not going."

"Then can we just run down and let her know we're not coming?" I knew I was pushing it.

"Tobit, go to the kitchen!" she exploded, with a flip of her shawl. "Do what you are told. She will manage without you. You are not that important."

The woman told us later that she had waited for us all afternoon and thought we had forgotten her.

In early 1975 the Fitzroy Council decided not to renew the license at the men's home at 101 Gore Street, as neighbors complained that the shelter was attracting drunks to the area. We closed it down and then worked to convert it into a novitiate. Some of the men went out to Corpus Christi; others moved to another shelter close by, run by the St. Vincent de Paul Organization. We cleaned and scrubbed 101, and some of the men from Corpus Christi repaired and painted it. For a while the professed and tertians lived there because Sister Regina didn't want to move the novitiate until after our profession in May, so that our spiritual preparation wouldn't be disturbed.

During Lent, a time of atonement, we gave up certain pleasures. One of the sacrifices we made was to wait an extra week before receiving our mail. In mid-February Mum rang, very upset, and Sister Regina allowed me to take the call. Something was very wrong.

"Did you get my letter?" Mum asked, crying.

"No. What's the matter?"

"I sent it last week. It should be there now," she replied, distraught.

"I'll ask Sister Regina. Maybe it's been delayed. What's happened?"

"Rod nearly died. He's still very sick. He had pneumonia and both his lungs have collapsed." Immediately, I wanted to be with her. A sense of panic rose in me, and I felt I had to go home quickly, worried he might die.

"Is he in Bowral Hospital?"

"No, they've transferred him down to Lewisham. I've been traveling to Sydney every day. He's had one operation and probably needs another one. I went to the court to find out where his father was. They wouldn't tell me, so I said, 'I thought he'd like to know his son was dying.'"

"So, could you contact him?"

"The court sent him a message. He came to the hospital once, and sort of took over. 'Don't you worry, I'll visit tomorrow,' he said. 'You can have a break from coming up from Moss Vale.' But he didn't show up. Rod was alone all day. His father never came back."

I didn't know what to do, so I consoled her as much as I could over the phone, then pleaded with Sister Regina to let me go home to be with my family.

"No, Tobit. You're making your first vows in two months, and no leave is allowed during the novitiate. If you give yourself to God, He will take care of those you love."

Preoccupied and distracted for days, I was torn between my chosen way of life and my family. I felt I was letting Mum down by not being there for her as well as the rest of the family. Sister Regina sent Rod and Mum a little note wishing him well and reassuring them that God loved him and Mum through it all. "The more God loves you the more He tries you," she wrote. All eight sisters in the novitiate with me then signed a note promising prayers for a quick recovery. After three weeks I received a letter saying Rod was home again with two "shark bite–like scars" on his back.

As the time of my first profession came closer, I knew I had to decide if I was able to make a commitment to God and the order, as I thought, for life. Clearly, there were going to be difficulties, but I was determined to dedicate my life to the service of the poor. This goal energized me; I thought it was the whole purpose of my life. Mother Teresa still inspired me. I wanted to reach out with her to those outside the gates of our society. Even though, as an MC sister, I was treated as a dependent child, I had come to believe that, if I gave all I had to God, He would use me to fulfill His purpose and help me overcome the problems and contradictions within the Society. No place was perfect, I reasoned.

On March 22, 1975, I received a handwritten letter from Mother

Teresa, confirming that I was permitted to make my first vows in May of that year and exhorting me to grow in prayerfulness and silence to learn to love others as Christ loved me. I was excited, thinking that soon I would be leaving the training house and starting the work I had joined to do. At recreation we talked about where we might be sent. I hoped to go to Africa or Asia.

Early that May a new intake of postulants included Doreen from New Zealand, Lacey from Australia, and three women from Singapore: Hua, Jun, and Mei-ying. Doreen had only recently converted to Catholicism, and the sisters from Singapore seemed very lost in a new country, trying to adapt to a very different way of life, but they were excited to know that Mother Teresa was soon to arrive and would welcome them into the Society.

Mother did come to Australia in time to make the preprofession retreat with us, which was to be given by the Cistercian abbot of Tarrawarra, Dom Kevin O'Farrell, at the convent at Corpus Christi. Before the retreat commenced, Mother spent a few days with us and gave us the news of the sisters worldwide. "The work in Africa is growing so much," she said. "God is good to us sisters. Already there are thirty African postulants in Addis Ababa and with them over a hundred Ethiopian aspirants. I will have to start a novitiate in Ethiopia to train them all. God cares for us. It's wonderful!

"In the Middle East, the situation is very uncertain," she continued. "In Amman our sisters were saved from being shot because, some time ago, Sister Damian and I picked up a man from the street who was suffering from gangrene. We sought medical help for him and the sisters nursed him back to health. The same man became a commander with the guerrilla fighters. He turned up at the place where the sisters were being held captive. He recognized Sister Damian as one of the women who had helped him. 'Let these women go!' he commanded. 'They do God's work.'

"There are many other stories I can tell you, Sisters."

She ranged over many topics in her talks with us. "Prayer is very powerful. In Gaza, the army was on the move and destroying everything—

burning houses and killing people. Our sisters and an order of Arabic-speaking nuns started a Novena [nine days of prayer] during which they said the Rosary constantly, night and day. On the ninth day, the army stopped just one street away from our convent."

She spoke to us of the lessons we should learn from this example. "Always remember, Sisters, 'Ask and you shall receive.' Soon, some of you will be making your first vows. If you really belong fully to God, you must be at His disposal to be used by Him as He pleases. Don't be preoccupied and worried. God is there. He will help you. The sisters in Gaza were very tense and worried. 'Should we leave, Mother?' they asked me. 'Many people are being killed.' 'No, Sisters,' I told them. 'Just let me know when you're dead!'"

I was taken aback by this seeming disregard for our sisters' safety, but Mother laughed and explained, "I knew God would protect them. From the time the sisters accepted this, they have been peaceful and happy, even in all the trouble. God will never forget you, Sisters. He is always there. He loves each of us individually and personally. He has carved you on the palm of His hand. Not even a sparrow falls to the ground without our Father knowing, so don't be afraid!"

Mother described herself and her sisters as the "spouses of Jesus crucified." By our consecration, we were to live out our vows and accept all suffering, sacrifices, and even death if it should come our way. Making our vows, she explained, was like making marriage vows; however, we were not committing ourselves to a human being but to Jesus crucified. I resisted reflecting on this marriage theme, because to me it was unhelpful and strange. I couldn't imagine myself married to Christ, and all that implied.

Mother also told us about Brother Andrew, an Australian who had been a Jesuit priest before joining with Mother to start the Missionaries of Charity brothers in 1963, of which he was servant general. Brother Andrew had sent all the brothers who had been working with him in Vietnam back to the safety of India because he feared Saigon would fall, but he remained to care for the people they had been looking after. One trainee brother refused to leave. "Even if you expel me from the brothers I will not leave you or the people," he told Brother Andrew. Mother said to pray for them because, if the troops broke through, they might both be shot. These stories make a deep impression on me.

We went out to Corpus Christi with Mother for the seven-day silent retreat, and I sensed she did not approve of the place, considering it too grand and modern to be part of the work of the MCs. There we listened to a talk each day from the abbot and another from Mother, and spent the rest of the time in prayer. We each saw Mother privately and made our confession to Dom Kevin.

During this time, I pondered why Mother was so sure that the sisters in the Middle East would be safe but was worried about Brother Andrew and his companion in Vietnam, who were under the care of the same God. I also thought of the people who had died before the ninth day of the Novena. They were as precious to God as the sisters; surely, they didn't die for lack of a few prayers.

On May 14, 1975, at the age of twenty-one, I knelt before Mother Teresa in All Saints Church Fitzroy, together with my group sisters Naomi, Laboni, and Elina, and committed myself to God and to the order. We dressed for the first time in a new blue *par* sari, which designated a professed sister, and then walked to the church, where everyone was gathered. Mum, Gran, Tony, Rod, and Judy drove down from Moss Vale for the profession. I was so happy to see Rod strong and well again. My friend Paul, who had become a brown-robed Franciscan friar, also attended, as did Naomi's family. Mother presented each of us with a cross, which we kissed and tucked into the rope tied around our waist. Along with the others, I made my first vows according to the prescribed formula:

> For the honor and glory of God . . . I consecrate myself wholly to Him in total surrender, loving trust and cheerfulness . . . in the presence of Mother Teresa MC, I, Sister Tobit Livermore MC, vow for one year Chastity, Poverty, Obedience, and Wholehearted and Free Service to the poorest of the poor according to the Constitution of the Missionaries of Charity.

Afterward I sat with my family talking and chatting in the front area of Gore Street, where the morning tea was held, and received cards and telegrams from my friends, uncles, aunties, and cousins. I had hardly seen Gran or the boys since I'd left home. We didn't go out because Gran couldn't walk far and the car was too small to take six. At lunchtime, while we in the community had a celebratory meal with Mother, my family was served their meal in the parlor.

Just before we took our places at lunch, Sister Regina called us sisters aside to say that Mother was about to announce our postings. After we had gathered and said the Grace before meals, Mother announced all the transfers, starting with the newly professed. Each announcement was greeted with shouts and clapping. "Sister Naomi, you will go to Katherine in the Northern Territory. Sister Elina, you are assigned to Bourke. Sister Laboni, you will leave for Port Moresby, and Sister Tobit, you will remain in the novitiate to help Sister Regina." I was dumbfounded. When I told Mum, she was happy that I was to remain relatively close, but I was devastated. I said nothing, but I felt that I was still waiting for my real life as an MC to begin. I wanted to prevent people dying from hunger and help those abandoned on the streets, not stay in the novitiate.

Our families left after lunch because two MC sisters were to make their final vows at St. Patrick's Cathedral and we newly professed were expected to attend. I wished I had been able to spend more time with my family after their 521-mile trip from Moss Vale, and I apologized that our visit was so rushed.

In contrast to our ceremony in the parish church, the final profession at the cathedral was less personal. Mother and our sisters were far away, up on the altar, and from where I sat were obscured by a pillar. The organ played, the congregation sang, but it seemed to lack spirit. When the sisters returned home, we formed an honor guard for them and showered them with flower petals. At night there were plays, songs, and dances. The novices put on a drama about St. Clare, the female equivalent of St. Francis, and a funny puppet show that had everyone in stitches. Mother said a few words, stressing the need to love each other, and gave her final blessing. The three others left with Mother that night to go to Corpus Christi.

I remained in the training house, feeling sad and flat. Mother had left, my family had come and gone, and yet, although I had attained my goal of making my first vows, I remained in the novitiate. After all the build-up, nothing much had changed for me. I sat on the floor at the back of the chapel trying to control my disappointment. "Apparently, Lord, it is your will that I don't escape from suburban Melbourne and the novitiate."

Sister Elina started out for Bourke at 4:00 the following morning; Sister Naomi went to Katherine a few days later; and Sister Laboni had to wait about two weeks for her flight to Port Moresby. Sister Regina, Sister Benedict, and I borrowed the parish priest's battered Cortina to see her off at Tullamarine Airport. Just before she disappeared into the overseas terminal I wished her well and hoped that one day I might join her. Father's car broke down on the way home. Sister Laboni was probably in Moresby before I reached the novitiate to assume my new duties.

CHAPTER FOUR

The Professed Life:
Still in Australia

*(Right to left) Mother Teresa, Pat Livermore and
Sister Tobit, Fitzroy, 1976. (Photographer: an MC sister)*

$\mathcal{I}$ had been looking forward to a new, exciting posting, but assignments in the MCs were never predictable. Nonetheless, it had never
crossed my mind that Mother would assign me to teach in the novitiate,
because those involved in training were usually experienced sisters, not

newly professed. Our assignments changed regularly, however, so it was self-protective to have no preferences. For instance one sister from the Bourke house had received a transfer to go to Manila and traveled down to Melbourne to apply for a visa to the Philippines. She returned to Bourke to work while she waited for it to be granted, only to find that, a few weeks later, her assignment was changed and she had to make the journey back to Melbourne to complete the paperwork for Papua New Guinea. This sort of thing often happened.

After our professions, the training house was moved into the two-story Gore Street site that had been refurbished after the men's shelter closed. Mother decided that Aspirancy, which is a six-month "come and see" period originally designed to help non-English-speaking sisters learn English, should be instituted in Australia. Naomi and I were exempted from this stage of training and had become postulants immediately on joining the Society, but Mother thought with sisters coming from different countries it was best to introduce it for all new sisters as a time of adjustment.

The five postulants, Sister Benedict, and I lived in one community. Within the same house Sister Regina stayed with the nine novices, four from India and five from Australia, in a separate community.

During the time of transition from halfway house to convent, several of the men who had lived at Gore Street climbed the front fence at night and tried to come up the external fire escape. Abby, who had completed her own training and become a well-behaved guard dog, chased them off.

Assigned to teach the novices and postulants what I barely knew myself, I taught three classes a day: Church History to the postulants and Church History and Moral Theology to the novices. I felt awkward teaching the novices because I had so recently been one of them, but after our term at the Assumption Institute no other group of novices did external studies, so I was asked to hand on what I had learned. Only a chapter ahead of them in the Church History, I had little time to prepare my classes. For a couple months I also fitted in driving lessons. One of the coworkers taught me. In spite of a few jerky starts, I got my provisional license within two months.

From 9:30 a.m. to 12 noon and from 3:30 to 7 p.m. I worked at the

St. Vincent de Paul Center for homeless men or went visiting with one of the postulants, usually Sister Hua, dutifully reciting the Rosary aloud with her at the traffic lights and doing work similar to what I had done as a postulant with Sister John. We visited elderly people who were basically trapped, alone in their apartments, and people with poor mobility in inner-city housing who had been referred to us by the St. Vincent de Paul Society or the coworkers. We did their shopping, washing, and cleaning and talked with them. Some were heavy drinkers, past caring.

I caught up again with Vince, the old chap from Gertrude Street, who still had no luck on the horses. Another regular was Bill. One day, while Sister Hua and I waited for another man's washing to finish at the Laundromat, we went to visit Bill up at the end of George Street. His room was still locked, which was unusual as he was always up early and sat at the front of his boardinghouse trying to catch the sun and chat with passers-by. He was unable to go out, as he could only walk a few yards. We called out and heard him grunt something in response. I couldn't see anything through the window and didn't want to have the door bashed down if he was just trying to sleep in, so I jumped up on the outside window ledge and looked through a crack at the top of the drawn blind. I could see his feet; he was lying on the floor, almost under the bed and wedged between the bed and the table. I jumped down and asked his neighbor to help us. He rammed the door open with shoulder charges and broke in so that we could attend to Bill, who was feverish and breathing fast. "Hang on, mate! We'll get you right again," I reassured him. "We're going to call an ambulance."

"Be buggered if I'm going to hospital!" he objected.

"I'm afraid you've got no choice, Bill, you can't stay here on the floor." He didn't put up much of a fight. He had collapsed with pneumonia, but after some antibiotics he was back to his wisecracking best when we visited him at St. Vincent's Hospital a few days later.

Another aspect of my work was to visit migrant families and help them adjust to life in Australia by putting them in touch with organizations that could help them learn English and find employment. Once a week I also went with the trainee sisters to relieve the professed at Corpus Christi for their day off. Fifty men lived there now, many of them old and sick, cared for by eight sisters. When we were there we helped prepare the tea, served meals, cleaned, and helped set up for breakfast. There was a nursing home in Collingwood that we visited as well, just to chat with the people there because many had no visitors. In addition, I was assigned to teach catechism at the Carlton State School for grades five and six and a first communion class on Saturdays.

For a while I took one of the postulants to help on a nocturnal soup run and try to warm up the men who slept in the wintry doorways of Melbourne's back lanes. They had only their coats as cover and newspapers under them to insulate their bodies from the cold concrete. One of them, an elderly Austrian man, had endured the concentration camps of the Second World War. I was sad that he was homeless in Melbourne after having survived that experience.

At the St. Vincent de Paul shelter we cooked and cleaned as we had at 101, but the place was much smaller and quite crowded for the twenty-five or so people who lived or ate there. One of the men there, called "the Captain," wore a Navy cap and walked around with all his belongings in a wagon, everything painted gold, including his TV and boots, except for some live chickens that roosted in the wagon and the dog he leashed to the handle. Once he lit a fire in the wastepaper basket in his room to try to cook a pig's head. We found him sitting on his mattress holding a fry pan over the blazing dustbin. We baked it for him in a more conventional stove.

In the wider world in 1975, Pol Pot came to power in Cambodia, Bill Gates was developing Microsoft, the Vietnam War was continuing as the Watergate scandal was rocking America, and Indonesia had invaded East Timor, killing tens of thousands of people, just four hundred miles from Darwin, Australia, the capital of the Northern Territory.

Our life at the convent went on largely oblivious to international events, except when Brother Andrew of the MC brothers arrived and alerted us to the fact that Saigon had fallen. He came to visit and say Mass for us, as he was originally from Melbourne, where his sister still lived. Thin, gaunt, and quiet-spoken, he told us about the MC brothers for whom we had prayed.

"The soldiers closed our houses and threw all our old people out onto the street," he explained. "Then I was expelled. One of our novice MC brothers, an American, was shot in Cambodia. It was a tragedy; he was only a young man. The others who had escaped earlier from Saigon were American and Dutch, but this fellow refused to leave. The others were only granted visas for three months in India and so couldn't complete their novitiate in Calcutta or have permanent refuge there."

"So where are they now, Andrew?" Sister Regina asked.

"In Los Angeles. The five of them have set up a house there. None of the brothers from India could accompany them, as they didn't have an America visa, so they left on their own. The most senior brother is only twenty-two."

"He must be one of the youngest religious superiors in the world," said Sister Regina, a little taken aback.

"I'd say that was a fair bet," replied Andrew. "I'm now organizing visas for some of our senior brothers to go over from India, but it all takes time. While I was in Vietnam, I couldn't do much as the situation was so unstable and I had no means of communication. But soon I'm hoping to start houses in Taiwan, Korea, and Japan."

After a short break he returned to Calcutta to resume his work.

In June 1975 the nurses in the psychiatric hospital at Kew, a large facility covering many acres and housing hundreds of patients with varying degrees of disability, went on strike for some days. We knew the Kew cottages as we visited there on Sunday afternoons, so all fifteen of us went to help, eight on the day shift and seven at night. Our classes were suspended, and the Kew central office assigned the volunteers their wards. Some of the patients were in a vegetative state, unable to sit or talk. I cared for women with Alzheimer's disease who, when we arrived in the morning, were cold, wet, and restrained. We bathed, toileted, and fed them. Even though they had no conscious memory of the day before, they seemed to have an emotional memory that kindled a spark of recognition when we greeted them again the following day. It was tragic that the culmination of the lives of these once vibrant, energetic people was this helpless, confused state.

• • •

In December 1975 Sisters Evelyn, Rosa, and Saranya were professed. My former postulant mistress, Sister Christine, came down from Katherine for retreat. I was happy to meet up with her again and to hear news of Naomi and her work among the Aboriginal people. Around this time Sisters Annie and Francesca came out from India to go through the novitiate with Sister Lara's group, which was to be professed the following December.

The day before the profession was the hair cutting and many squeals came from Sister Regina's "barber shop room." It was such a big thing, especially for an Indian woman, to lose her hair. Evelyn's large family drove up from Sale and packed into the church. The Indian sisters had only their MC community to celebrate the day with them. After Mass we had about a hundred to serve for morning tea. Then all the sisters in Melbourne came to share lunch, after which Sister Regina announced that Sister Rosa was assigned to Hanuabada, in Port Moresby, to join Sister Laboni; Sister Evelyn went to Bourke, where Elina was working; and Saranya went back to Katherine with Sister Christine. I sent a letter back with her to Naomi telling her all the news from Melbourne.

At Christmastime we prepared for a party for the poorer children from the inner city, many of whom were of migrant background. We wrapped a hundred donated presents in four different colors to denote age group and sex so that they would be easy to distribute. Then we set out in several hired buses to the Salesian Agricultural College at Sunbury, where the children had a great time participating in races, playing games, and jumping on the trampolines. They loved the spaciousness of the grounds and contact with the animals, patting the horses and watching a quail and her tiny chicks. After the party was over we packed and distributed seventy or so care packages for our oldies, including Vince and Bill.

The coworkers were busy helping us for the Christmas celebrations, as well as collecting funds and goods to send to people suffering from a famine in Gujarat, a state of India. Sister Augustine asked me to speak at a fund-raising night along with a companion. We showed a brief documentary film, and then I described what the sisters were doing to help in the famine. This stirred up strong feelings within me as I wanted to be working in Gujarat, not talking about it. After two and a half years with the Society I felt no closer to my original goal of helping the poor. I went to talk to Sister Regina. "I don't feel like I'm doing the work I joined to do. I felt upset talking to the coworkers about people starving in India, while I'm quite comfortable here in Australia."

"Tobit, you are not a Missionary of Charity to do a particular type of work, but to give yourself wholly to God. You just have to be patient. Your time will come. You have surrendered your mind and will over to God, to be used by Him as it pleases Him. Be as faithful as you can where you are. Bloom where you are planted. Don't seek to do your own will."

"Yes, Sister," I said, doing my best impersonation of an obedient nun, though I didn't feel I was making any contribution to redressing the inequality in the world. Sister Regina asked me to say the Prayer of Abandonment of Father Charles de Foucauld to learn "total surrender." Father Foucauld had lived and worked among the poor for a time as a manual laborer. For him and for Mother's patron, St. Thérèse of Lisieux, the ordinary tasks of everyday life were imbued with holiness if done with love and attention.

> Father, I abandon myself into your hands; do with me what you will. Whatever you may do, I thank you: I am ready for all, I accept all. Let only your will be done in me, and in all your creatures—I wish no more than this, O Lord. Into your hand I commend my soul. I offer it to you with all the love of my heart, for I love you, Lord, and so need to give myself to surrender myself into your hands without reserve, and with boundless confidence, for you are my Father.

My frustration continued, in spite of my prayers, as the postulants, novices, and I helped pack fifty tea chests full of the canned milk, clothes, and soap that the coworkers had collected. I dreamed of getting closer to the action rather than acting as a dispatch clerk for goods to India, but I continued in my duties, teaching and visiting those living on the margins of inner-city Melbourne.

Sister Regina reinforced her message to me that doing God's will was more important than doing difficult things. Jesus, although He was God, had remained in the backwaters of Nazareth, obedient to Mary and Joseph until he was thirty, doing nothing noteworthy. All this time, He was being prepared by the Father for His public ministry. Sister Regina felt that I needed further "purifying" before I was let loose on the world.

During the Chinese New Year Sister Regina and I dressed up as Chinese elders, complete with ponytails made from our sisters' hair that had been kept from the hair cutting, to deliver little red gift packets to our homesick Singaporean postulants. They laughed so much at our beards, moustaches, and walking sticks that they forgot to wish us long life and good health, as was customary when visited by persons of such venerable age.

In May 1976 I renewed my vows for the first time in the chapel at the Corpus Christi center with Sister Karina and Annette, who were working there and who had been professed a year before me. Sister Karina had been quite sick since her profession and had spent time in hospital with a blood disorder and then a broken leg. Sister Jasmin, the classical dancer from Kerala, left quietly and returned to India, having decided not to renew her vows. I didn't get to say good-bye and I have often wondered if she fitted back into her traditional fishing community, a beautiful young woman with very short hair that would have branded her for a time with the stigma of being an ex-nun.

In June Sister Benedict, or Spitfire, was transferred back to India after seven years in Australia. We took her to the airport carrying three large pink-and-white teddy bears that the prisoners at Pentridge Gaol had made for her. Her mother was dying, which may have been why she was allowed to return home. The men at Corpus Christi, the prisoners, and those on the streets respected Sister Spitfire, whose small frame often shook with laughter and who never shirked hard work.

There were other comings and goings among the sisters. The Kiwi postulant Doreen and the Aussie Lacey left the Society, but Hua, Jun, and Mei-ying were to be received as novices when Mother came. Two Australians joined for a few months but decided the MC life wasn't for them, and Sister Evelyn, who had been in Bourke, left unexpectedly. Just before

Mother arrived five new aspirants joined us: Ling from Hong Kong, Reka from New Zealand, Marion from Sydney, Ann from West Australia, and Madeline from the Philippines.

That October we learned that Mother Teresa was in the Philippines opening a house in Manila to care for sick children, as well as a new novitiate, which meant our Australian novitiate would close and the Australian trainees would move to the Philippines to complete their formation. Because there were many young women in the Philippines seeking to join the order and few in Australia, this change made sense. Mother planned to come to Melbourne after her visit to Manila to receive the December group's first vows and to hand over Corpus Christi Men's Center to the Jesuits.

Sister Dolores assigned us sisters to pack tea chests with donated toys for a new foundation, called Kerema, in the remote Gulf province of Papua New Guinea. I didn't know what conditions the sisters would face there, but from what I had heard at school they were very basic. I thought soap, clothes, flashlights, tools, mosquito nets, notebooks and paper, pencils, and balls might be more useful than the white dolls, plastic novelties, and trucks that we were packing. I asked Sister Dolores, "Sister, do you think these things might be out of place up in New Guinea?"

"No. Why do you think that?"

"Well, the village children might have never seen toys like this."

"How do you know that? Anyway, don't you think poor children deserve a little happiness? The sisters can give them out at Christmas." She frowned as she stood erect and straightened the blue border of her sari. "Can you ever just do what you are told?"

I returned to my packing in silence, and the goods were shipped off to Kerema to await the new foundation.

Toward the end of 1976 I knew I was about to be sent somewhere, because I was asked to write home for my birth certificate in order to apply for a passport, and some time later, I signed the last page of a visa application.

Mother Teresa's visit and the professions generated the usual excitement, but her own frequent change of plans and dates made it difficult to organize the retreat and travel plans of family and friends attending the profession. In the end, she came in late November and five sisters made their first vows before her at All Saints Church. The Essendon parish choir sang the Mass, livening up the inner-city parish with many guitars, drums, and a glockenspiel.

We had a special lunch of Vindaloo curry and rice and a sweet called halva, and Sister Regina made a trifle with liberal use of some altar wine. A relative of Mother's who had immigrated to Australia, and whom we called Auntie, also brought special food, including stuffed hot peppers, baked potatoes, and chicken. Mother had previously scolded Auntie and told her not to spoil us, but fortunately she took no notice and often brought us treats.

Mother announced the assignments after lunch, when I found out that I was going to the new house in Kerema. Sister Karina, who had been my companion in the novitiate, was also assigned there, and Sister Margaret, a gentle woman from Bombay who had made her final vows in Australia, was to be our superior. I asked Anthea's parents, who were visiting from Sydney for her profession, to ring Mum and tell her where I was going. I was very happy to be leaving Melbourne.

In the evening the novices, postulants, and I put on a play and performed songs, dances, and skits for Mother and the other sisters. The play was based on the life of a Polish priest named Maximilian Kolbe, who had died in a German concentration camp in Auschwitz. Three prisoners had escaped, and so the Nazis randomly selected ten men from the assembled inmates to die. A Polish sergeant who had been selected for execution cried out, "My poor wife and children!" At that, Kolbe stepped forward and volunteered to go to take his place. His offer was accepted and the commandant sent him, with the others, to the starvation block. After several days, the nine others had died of hunger and dehydration, but Kolbe hung on and had to be finished off with a lethal injection. The Polish sergeant whom Kolbe replaced survived the war, and Kolbe himself was later canonized in 1982. Mother liked the play and its theme of giving up one's life for others and said she would take a copy back to Calcutta.

As we made preparations to leave for Papua New Guinea, I asked Sister Dolores if I should take something to prevent malaria, because my high school friends from there, Peggy and Agnes, had suffered periodically from attacks of malaria and said people had died from it in their villages. Sister Dolores thought it wasn't necessary but said I could ask Sister Felicity when I reached Port Moresby.

While Mother was in Australia for the profession we held the ceremony to hand over Corpus Christi to the Jesuits, which was difficult for us sisters, as we had become attached to the men. It must have been particularly hard for Sister Augustine, for she had worked on the project since the time I'd joined.

I had worked patiently in Melbourne for people whom the Society called the "spiritually poor." I had never been sure what the term meant, as we were all spiritually poor. I had joined the order to work with people who were lacking basic necessities. I wanted to bridge, in some small way, the chasm between the lifestyle we experienced in Australia and the hardship encountered in other parts of the world. I felt underemployed teaching catechism and visiting. Mother said, "It's not how much you do but how much love you put into the work." Nonetheless, I was not satisfied. I wanted to do the work that she had done in the beginning, the work I thought she had founded the order to do.

Soon, I hoped, I would be.

CHAPTER FIVE

Bilums and Betel Nuts

*Arrival in Kerema, 1977. Archbishop Copas (far left),
Mother Teresa (center), members of the MC community, and
students of St. Peter's Extension School.*

On January 27, 1977, Mother and a carload of sisters said farewell to Sisters Margaret, Karina, Samantha, and me on the Air Niugini flight from Tullamarine to Papua New Guinea. We were to wait in Port Moresby for Mother to join us in a few weeks and then go with her to Kerema. Our visa conditions stated that we had to enter the country by February 1, so we needed to go on ahead of her.

As we flew over the mountains close to Sydney, I scanned the country-side for a glimpse of home, wondering when I would see my family again. When we disembarked at Jackson's Airport in Port Moresby, the heat was like an oven blast. Our group was the last to approach the customs bench, our boxes and bedrolls fastened with rope, and the tired officials waved us through. The waiting sisters greeted us excitedly, among them Sister Felicity, whom I had first contacted in Bourke about my interest in joining the Missionaries of Charity; Sister Laboni, my group sister; and Sister Rosa, who had been with us in the novitiate. Sister Anthea, who had only recently been professed, had arrived a few weeks before us.

We piled into the back of their truck onto wooden benches covered by a canopy for our trip from the airport to Hanuabada, a seaside suburb of Moresby. I hung on tightly as we careered around hills at high speed. Coconut palms, chili bushes, and utes packed with people flashed past as we negotiated the winding roads. Gardens of bananas, papayas, and tapioca dotted the steep hillsides on the town's periphery.

We slowed slightly on the crowded streets around the markets, where vendors guarded little mounds of vegetables displayed on the ground. The women were dressed in their distinctive, brightly colored *meri* blouses—long, loose blouses with round necklines and short puffed sleeves, and lap laps—lengths of cloth tied at the waist like a sarong. Both were made of colorful prints depicting birds of paradise, fierce warriors, *kundu* drums, and hibiscus flowers. They carried babies or heavy loads in *bilums,* or string bags hand-crocheted out of natural fiber and slung over their heads. At first I mistook the red betel nut stains around their mouths as a sign of illness. I was fascinated to see that the Papuans' tightly curled hair was used to store all sorts of things: pens, combs, and even the car mechanic's tools.

The sisters at Hanuabada took chloroquine each Sunday to prevent malaria, though it wasn't as big a problem in Port Moresby as in the rest of the country because the city had a mosquito eradication program. They lived in a two-story house on the edge of the bay with a stony beach for the front yard. The sound of the gently lapping waves and an occasional sea breeze filtered through the louvered glass of the chapel windows. The adjoining thatched, raw wood, stilt houses were built out over the bay on both sides of a rough jetty. Groups of children jumped and dived into the sea while others fished from dugout canoes.

Papua New Guinea is divided into two areas by a central mountain range. Northern New Guineans use mainly Tok Pisin, or Pidgin English, as their lingua franca, while Papuans in the south use a simplified form of Motu, the language of Hanuabada. Not knowing what language was spoken in Kerema, we started to learn some Pidgin and Motu words while we waited for Mother. These linking languages are very necessary in the culturally diverse, mountainous country, which has over seven hundred indigenous languages.

The sisters who had already been stationed in PNG when we got there expected changes in their assignments and thought they might be going to Kerema instead of us, so I started to feel insecure about my posting. The powerlessness I had felt back in Melbourne returned, knowing that my fate was always in the hands of others.

After a few weeks Mother arrived to much rejoicing, and we left for Kerema as originally planned. The five of us waited for hours on a grassy airstrip, surrounded by our bedrolls and boxes, scanning the sky for the plane to arrive. Mother said that if we prayed with faith the plane would come, and it did finally arrive, but in Papua New Guinea time—very late. Prior to boarding, the pilot weighed all the passengers and their luggage. I came in at 114 pounds.

We flew low over serpentine rivers, coastal islands, and groups of huts perched on bare clay mountaintop clearings, the brown of the bare earth contrasted with the intense green of the surrounding jungle.

At last, I thought, this is the real thing.

When we reached Kerema, Archbishop Copas, a tall, erect man with unruly white curly hair, and a group of young Papuans waited to greet us, having heard the light plane as it circled overhead. As we scrambled out of the hatch the students helped unload our boxes and bedrolls. The bishop warmly welcomed Mother as the students sang a welcome song and wreathed us with garlands of hibiscus. We then piled into the bishop's four-wheel drive for the short trip up to St. Peter's Extension School, where we were to live and work.

Our convent was on the smaller, top floor of the airy wooden building. On the second floor were classrooms and our bathroom and kitchen facilities. The bishop's quarters were also in a walled-off section of the second story. He lived a simple life and welcomed visitors from the rural areas who often camped at his place overnight. The school and boarders' quarters occupied the ground floor. At the back of the school beyond the playing fields was the church, a wooden building with rough benches and open windows all along the side walls. The backdrop to the altar was a Papuan Christian mural with traditional designs and colors.

The church buildings were on flat, elevated land rimmed by coconut palms and overlooking Kerema Bay. The village market was close by, and there was a store in town run by Chinese merchants. Below us, hugging the shoreline, were thatched huts erected on poles and accessed by rough ladders. Dugout canoes ebbed back and forth on the gentle waves and fallen coconuts bobbed up and down like buoys. Chickens and pigs foraged under the huts. Small boys scampered up nearly vertical coconut trees and sat up in the palms, shaking the tree until the coconuts fell.

Our bishop was compassionate, conservative, and emotionally contained. He had been archbishop of Port Moresby, but in 1975, just after Papua New Guinea attained independence from Australia, he resigned in favor of an indigenous bishop. The Vatican then appointed him bishop of Kerema, but he retained his title of archbishop. In his early sixties, he still went on foot throughout his diocese, meeting villagers who had never seen a European before.

The bishop had started St. Peter's, with only one national teacher, in order to train the many teenagers from the tribal areas who had dropped out of school after only one or two years and so had become too old to attend a regular elementary school. The surrounding area was dense jungle with only a few poorly maintained roads. It was a long walk from their villages to the school, and there was nowhere for them to stay in town, so the bishop started a boarding school for them. The Kerema youth were drifting into Port Moresby, into the hands of the "rascal" (criminal) gangs and trouble with the law. Upset that his boys were ending up in jail convicted of theft, assault, and murder, the bishop thought that if he could help the young people become literate and learn math and English, they would have the skills to start local industries and wouldn't feel they needed to leave Kerema. In their own province, family networks, traditional taboos, and culture supported them, but in the anarchy of

Moresby's urban sprawl, customary law broke down and the newly independent government was struggling to cope.

The students at St. Peter's School generally had a poor grasp of English and spoke a collection of tribal languages. Both boys and girls attended the school, but the boys were in the majority, and only boys were boarders. They were tough, athletic, and good at ball games. They ran up nearly vertical slopes with ease and climbed trees in pursuit of the possum-like creature called a cuscus, which they then added to their dinner menu. They also had their own gardens for vegetables but otherwise the bishop provided the boarders' food, which they cooked themselves.

The bishop, Mother, our superior, Sister Margaret, and the national teacher discussed how the sisters would work in the school. I was assigned to teach two to three classes a day of English and math, at about the fourth-grade level. I was also to teach an agricultural subject, which included on its syllabus copra production, a process by which the white flesh of coconuts is sun-dried on mats to prevent spoiling, then bagged and sold for oil production. Crocodile husbandry to produce skins to make shoes and handbags was another topic I needed to cover. My knowledge of these two subjects was nonexistent; I had never seen a crocodile and had only recently discovered that coconuts had outer husks. I was grateful that the national teacher could provide some printed teaching material and student notes.

I taught eleven periods a week and kept an eye on the self-sufficient boarders, encouraging them to study and practice English, and helped sort out any conflicts they had among themselves. They were managing independently when we arrived, but I made sure none of them was sick, that their dormitories were clean, that they had all they needed in the way of soap and other basics.

When we opened the tea chests containing the toys that Sister Dolores had shipped ahead of us, Mother was annoyed. I was there helping her unpack them and she was cross with me, pushing the chests angrily across the room. "Did you pack these things, Sister?"

"Yes, Mother. I helped pack them."

"Look at these toys—white dolls in lace clothing. What were you thinking of? Do you think these children are Australians? This is a terrible waste sending toys like this over here, and it will not be good for the people. They are not to be given out."

"Yes, Mother."

It was not a good time to remind Mother of her teaching: "A superior can make a mistake in commanding, but you cannot make a mistake in obeying." She must have known the decision was not mine. I was soon in trouble again as I hurriedly prepared tea for the community and left the kitchen untidy. Mother liked tidiness. "Do small things well, Sister," she chided.

Sister Felicity had given us only a few chloroquine tablets from their supply, so I approached Mother. "Mother, could we get some more tablets from the hospital to prevent malaria?"

"I don't take anything," she said. "I leave it in God's hands. But you take it if you need to."

I thought, *God provided us with chloroquine,* so I went to the hospital with Sister Karina to get the tablets. The doctor told us that the Gulf Province had a lot of malaria of the more serious *falciparum* or cerebral type, which could be fatal.

Mother returned to Port Moresby and we newcomers set about exploring our environment. The PNG culture was fascinating: betel nuts, *bilums,* men's houses, penile gourds, and fierce, masked dancers. On special occasions, *sing-sings* were held on the local oval where grass-skirted warriors with feather headdresses chanted and danced to the rhythm of the handheld *kundu,* an hourglass-shaped drum made from one piece of hollowed-out wood, with a handle carved at the side and lizard or goanna skin pulled tightly over the top. Singing was a part of life. Most of the violent tribal wars that had characterized the nation had stopped, and young men from rival clans now studied at the same school. Sometimes at night the boys would sing around a fire to the beat of their drums.

Every night in the wet season violent tropical storms erupted. Lightning flashed and a heart-stopping thunderclap followed immediately. Despite the heavy rainfall that we collected in water tanks, we often ran short. The demands of the school, plus the needs of the boarders and the villagers borrowing water, exceeded what we could collect. The situation worsened when a rat drowned in our big tank and we had to discard all the water. For a short while we had to bathe and clean the house with seawater that we bucketed up from the bay, and we reserved the rainwater only for drinking and cooking.

At first I found it incongruous to hear the bishop's cultured voice say the Pidgin English Mass at our local church. He used *bagarap,* from the Australian slang "buggered up," which meant, in pidgin, damaged or tired and not well, to describe the sufferings of Jesus; the term "fruit of the vine" was translated as *pikinini bilong grape,* or "child of the grape." When learning Pidgin the temptation for English speakers was just to add *-im* to the end of the English word, but that could cause real misunderstandings. One day our car got bogged down in the mud road and I called out to the boys who had jumped out to help us push, "Pushim!" They fell about laughing, and only then did I discover that the right word was *siubim,* from "to shove." What I had said sounded like *pusim,* "to have sex." The word for "to get" is *kisim,* and at first I was amused to hear the boys saying "Kisim buk bilong mi" (I will get my book).

I was often confused as I tried to learn the language. A little boy I knew had malaria, and I was told, "Sister, em i dai," and became upset because I thought that he'd died. But the expression for "to die" was *dai pinis.* The child had only fainted.

Along with Pidgin and Hiri Motu we were trying to learn Torapi, the language of Kerema Bay. Initially we didn't realize that the students originated from several different areas and spoke nine different local dialects and languages. Some were from the mountain regions and others from the coast, but we didn't know the difference, so the words for simple objects kept changing depending on whom we asked. A young woman, Uva, who attended the school, became my main teacher of Torapi.

Sometimes we visited Waripi, on the other side of the bay, by motorized dinghy skippered by one of the students. After we beached the dinghy we set out along a bush road lined with coconuts, wild pineapple, and sago palms. The sea was often rough, and I walked with a soaked sari clinging like an octopus around my legs. To the side of the bush roads women dug sago pulp from felled palms to make a form of starch used in cooking, while in the villages they sat in front of the huts and rolled out soaked tree bark fiber on their thighs to make string. They then skillfully knotted it into *bilums*. Often only children, women, and old men inhabited these villages, because the younger men had strayed to the bright lights of Moresby. After one of these trips, Sister Margaret decided that Sister Samantha should start taking sewing lessons at Waripi so that the women could make clothes for their families and thus save money, as goods were very expensive in the town store.

We visited the Kerema Hospital on Sundays, where I saw my first person with leprosy. The hospital was crowed and chaotic, the mattresses dirty and without sheets or pillows. Family members slept on the floor near the patients to care for them and provide food.

The women in Kerema attributed illnesses such as pneumonia, malnutrition, malaria, and problems associated with childbirth to black magic, or *puri puri*, and feared sorcerers who, they believed, had power over their lives. Ancient spells were generally credited with giving shamans the ability to travel from one place to another in an instant and to have a watching eye everywhere, able to witness events without being present. Often these beliefs prevented the women from seeking medical help for themselves and their children, so deaths from treatable illnesses such as malaria were common. When we visited villages with our students as translators we tried to convince the parents to take their sick, malnourished children to the hospital clinic for medicine. We were able to give extra milk and food to some children who received treatment for tuberculosis. Even though they lived close to the sea, not everyone had access to fish; cassava and sweet potato supplemented by seasonal vegetables weren't nutritious enough for the young children.

Following the example of the locals, we sisters made a garden on the side of the hill next to our house for native crops such as paw-paw, bananas, sweet potato, and tapioca. I also planted seeds Mum had given me to grow beans, tomatoes, and squash. Long white habits and saris are not ideal clothes to wear while clearing steep muddy hillsides. Already renowned for my unique standard of neatness, I now had a sari adorned with rust, banana, and coconut stains.

About a month after we arrived we heard that Sister Lara, a nurse who had been professed the previous year and assigned to Bourke, was coming to join us. She was to join Sister Margaret in starting some dispensary work in remote communities on the other side of the bay.

One night I awoke shivering and shaking violently. "Samantha! Wake up!" I tried to rouse the sister next to me in the dormitory, but she shrugged me off as a *klama* (ghost). I got up to search for blankets, and finally Sister Samantha stirred.

"What are you doing, Tobit? It's stifling. Take those blankets off."

"I'm freezing. Colder than I've ever been in my life. My head feels like it will explode."

"You've got a fever. I'll call Sister Margaret."

My teeth chattered, my body shook, and a searing pain exploded in my head. The sisters gave me some paracetamol for the fever. The next day I was alone in the third-floor dormitory, vomiting, feverish, and too sick to work. The pain in my head and back was unrelenting. My tongue started to protrude involuntarily and my back and neck arched in spasm. I was frightened and thought I was dying. I could see the sisters down at the markets; I was conscious but couldn't call out. When they finally came home and saw what I was like, they rushed out again to call the doctor from the hospital. He diagnosed cerebral malaria and gave me an intravenous injection to stop the seizures and a quinine infusion. Rather than take me to the hospital he hung the drip right in the room and Sister Margaret, who had done some medical work in India, looked after it. She told me later that the doctor said I was having seizures because of the large number of parasites interfering with blood flow to my brain. He also said I was in danger of having a stroke or damaged kidneys. She called for the bishop to give me Anointing of the Sick, as there was some concern that I might die.

Our ceiling was not lined, and lying in bed under the mosquito net I imagined I could see rats scurrying along the rafters and hiding behind the silver insulation. I thought a rat had fallen onto my mosquito net and I felt a rat on my back as I opened the toilet door. I could see and feel them, but the sisters told me that I was delirious. There were no rats.

My immunity was impaired and I contracted pneumonia, had tropical ulcers on my legs, anemia, and an infected, swollen knee. The concerned students said someone must be working *puri puri* against me and warned me not to let any of my clothing or personal belongings go astray.

During my recovery I went to the public outpatient clinic, where I felt like a rare zoo exhibit as everyone crowded around to see the doctor check my white chest. The sisters from India had some immunity against the malarial parasite, but I seemed to have no defense. I went back to work after about two weeks, but was very weak. The initial illness seemed to have changed me; I was more emotional and had surges of anger that I battled to control, such as when I was accidentally locked out of the convent after night prayer when I went to check on one of the boarders who was sick. I felt inexplicably upset and frustrated and began to cry, which was unusual for me. It may have been because I was just run down, but I felt different.

I returned to my teaching and visiting routines, but over the next few months I became ill several times with recurrences of fever and shivering, though no attack was as bad as the first one. Sister Karina was also sick, so in early May we were both sent to Port Moresby in a single-engine mission plane, the pilot a priest from the mountain station of Kanabea. We encountered a storm and flew through lightning, the turbulence tossing the plane up and down like a yo-yo. My heart thumped with each clap of thunder. Eventually we landed safely and Karina and I were admitted to the infectious diseases ward at Port Moresby Hospital.

After a course of quinine my blood films were negative, so the doctors said I could return to Kerema on chloroquine. If I contracted malaria within a month of returning I was to take a ten-day course of quinine, and after that a double dose of chloroquine each week. Sister Karina was discharged as well.

Sister Felicity was angry that we had to pay for our treatment, probably because we were not PNG citizens, because she had thought it would be free. Embarrassed, I stood listening to her argue heatedly over the bill. I don't know if, in the end, we paid it or not.

I enjoyed what I was doing in PNG and wanted to continue with my work, but the repeated attacks had weakened me and made me anemic.

My greatest fear was that I would be sent away from Kerema and back to Australia. Sister Felicity kept both Karina and me in Hanuabada for a week, where we were to sleep in until six each morning and have an egg for breakfast each day. I was uncomfortable with this special treatment, but unfortunately, very soon after going back to the Gulf, I again contracted malaria. Instead of allowing me to follow the doctor's plan for quinine and then a double dose of chloroquine, I was sent back to Moresby in case I got worse. After my seizures during the last bout with the parasite Sister Margaret had wanted me to leave, but Sister Karina, who also contracted malaria again, followed through with the planned treatment, and recovered. I was disappointed that I wasn't allowed to do the same.

The malaria parasite's resistance to chloroquine was not reported in the medical journals until the 1980s, but it may well have started to manifest itself in the late 1970s there in Papua New Guinea. I fully recovered in PNG and did not suffer many long-term effects from my encounters with malaria, apart from ongoing headaches that were sometimes quite severe. Much later, in 2005, a scan detected damage to the white matter of my brain.

I flew back to Port Moresby in a Douglas Airline mail plane in early June, and as I was the only passenger, I occupied the copilot's seat. The pilot had to go up to Kanabea in the mountains behind Kerema rather than straight to Moresby. From the air I could see small brown figures making the steep ascent to their mountaintop villages. At first I didn't recognize them as women, as they wore bark veils that shaded their babies, who lay in the fetal position in a *bilum* slung from their mother's head. Holes in the sling bags provided a natural air-conditioning for the baby. It was customary for a woman to carry huge loads on her head while her husband walked, unencumbered, carrying only a spear.

The hillsides were dotted with gardens of *kau kau* (sweet potato), bananas, and cassava, and the villagers had cut the landing strip out of the side of a mountain. It was short and had a precipitous drop at either end. "They're bloody treacherous, these highland strips," the pilot, Jim, said as he lined the plane up with the rough runway.

"Because of the weather?"

"Yeah, there's that too, but these mountains have tricky downdrafts. If we cut our engines off too early, we might fall short, but if we approach too quickly, we could overshoot at the other end."

I nervously eyed the steep, jungle-clad slope.

"Happened to me once," he volunteered. "It was a bloody close thing. I went over the edge at the other end and had a hell of a time pulling her up. I'd lost my revs. Had a holiday after that little trip!"

Thud! We were down. We bumped along the strip as huts and an elongated European-style building sped past.

A lanky Australian priest named Father Flynn came down to meet the plane with a swarm of children. The highlanders who gathered around the plane were short and muscular, with cropped, tightly curled hair. Some dressed in Western T-shirts and shorts, while others wore grass skirts and strings of fine, brown beads. "I reckon the weather's coming in," the priest said, gesturing in the direction of the low-lying clouds. I had met Father Flynn before, when he had filled in for our bishop on a few occasions, and he showed me around the medical clinic and school.

The fog rolled in as predicted, and since there was no possibility of taking off, we settled down to a cup of black tea and baked sweet potato. After about four hours there was a break in the weather and we used the opportunity to become airborne again. On the way back to Moresby Jim asked me to hold the controls while he went to the rear of the plane; thankfully, I didn't have to do anything, and Jim returned to take over again. We talked a lot during the flight, and he invited me to a meal with his family in Moresby. He couldn't understand why I didn't accept his invitation.

The sisters had been at the airport to meet me, but when I failed to arrive they assumed I wasn't coming and returned home. Because I couldn't contact them when we finally did land, Jim offered to drop me at Hanuabada and I accepted. I arrived very late, and Sister Felicity was angry because I had not asked permission to visit Kanabea! But I had had no choice in the matter: I was in a plane and it was going to Kanabea. I was in trouble too for being alone with Jim in the car. *No different from the plane*, I thought, but didn't say anything. It wasn't a good start to life in my new community.

• • •

The Missionaries of Charity are often criticized by other religious orders and medical practitioners for their lack of training for the work they undertake. At least those of us in Papua New Guinea could have been much better prepared for our work. If, as soon as our assignments were known, we had been told where we were going and what we were expected to do, we could have researched information about the language and the general conditions we were to face. But we were not given the time or resources, such as permission to use the phone, to do this. In Melbourne several other religious orders had branches that were already working in the Gulf province and could have advised us how to prepare for our work. Even if we had only bought Pidgin English and Hiri Motu books, which were easily available, it would have been such a help. But we lived in a culture of deprivation and isolation. Relying on Divine Providence seemed to mean that we didn't buy items such as books to help with our work, even though money was donated to us for this very purpose.

It also seemed to mean that our health as sisters was to be put at risk unnecessarily. I almost did have to make that call to Mother Teresa to let her know I was dead, just as she had joked with the sisters in the Middle East. If I had died or become disabled, the order would have said, "It's God's will," yet simple measures such as seeking medical advice, taking chloroquine two weeks before we left Australia, using mosquito repellents, becoming informed about malaria, and having a readily available treatment dose for the disease if the preventive measures failed could have averted the whole scenario. The assumption that God's loving care would protect us was used by the order to justify a dangerous lack of foresight and sloppiness. All of us sisters should have gone to the doctor for travel advice and vaccinations and learned all we could about the diseases present in the Gulf, so that when I woke up shivering with fever and classic symptoms of malaria, I could have started treatment doses of chloroquine or quinine immediately, before the parasites had built up to dangerous levels. But none of us realized how dangerous cerebral malaria can be, and I was left untreated, to have seizures alone.

With minimal effort we could also have obtained necessary resources for the school, such as simple sporting equipment (soccer balls and bas-ketballs) and other educational materials they badly needed. Wall charts, globes, readers, books, chalk, blackboard paint, and pencils could have replaced the useless plastic dolls with just a few phone calls to the co-workers. Yet there was no planning for our work and we were prevented from using our individual human talents in preparing ourselves to do that work. We were kept in the dark, even forbidden from asking intel-ligent questions or offering constructive suggestions. Mother taught that God uses the weak, despised, and ignorant to confound the clever of this world, so professionalism and initiative were suspected even though Mother herself was a teacher. Our superiors behaved as if we had no money to afford a doctor's consultation or a language book. We had plenty of money, but in the name of poverty we didn't want to use it.

Sister Felicity rang the Mother House to ask what to do with me as I had been sent back to Port Moresby. Mother wasn't in Calcutta, so the councillors, who made decisions in her absence, said I should go to Bourke. I had my ticket to fly back to Australia on July 1, 1977, but Sister Felicity wanted me to stay in Port Moresby. Sister Annie, from the other house in Port Moresby, Tokarara, was going to India to prepare for her final vows, and there was no replacement for her. So Sister Felicity kept me in Hanuabada and wrote Mother a letter saying that I was needed to replace Sister Annie, that there wasn't much malaria in Port Moresby, that I was no longer sick, and that I was taking extra chloroquine each week.

I still wanted to return to Kerema on the double chloroquine, but I wasn't allowed, and it seems superiors did have my best interests at heart in this regard. However, I was extremely disappointed as I felt that if I had been on the correct prophylaxis in the first place and allowed to fol-low through with the doctor's instructions, I would have been all right. Living and working in Kerema was much more interesting than dealing with the tense atmosphere of the Hanuabada community. I was clearly not "totally surrendered" to God's will; to me surrender meant defeat.

It took more than a month for the Mother House to advise Sister Felicity of my posting, and so I remained a supernumerary in Hanuabada, the seventh member of the community. I had no assigned work, as it was unknown if I would stay or go. I cooked in the mornings and helped Sister Rosa with her preschoolers in the afternoon. The children didn't understand the Motu I'd learned because they spoke a grammatically complex, purer form of the language; the difference between Motu and Hiri Motu is similar to that between English and Tok Pisin.

I sometimes accompanied Sister Rosa in the afternoon when she taught sewing and "natural" family planning, also known as the rhythm method, as contraception is not allowed by the Church. Sister Felicity told me to learn embroidery, which I disliked and had no aptitude for, to fill the time. I was also on standby to go in the car as Sister Felicity's companion begging for food at various shops and doing routine business, such as paying bills, applying for visa renewals, and collecting mail. I felt awkward and uncomfortable with the way she dealt with people, and her driving around Port Moresby was nerve-wracking, but she refused to allow me to drive as she had heard I was a bad driver. This stemmed from an incident in Victoria, when I had driven off the road on the way home from a picnic. My front seat passenger had left an open can of drink on the dashboard in front of her. As I rounded a corner, it slid across the dash and spilled into my lap. Startled, I veered off the road, but didn't damage the car. Yet Sister Dolores also hadn't allowed me to drive for many months after that.

Word finally came from Calcutta that I was to remain in Papua New Guinea as part of the community in Tokarara, a new suburb of Port Moresby, where identical, mass-produced houses were interspersed among grasslands dotted with gum trees. We lived in a pole house with the living area above and a carport underneath. There I taught about sixty preschoolers, ranging in age from four to nine, providing them with a bridge into mainstream education. At first my classroom was the parish priest's carport; later it was moved to a concrete slab under our house. In the afternoon we drove to the nearby suburb of Gerehu, where I taught a similar number of children. The owners of the house were at work during the day so we had use of their carport. The children were crowded together on the floor and I had very little in the way of aids to teach and entertain them. While I taught, two other sisters went visiting and encouraged the parents, who had come into the city from the provinces, to bring their children to our classes to learn English.

I did my best to teach rudimentary English, numbers, and the alphabet and we entertained the surrounding houses with moving renditions of "Kookaburra Sits on the Old Gum Tree" and the Papuan National Anthem. Some of the parents taught the children language songs in their own dialect. We could be heard blocks away, and neighbors told us that their two-year-olds were picking up the songs "from the air." I collected bottle tops and sticks to start a preschool band and was on the lookout for a *kundu* drum. I had to keep a close eye on the colored chalk because the children loved to use it for face and body decoration. I occasionally allowed them to go for it, and we had a preschool *sing-sing* that included singing, drumming, dancing, colored chalk for body paint, and paper streamers in place of feathered headdresses.

At the end of the year we helped the parents fill out the forms and went with them to enroll their children in the primary school. This was the most important part of our work: to give the parents and children the confidence to enter official buildings to get into the educational system so that they wouldn't end up unskilled and illiterate. These Papuan villagers had earned enough for the plane fare to Moresby by selling a good crop of betel nuts or some carved artifacts, but once they arrived in the city, they were trapped, as they had no land, work, or resources and couldn't afford the fare home. They had arrived from remote places with ancient customs but no modern skills, and they ended up living in crowded houses together with *wantoks,* people of the same language group.

Young, unemployed men, separated from their traditional lands and families, felt belittled, as they had no status in the city. They desired Western goods but lacked the skills to attain them, so some joined the rascal gangs, which divided into rival tribal groups. Once a Chimbu man stabbed three Kerema men so the Keremas felt obliged to pay back the crime and stabbed three Chimbus to death. Their kinsmen in turn made revenge attacks, and so the cycle continued.

Often in Moresby a man would have a few children with one wife, and then decide not to pay the bride price that he owed to the woman's family to finalize the union. In a traditional setting, surrounded by the woman's relatives, he couldn't have deserted the mother of his children, but in the city it was easy to seek a new partner, leaving his first bereft. There was a lot of domestic violence in the city too, which we did not see as much in the villages, where traditional taboos were in place. One of the women we knew delivered a baby girl, but just after labor her husband beat her viciously because he wanted a boy. I had an angry exchange with him, saying it was out of anyone's control that his wife had delivered a girl, but if he wanted to blame someone it was up to the father to pass on maleness. My Pidgin didn't extend to the Y chromosome.

At Christmastime the preschoolers put on a Nativity play with lots of singing. A cute, curly-haired drummer boy, playing a *kundu* drum, led in the actors in the pageant. Draped in towels and sheets, the children acted out the Nativity story with a newly born Papuan Jesus sleeping peacefully through the performance. Singing and traditional dances followed. Preparations for the Christmas feast had actually started the day before, when all the women who attended our sewing class came with *kai-kai* (food) and dug out a traditional *mumu* (cooking pit) in our backyard. They lined it with large stones covered with banana leaves, then put in tapioca, sweet potatoes, scraped coconut, cooking bananas, taro, and chicken and covered the food with more banana leaves. Soil and stones sealed the pit, and we lit a fire above it that burned all night. The next day there were many races and games, including a tug of war between the women and the sisters. Being the heaviest sister, I was the anchor-nun and ended up flat on my face as the sisters were unceremoniously defeated by the stronger, bigger Papuan women. After the games we broke open the *mumu* and had a feast, using banana leaves as plates.

My friend Rell, who had finished university and had been teaching for a year, was on an adventurous road trip through PNG using the local vans as transport. She rocked up in skimpy shorts and a T-shirt to the Christmas *mumu* with another friend, Michelle, who was still a uni student. Rell was worried I would suffocate in the heat and humidity with all my nun garb on; I reassured her I was okay. It was brilliant timing as all the rules were relaxed and there was plenty of *kai-kai*. Rell thought my new accent was ridiculous and was still puzzled over my decision to join the MCs. She was gobsmacked when I told her I taught a preschool class, which had grown to ninety students, on the concrete slab under our house, and had a go at me when I said something pious like "This is what Mother wants me to do to serve God's will."

"You're losing your sense of humor, Clot. You were never such a goody-two-shoes at school!"

I have great friends. They pierced the shell of my MC existence and reminded me that there were other possibilities. Then they went on their irreverent way north to Lae and Mount Hagen, where there was a riot on New Year's Eve. I felt a bit sad when they left and believe they must have had a drink to celebrate that they were not nuns.

After Christmas our convent returned to our regular routine, and we often acted as facilitators, trying to find solutions to the people's problems. For instance, one of the children I taught was wasted and coughing a lot, so we arranged a doctor's appointment. He was diagnosed with TB, as was his younger sister. The doctor wanted the whole family admitted to hospital, but the parents believed the sickness was the result of *puri puri* and thought that Western medicine would be powerless to help them. Eventually we convinced the whole family to accept treatment for tuberculosis, which is very contagious and destructive if not treated early. We visited the family each Sunday in the hospital to encourage them not to run away, but to stay until they were no longer contagious and were able to receive outpatient treatment. One day, in my poor Hiri Motu, instead of telling a sick little girl to eat the food I had brought because it was good for her, I said, "You are good food." This entertained the entire ward.

Mum came to visit me for a few weeks. My young superior, Sister Claudia, allowed her to eat with us sometimes, though I had to remind her not to keep talking after meals. She was always a great talker. The children were fascinated with her stockings, which they had never encountered before, and kept pulling her "second skin." Drawing on her nursery school experience, she helped me by teaching the children games to help them learn new English words. She also knew many songs with actions that the children loved, like "Teensy Weensy Spider."

When Sister Margaret came down to Moresby for business I heard lots of news from Kerema. Sister Karina had no trouble with malaria on her extra tablet of chloroquine each week. Sister Lara, another Australian, had not succumbed to malaria on the right medication and was now driving along the beaches in a four-wheel-drive tractor working as a nurse operating mobile medical clinics. I was a bit jealous of her! The sisters from Kerema also wrote, saying that the Salesians, a male teaching order, were going to take over St. Peter's and that the sweet potatoes I had planted had yielded a big crop.

New sisters arrived from Australia, including Annette, the Croatian Australian, and Hua and Mei-ying from Singapore. We had a great reunion at the Easter picnic in the Botanic Gardens in Moresby and heard that Mother had opened the novitiate in Manila and all the sisters training in Australia had moved over there.

At this point I began again to have doubts about my vocation and often thought of leaving. I sought to live a life of prayer and compassion, but my main attraction to Mother Teresa had been her work and her identification with the very poor. I wouldn't have become any other sort of nun. It was the work that had lured me into religious life. I found it difficult to persevere in my rough and ready preschool teaching and family visiting. I was attracted to medicine or nursing and wanted to study. I felt inadequately trained, constrained, and stifled in the order. In the middle of these reflections, however, I was struck by the reaction of Sister Sara, one of the members of my community in Tokarara, to the news that her own sister had left the convent. Sister Sara was so upset that it was as if her sister had died; she felt that by breaking her vows her sister had turned her back on God. Nonetheless, I kept thinking of taking control of my own life again, after only five years in the order.

But then I received a short note from Mother Teresa saying that she was sending me to Manila. I was glad to go.

CHAPTER SIX

The Garbage Mountain

The Garbage Mountain at Barrio Magdaragat, Manila.
(Photographer: Pat Livermore)

Live simply that others may simply live.
FORCE 10 (AN AUSTRALIAN
CATHOLIC-AID ORGANIZATION)

*T*wo sisters waited in the throng outside the guarded doors of Manila Airport. Our uniform allowed instant recognition; no one else in Manila wore the incongruous blue-and-white sari in the Bengali style. We threaded our way through the crush of people to where the MC driver, Mang (Mr.) Patrin, had double-parked a distinctive blue van with

99

"Missionaries of Charity" emblazoned on the side doors. Even around the airport, squatters camped under bridges and on any vacant land, despite President Marcos's attempts to move and conceal them.

As the MC van drove along the palm-lined Roxas Boulevard we passed tourist hotels and showy government buildings built on reclaimed waterfront land. Manila aides in their conical straw hats, red shirts, and yellow scarves were continually sweeping and cleaning this part of town. Jeepneys, crammed with ten to twelve passengers and decorated with flashing lights, ornamental horses, and religious pictures weaved chaotically through the traffic, their radios blaring. We passed Rizal Park, the Old Fort, the imposing white Manila Hotel, and the fortified, heavily guarded American Embassy. In 1979, during the Marcos presidency, there was a stark contrast between the very wealthy and the very poor and consequently a great deal of crime, so most government buildings and even supermarkets had obvious security.

As we approached the dock areas the scenery changed and the traffic became gridlocked. The canal waters were black and choked with rubbish; little stalls fronted unpainted shacks. People used the railway lines as a sidewalk to get to a maze of drab dwellings that crowded each other parallel to the tracks. Here the poverty of the people was apparent, in stark contrast to the tourist strip, with its flash buildings. As our van crawled to a halt, young boys swooped in to wash the windows and sell single cigarettes to the driver or sweet-smelling garlands of *sampagita* flowers.

We passed the Pritil markets, where fruit and vegetables were sold, and turned right down the traffic-choked Tayuman Street, one of the main roads in the area. Soon after, we entered the driveway to our house, which was between a church and a school. Mang Patrin blared the horn, and in response a large iron gate in front of us swung open. A party of novices and professed ran outside as the bell clanged to signal our arrival. Several familiar faces welcomed me, including the postulants who had started their training in Australia: Ling, Reka, Marion, and Ann, who had become sari-clad novices. There were about forty trainees altogether, from Singapore, the Philippines, India, Australia, and New Zealand.

I was introduced to the superior of the professed, Sister Aloysius, who had been one of Mother's first companions. Sister Gabrielle, the first-year novice mistress, was tall, fine-featured, and a talented musician. The second-year novice mistress, Sister Barbara, was from southern India.

The Tahanan, "home" in Tagalog, the language of Manila, was just being completed when I arrived and consisted of three long buildings lined up side by side and linked by a covered walkway. Here the sisters had just started their work caring for poor people with tuberculosis and other illnesses. The square wooden convent had a grassy central courtyard, its four sides formed by a chapel with wooden shutters, two large dormitories, and the refectory. At the back was a cement washing place and a large, open water storage tank for all household purposes. The sisters' numbered buckets lined the side wall in the familiar way; the cooking fires were at the back. The professed house was a two-story building located near the gate, separated from the novitiate by a large covered carport, which was used for feast day gatherings when not housing the van.

The floors of the convent were a shiny red concrete, which we polished by rotating a coconut husk under one foot and a rag under the other. I was clumsy and fell over when I first tried this maneuver, but everyone else managed it gracefully. In every house life followed the same rhythms. From house to house, wherever I was assigned, I carried my three sets of clothing, apron, metal plate, serviette, cutlery, bucket, soap tin, ten pegs, discipline bag (containing the rope discipline and chains), and devotional books.

The twenty or so novices, a similar number of postulants, and about ten professed made this the largest house I had stayed in. I mainly worked in the Tahanan cleaning, changing the linen, washing and dressing the patients, and feeding them, but before going out in the afternoon, I taught a class to the novices and also went visiting the shanties along the railway line two afternoons a week. After about a year my classes increased to take up the whole morning. Over the three years I was there I taught English, scripture, moral theology, and Church history. At first I lived with the professed, and at one stage was the sister responsible for the Tahanan work so that in addition to my usual work, I made lists for the marketing, supervised and worked with the novices, and organized visits to our patients by

local doctors. Then I became Sister Gabrielle's assistant and was based in
the first-year novice community. I taught in the morning and went visiting
in the afternoons. I was no longer responsible for the Tahanan, although I
still worked there with the novices on Thursdays and Sundays.

Novices, postulants, and the professed worked in the Tahanan, dispensary, and feeding center, which was situated in a covered area to the
side of the Tahanan. We also visited the various barrios. At the other MC
house in Manila, called Binondo or Del Pan, the order cared for sick and
malnourished children. Sister Naomi had been transferred there from
Katherine, and it was great to see her again.

When I first arrived there were only seventeen patients in the Tahanan,
many of whom were young and suffered from tuberculosis. Some were
bedridden and too weak to walk. Initially I worked alone to help them
because the other sister assigned there was sick, although a woman who
lived in the slums along the railway track did the cooking. I struggled to
learn Tagalog and carried a notebook in my apron pocket with lists of
words.

Treatment was meant to be free, but our patients told us that some
of the government clinics were asking for money for the anti-TB drugs,
which we were able to provide free of charge as we received donated
medicines from Germany. The treatment lasted six to eight months
and if patients took their drugs intermittently the tuberculosis bacillus
became drug-resistant and made treatment even more expensive and
difficult. The TB patients walked laboriously on thin, stick-like legs with
swollen feet. They heaved for air, were wracked by coughing fits, and
spat up blood. I had never seen people as ill as this. Nonetheless, I loved
to work with them and see them recover, and finally felt I was doing the
work I had joined the order to do. But at the same time I felt untrained
and inadequately prepared. As Dostoyevsky wrote, "Love in action is a
harsh and dreadful thing compared to love in dreams." The practical
service that love required was far from lofty or romantic, but consisted
mainly of endless, simple tasks of feeding, hand-washing linen, cleaning,
and toileting. I was happy to be doing these tasks, however, and felt a
sense of purpose that, until now, had eluded me.

One of our patients had a large, open, cancerous wound extending from his arm socket along the side of his chest wall. I could see the lung moving up and down when I did his dressing. He asked to go back to his village to die when his condition deteriorated, so we arranged for his family to come to collect him so that he could spend his last few days at home. They were reluctant to do so because they were frightened of managing his gaping wound and because he had become angry and hard to please from being in pain.

Another patient was discharging so much thick, dark blood from the rectum that I didn't know how he could live. A cauliflower mass of cancer was eroding his face, mouth, and throat. He would pull out the feeding tubes we had inserted to give him fluids but then would become very thirsty, so we trickled milk into his mouth to keep him hydrated and give him some nutrition.

Every day there were new admissions, and the number of patients grew to over sixty. More sisters were assigned to help, and all three wards were opened. A priest brought in a woman who had a cancer eroding her skull. Her hair was full of lice and she had maggots in her leg wounds. We showered her and made her comfortable; she stayed with us until she died.

Sometimes our patients became difficult. One woman with tuberculosis and liver disease was alternately withdrawn and then violently delirious, mistreating both the sisters and the other patients; she refused to eat and threw herself on the floor. We took her to a hospital hoping the medical staff there could help, because she was so hard for us to control on an open ward. When we returned to visit her a few days later, however, she looked worse; her lips were parched, and no one had bathed or toileted her, so she sat in her own mess. The staff had tied her to the bed so tightly that her hand was swollen. She tried to jump up from the stretcher when she saw me and shouted, "Sister Toobig! Sister Toobig!" In the Philippines, my name, Tobit, was often confused with *toobig*, the Tagalog word for water. We took her home again and gave her a little milk, and she died peacefully a few days later.

I became close to Felicitas, a gaunt woman with tuberculosis who had been in the Tahanan for a long time. Her husband, Reynaldo, also had TB. After a worrying pregnancy she gave birth to a little girl, whom she named Obit, after me. I felt sorry for that child who had to bear such a name all her life. Mum and my brother Rodney sponsored Felicitas, Reynaldo, and their family by contributing to their rent and the expensive treatment for her resistant TB.

Each day at noon malnourished children came in for lunch from surrounding areas. We cooked outside on wood fires because it was too difficult to prepare lunch for the patients and eighty children on the two little gas cookers in the Tahanan kitchen. They received their food in a shaded area at the back of the Tahanan or on the veranda if it was wet. If any of these children were severely malnourished or were suspected of having TB, we talked to their parents and then took them to the children's home at Binondo, about twenty minutes away, to receive treatment. Many were badly infested with roundworms, which they passed in large balls after receiving worming medicine.

After working in the Tahanan for a while I could see ways to improve conditions there. For instance, I wanted to provide the patients with mosquito nets and improve their diet from the usual dry fish and rice by adding more fresh vegetables and meat. Sister Aloysius said they weren't used to such foods, but I believed that their poor diet weakened them. Impoverished and undernourished, they couldn't resist disease, and I knew that they would recover more rapidly with better nutrition. I was able to make small, gradual changes. We had enough money from donations to increase the patients' comfort, but the superiors seemed to fear making even minor changes and allowing any sparks of initiative. After some months the superior arranged for us to pick up leftover food from the airline caterers at Manila Airport, so we were able to supplement the patients' diet with cheeses, cold meats, and the like.

Because medical treatment in the Philippines wasn't free, in general patients had to buy their own needles, drips, and medicines. Poorer people came to us for expensive prescriptions, and often we were able to help them, at least with an equivalent medicine from our donated stock. One day, when we were having afternoon tea, there was an urgent knock at the door. The portress reported, "A little boy is having trouble breathing." I started to get up because I had access to the Tahanan medicines and thought I should go to help.

"Sit down, Tobit, there is no hurry. We are not running an emergency hospital," the superior reminded me. I thought to myself, *Is afternoon tea more important than assisting the boy and giving comfort to his parents?* Yet I obediently waited until after tea to get some salbutamol to relieve his distress.

Petty things often became big incidents. On one occasion Mum sent me a newspaper clipping about Mother, which I pinned up on the community notice board. "Didn't you learn anything in the novitiate?" my superior asked, angry that I had not sought permission first. The level of control was Orwellian.

We found a woman with active leprosy living in a bus stop shelter after her family had thrown her out. She had many bleeding sores on her legs and part of her face was eaten away; where her nose should have been was an open cavity. I knew of a village-like settlement, about ten miles north of Manila, called Tala (Star), that cared for people with Hansen's disease, or leprosy. I suggested that we could get her there for treatment, so she agreed to come back with us to the Tahanan. I washed her and gave her something to eat, then went to speak to the superior. "Sister, we have found a woman with leprosy in the bus shelter. We've brought her back with us. Can we take her up to Tala?"

"Leprosy is not our work here in Manila. You shouldn't have brought her here. There are other people who could have looked after her."

"I know we don't have the facilities to care for her, but I thought we might be able to take her up to Tala. She's in terrible condition, and I thought it was wrong just to leave her there. I've kept her separate, and have put all her clothing and towels aside. I will boil everything."

"I can't understand you, Tobit," the superior replied, angrily. "You are often doing things like this. You try to force me into doing what you want. You had no business bringing her here. How much petrol are you going to use to go all the way up to Tala? Now you have made this problem for yourself I am forced into a position where I will have to let you take her to Tala."

Sister was furious, which I found hard to understand. To me, responding to an abandoned person on the street was the quintessential reason for being an MC and I found her response incomprehensible. I felt upset and angry. Grudgingly, she gave me use of the car and a companion, and we took the woman to Tala, which took about an hour. I daydreamed about stopping the car on the way and asking people for donations to buy petrol, even though I hated begging, and then flinging the money at the superior, saying, "Here's your money you're so worried about." Such an outburst was unthinkable in reality, and my thoughts became the subject of self-accusation at the next general permissions: "I speak my fault for being angry, and having rebellious thoughts." I hoped that the sister wouldn't ask for further information.

When we got to Tala the receptionist received us with an air of suppressed boredom and motioned us to a stretcher on which to settle the woman. I gave her name and other details, and then the receptionist asked, "Where are her belongings?"

"She's from the street and does not have many things. We have put together some clothes, towel, and soap for her."

"She needs her own blanket, plate, bucket, and cutlery or she can't stay."

Fortunately there was a little shop on the grounds, where I burned through some more money to purchase these supplies for her, thinking that would no doubt cause further recriminations when I returned home.

This sort of scenario played itself out on many occasions throughout my life as an MC. Our timetable and structure were so unyielding that we weren't supposed to respond to the random requests of the desperate, but I believed we had no other reason for existing. I still did not fully accept that obedience to our superior was considered more important than our service to the poor. Because of this overriding philosophy, a sister's happiness, in large part, depended on the disposition of the superior who had power over her.

I struggled to be humble, to curb my anger and my tongue, with varying success. I struggled to pray, repeating over and over during the day the short phrase "Lord Jesus" as a mantra. I plowed through the daily vocal prayers as an obligation that, when completed, allowed me to retreat into silence. My notebooks of scrap paper, sewn together with string, were full of critical self-admonitions, such as this entry: "Holiness is to pray often to God, to rely on Him, to love everyone and to be able to suffer and bear the anger and hurt of others or difficult circumstances without ourselves getting angry or bitter." Simple! I felt a bit like a horse in harness, able to run sometimes but always under a tight rein.

A little while after taking the woman to Tala, we found a man with leprosy in Tondo. He had lost two toes and a finger and had a badly infected hand. This time it wasn't an emergency, and I approached the superior for permission before moving him from his house. She was less resistant on this occasion, and we went to Tala better prepared with all he needed. On several other trips to Tala with new patients we visited our old friends and brought them gifts of clothes and extra food.

I became friendly with Sister Emilia, a Franciscan sister who cared for the children of the leprosy patients until their parents' disease was inactive and the family could be reunited, as well as a Dominican priest, Father Hofstee, who was an Army chaplain during the war. He had come across the leprosy colony and for the next thirty years worked to improve conditions there, starting a school and a hospital on the site. Elderly and missing part of his ear, he still plodded around in his gumboots and white cassock. When I met up with him on my second visit to Tala he had just officiated at a burial. "Be careful in those sandals of yours!" he told me. "You'll slip into one of those graves and I'll have more work to do!"

"I went to a Dominican school," I told him, implying that I knew better than to fall into burial holes.

"Then what are you doing dressed in a blue-and-white tea towel? You should be in black and white, the Dominican colors," he quipped. He was a man who lived up to his motto, *Veritas* (Truth). His deeds matched his words, and he made everyone around him laugh.

One of our coworkers, Ate Ester, first showed me the path into the slum at the base of the *tambakan* (garbage dump). Hidden behind large buildings and factories, the track was invisible unless you were shown where to look. On the first day I was overwhelmed by the smell, the grinding poverty, and the acrid smoke issuing from the mountain of refuse, but I began to visit Barrio Magdaragat (the Place of the Seafarer) regularly.

Many shanties were crammed into a triangular space between the garbage, the factories facing the road, and the flat, brown waters of Manila Bay. Narrow passageways wove through the flimsy huts made of tin, wood, and plastic. There were no sewers or plumbing, and ditches of black water snaked between the houses. Flies formed a thick coat over the clotheslines, and the pervasive smoke from the garbage seeped into my skin and clothes and made my eyes water. The skies above the dump were silent. I never heard a bird's song in that polluted place and regretted that I had taken for granted the warbling conversations of the magpie family in our trees at home.

On the garbage mountain, towering above the squatter's village, people worked bent over, their mouth and nose covered with a bandana to protect against the toxic fumes and stench. Their feet sank into the rubbish as they scratched at the soggy debris with a hook; they threw anything salvageable into a wicker basket slung behind their backs. These families had come to the city hoping to find work or to escape the violence and poverty of the provinces. They lived beside black, polluted canals, along railway tracks, or at the bottom of the garbage dumps on which they depended for survival. Smoke, pounding typhoons, and suffocating odors were a part of life.

Amid this poverty and filth, however, there was life, comradeship, fiestas, joy, and the usual conflicts. The people worked hard to survive, and nothing was wasted. They gathered up discarded newspapers, tins, plastic containers, bones, and glass to sell. Yet even this government controlled, at one time posting soldiers to guard the dump and to force scavengers to sell to particular merchants at a cheaper price.

There was an old blind man in the barrio who was always very cheerful and rowed for the fishermen while he was still strong. In return they gave him part of their catch. When I met him he could no longer work due to a heart condition, but his old mates continued to help him with regular gifts of fresh fish.

A widow and mother of eight children asked her son to climb up the mountain to look for something for them to eat. He found nothing worthwhile, and so lay down to wait for a new truck, but fell asleep. An avalanche of tins and decaying vegetables falling onto him woke him, as a yellow dump truck emptied its contents. When he got home with the food, his mother scolded him, saying, "You could have been killed."

"At least I got there first!" he replied.

During the wet season the barrio was regularly flooded. As we waded through the streets in knee-deep, opaque water, I fell up to my waist into a submerged ditch. *Why did Mother choose white habits?* I asked myself as I tried to gain my composure. The onlookers cried out, "Madre!" My face blushed red, while the rest of me was gray and wet.

In the torrential downpours the dump became a quagmire. Many people near the water lost their huts during the monsoons. Once, there was a landslide along part of the dump and the falling rubbish crushed and killed two men. During these times of flooding we gave out cooked food and a dry ration of rice, mung beans, milk powder, and tinned fish to the families most affected by the storms. Whole families sat up all night in their leaking lean-tos, frantically moving their babies from place to place to keep them dry. Often, the water rose quickly and families had to put all they had on the table for safety. If the water rose higher still, they crossed over the main road to the Tondo Hospital or to schools built on higher ground, and because it was an emergency their presence was tolerated. When it rained for days all the firewood was wet and the people went hungry because they couldn't cook their rice. The *lavenderas* (washerwomen), who lived from day to day, were unable to work, and the hawkers had difficulty selling their wares.

During the monsoons disease increased, as even the drinking water, carted in from outside the barrio, was polluted. Outbreaks of dysentery, hepatitis, pneumonia, and conjunctivitis ravaged the population. Polio, tuberculosis, and leprosy were all present, and outbreaks of *tigdas* (measles) killed many children and left others blind. The sisters and I found children in the small, low, corrugated-iron shacks, who were feverish, dehydrated, and close to death with pneumonia. Many had discharging ears and sores. We took sick children by jeepney to the children's home at Binondo.

A Filipino priest, Father Beltran, just back from studies in Rome, where he had completed a learned theological dissertation, was assigned to teach at the seminary at Tagaytay and began to work with us. He said Mass for us in the Barrio Chapel of the Resurrection. During the floods we met him at the entrance to the barrio carrying wading boots for him to wear. Later, the student priests whom Father Beltran taught came with him, dressed in their pristine white cassocks. At first they held handkerchiefs over their mouths and noses to ward off the smell of the dump, which was very different from their seminary, located in a beautiful area near a volcanic lake.

After working with us for a few months, Father Beltran invited some of the people from the *tambakan* to come to Tagaytay for a picnic. The twenty-mile bus ride brought them to another world, free of smoke, filth, and flies. The mountain air was cool and clear, and the barrio people gasped in delight at the vistas of green. From the ridge near the seminary they could see the small, powerful Taal volcano, which looked innocent and beautiful in the center of the lake below them, even though it was packed with menacing subterranean power. Transformed and invigorated by the beauty of the unspoiled country, the visitors ran through the gardens, played raucous ball games, and ate ravenously the lunch we provided.

Some time after I left Manila Father Beltran fell out with the MCs but continued to act as an advocate for the people of the garbage dump. He fought to have their issues addressed when, in 1983, the government, wanting to develop the Manila Bay site, relocated the people of the barrio into a crowded settlement on the outskirts of Manila with no work, water, or power.

I dreamt of living in Barrio Magdaragat with a small group of sisters close to the people rather than in our walled compound. I thought that if we were there with them, facing the same obstacles, we would learn how to respond. The problem was that because we had resources, we had power. Then we needed gates, locks, walls, and distribution timetables to protect our resources. There had to be rules about who was eligible and when. Before we knew it, the barriers were up and the really poor were outside the gate again, in the wrong place, at the wrong time.

. . .

The week before Christmas we stayed the whole day in the barrio, going from house to house to give out tickets for a gift distribution and children's party we held at our house. On one of these days we found a very sick young man, in a house near the dump, with advanced TB. He was thin and pale with swollen feet. His old *lola* (grandmother) sold flowerpots to support him, but there wasn't a big market for potted plants in a garbage dump slum. We took him to Tayuman by van, because he was too weak to go by jeepney, and after a long time he recovered, although his lungs were permanently damaged.

Filipinos observe the *aquinalo,* for the nine days before Christmas. The churches were crowded for the 4:30 a.m. Mass, and Christmas carols, especially "O, Holy Night," filled the air. The novices were busy for weeks during recreation, packing buckets with canned fish, soap, rice, a towel, and other goods as they laughed and chatted. We distributed the gifts on the Monday and Thursday before Christmas to about 550 people each day, then had the children's parties. We thought that a thousand children, 175 of whom were from Barrio Magdaragat, might be too difficult to manage all at once, so we had two parties: first, five hundred children from Binondo had their party, and on the next day five hundred from Tondo had theirs. The sisters organized each group around their own banner and the children wore a ribbon of the same color to identify their barrio group. They had lunch in our compound and then went in buses to the zoo. It was a bit hard keeping track of them, but they had a great time.

On Christmas Day Sister Reka's cousin, a Kiwi, said Mass outdoors in the barrio under an awning, and in place of the Gospel reading the children acted out the Nativity scene, complete with the drummer boy. After Mass we gave out sweets and presents to all the children under six, as the little ones had not been included in the Christmas picnic. We had some leftovers and so we climbed up to the top of the garbage mountain to give them to the children who were scavenging. Even on Christmas Day we found one very sick child whom we took with his mother to Binondo. Once we were back home we helped serve a special Christmas meal in the Tahanan. I enjoyed working that day, still feeling that I was fulfilling my purpose.

In the middle of 1978 I was moved into the novitiate to work more closely with Sister Gabrielle and the first- and second-year novices, a great bunch of people. Sister Eva was a senior second-year and would be the first Filipina professed as an MC. The Kiwi, Sister Reka, had a strong, compassionate personality and was often in trouble, as she fought for what she thought was right, but she weathered it well. Sister Ling from Hong Kong was prayerful and obedient, yet both she and Reka seemed to understand the essence of the work and lived in a way consistent with their inner being. I hoped that they wouldn't surrender that inner part of themselves that made them who they were.

I taught mostly religious subjects, but also English to the non-English-speaking aspirants. Since Mum taught adult literacy classes and had told me that basic words at the core of the language should be taught first, I asked her to send me any notes she had, which were very helpful. My other subjects were Church history, biblical studies, and the MC Constitution. I still worked in the Tahanan on Thursdays and Sundays and visited in the afternoons.

During one rainy season the road leading to our compound flooded, and the mayor of Manila sent seven huge lorries of road base to help solve the problem. However, the dirt and rocks were dumped at our gate on a Saturday night, blocking the road. Eight men working all Sunday morning made no impression on the large pile of dirt. Then they went home to rest in the afternoon. Therefore, on the Sabbath, scandalizing all attending weddings and funerals in the church, the novices and I set out, shovel, pick, and metal bucket in hand, to level the ground so that our van could get through. A visitor said, "I've never met nuns like this. Last time you were unloading two thousand bags of milk from a container van, and now you're making a road!"

I had continued my habit of seeking out news of the outside world at any opportunity, and in late September 1978, after returning from visiting, I learned and announced at mealtime that the pope had died. "That's old news," Sister Gabrielle replied. "Paul VI died in August."

"No, it's the new pope, John Paul," I insisted. "He's dead after only a month in office."

"That can't be."

"I'm sure it's true. It was on a newspaper headline sheet outside the *tindhan* [shop]."

Sister Gabrielle went straight over to the professed house to see if anyone else had heard. No one knew, so Sister rang the cardinal's office and confirmed that the pope had indeed died.

In early 1979 we had a terrible fire in the Tayuman neighborhood, which destroyed the whole block behind our convent and left about seven thousand people homeless. It started at about 8:30 at night, and by 9:30 the flames threatened our buildings. As the fire crackled and exploded its way through the shanties, it created its own wind and made a low-pitched roar like a bush fire. Acrid black smoke billowed toward us. The cement wall behind the convent was about ten feet high. People trapped in the houses behind us were screaming. They broke the wooden shutters of their windows to get out and threw sewing machines, bundles of cloth, and other personal possessions over the wall into our yard. These were in danger of catching fire from the sparks and flying debris, so I hauled people's possessions away from the fence to maintain the firebreak. Firefighters stood on the roofs of the houses, silhouetted by the red glow behind them, but they worked with very low water pressure and so had little chance of controlling the situation. As the other sisters evacuated the patients from the Tahanan to Tayuman Street, I heard a frantic scream from where I was keeping the firebreak. "Madre! Madre!" I stood up on the cement footings of the wire side fence where it intersected with the back wall, and called out, "What can I do?"

A woman answered frantically, "Anak ko! Anak ko!" (My child! My child!) She was standing on boxes pushed close to the other side of the wall, holding up her infant. I managed to reach the child and lift him to safety. Other sisters came to help and took the baby. Then I assisted the mother, who had pulled herself up onto the wall, to get down safely. Hot cinders rained down on us near the wire fence, and adults and children scaled it to jump into the yard. We comforted children, who were crying hysterically after losing track of their parents in the dark and smoke, and had them stay with the sisters on the street, where their parents could find them.

The houses along our boundary began to catch fire and the heat was intense. The men's ward caught fire in places, but fortunately was made mainly of concrete and the fire didn't take hold. However, the intense heat warped the gutters and shattered the glass windows. At that point, the firefighters charged in. "Sisters, get out of here immediately!" they yelled in Tagalog. We went out on the road, where the flames looked so high that the convent appeared to be on fire.

A family named Abad lived close by and helped us in many ways, offering to accommodate our patients overnight. Tayuman Street was nearly impassable even on foot. Slowly we moved twenty-five of the sickest patients to the neighbor's house. Sister Esther and I stayed with them, crammed into the two downstairs rooms, while the family retired upstairs. In the rush of the evacuation we had forgotten the bedpans and so had a very difficult situation on our hands. Neighbors had given our patients sandwiches and coffee. One retarded girl, Aurora, was very agitated, clapping, shouting, and wandering around the unfamiliar surroundings, stepping on the others who were trying to sleep. It was a long night.

The emergency services allowed us sisters to return to our compound at about 4 a.m. the next morning, and we began cleaning up the water damage in the convent and Tahanan. Homeless people from the surrounding slums had already taken over the wards, but we had to ask some to leave so that our patients could return. For a short time we allowed mothers with infants and the elderly to stay under cover in the women's ward, away from the infectious TB patients. The Tahanan was in a terrible condition, but our storage room, the "bodega," was not water damaged.

All the sisters, postulants, novices, and professed, about sixty in all, were mobilized to clean up and also to cook huge dishes of rice and curry for hundreds of people who had taken refuge in our yard. Our stoves were campfires made of three large cement blocks on which we supported a very large pot. We prepared two meals a day for three days. In a vacant lot behind the school, which the children normally used as a playground, the Army erected large tents as temporary shelter and organized sanitation. Water was pushed in on carts, as in other squatter settlements around the city. Families started to erect their own rough shanties. Once an alternative place to stay had been made available, we asked everyone to leave our compound; we were beside ourselves with people all over the wards, in the kitchen, patient bathrooms, and the yard. This unhealthy situation couldn't continue because some of our patients had active TB and had to be kept quarantined. Nonetheless, for over a month we cooked lunch for the tent city and then gave out dry rations for a few more weeks to allow the people time to recover.

Sister Gabrielle received a large donation from her family and friends and used it to give the people galvanized iron sheets, timber, and large, locally made, wooden double beds to reestablish their homes. It required a lot of organization to prevent families and individuals from double dipping. A frozen butchered steer arrived as a donation from New Zealand via Sister Reka's connections. After a little trouble from customs, we were able to have it released tax-free and could use it for the people's curry. Meat in the Philippines is very expensive, so the poor rarely ate it.

The first MC profession ever to be held in Manila was scheduled for May, and Mother sent a message on March 17, 1979, saying that she would arrive *seven weeks* early, on March 31, in order to be present at the professions as well as the reception of the new novices and postulants during the first week of April. Prior to the professions there was always a lot of activity and excitement. But at that news there was pandemonium as we scrambled to arrange the preprofession retreat, make new habits, and organize the work to cope with the loss of nun power since the sisters on retreat did no outside work. The novices began preparing congratulation cards and plays for the evening entertainment. In the midst of all this, we had nearly continuous blackouts and water shortages.

Five sisters—Ling, Ann, Eva, Charlotte, and Jyotini Asha—made their first vows on April 3 at our parish church of the Immaculate Conception. The main celebrant at the Mass was Cardinal Sin. Mother tried in vain to get our parish priest's dogs off the sanctuary, but they had made no vow of obedience and weren't shifting from Father Piñeda's side. After the profession, Sisters Ling, Jyotini, and Eva stayed in Manila and Sister Ann left for Bourke; Sister Charlotte went to PNG.

Gran died while I was in Manila; she was eighty years old. The sisters' words of comfort left me feeling strangely hollow. "Well, she was very old, and now she's with God. It's silly to be sad. You should be happy. She'll be in heaven looking out for you." I felt empty and alone, wanting to be with Mum and Judy and the rest of my family to grieve our Gran. It's strange how we are never quite ready even for an expected death.

On two occasions, just as I was falling asleep, I felt paralyzed, as if I were locked in, not able to move or call out. I felt I was going to die, and was afraid to go to sleep. Perhaps these were anxiety attacks. Our compound and convent were very crowded, and in my mind I'd escape to the bush trails and hills around my home. In Tondo there was only cement, mud, and people crammed together. Nothing was green. It seemed unfair that some people would live and die never having seen natural beauty and have to live in polluted slums where they could never be alone.

During a United Nations Trade Conference in Manila a German television crew came to see Sister Gabrielle, who sent me to Barrio Magdaragat with them. I tried to reason with her. "Sister, please, could you go with them, yourself? I don't want to be on film."

"Go, Sister Tobit! Just show them around, you know the area. They can speak English well."

It was incongruous driving to the barrio in a shiny black LTD. The crew followed me everywhere with their cameras, first to the barrio chairman, to ask permission to film, and then to visit different families living amid the mud and smoke.

The documentary makers wanted to get an overall shot of the area, so I advised them to climb up the garbage dump because from there they could see the whole barrio, the bay, and the distant horizon. Just at the edge of the *tambakan* I checked on a child we had taken to hospital two weeks earlier. Measles had recently killed many in the barrio. There I found a six-year-old girl whom the doctors had discharged three days earlier lying on the floor gravely ill with dysentery, pneumonia, and dehydration. Her mother was eight months pregnant and nursing a sick three-year-old and had sent another child to find her husband, who was scavenging up on the dump. I decided to take the child straight to Tondo Hospital, explaining to the TV people that we needed to leave them and arranging a later meeting place outside the hospital. We rushed to the nearby hospital, carrying the child while the film crew climbed to the top of the garbage mountain with the barrio chairman, where they took a few shots. One member of the group became unwell due to the heat and smell. The crew donated money to buy medicine and fluids for the little girl, but despite their generosity, she died that night.

In May 1980 it was time for Sister Naomi and me to go to Calcutta for our tertianship, the year of preparation before final vows. It wasn't certain if we would be granted visas to enter India, but eventually they came through. All MC sisters make a visit home before their final vows, but Naomi and I didn't go back to Australia because of the distance and expense.

Prior to leaving for Calcutta we renewed our temporary vows for the fifth and last time before our final commitment. The novices and postulants put on a play, which told the story of the two of us arriving in Calcutta with a great crash and bang. I had a touching farewell with many tears and hugs from the patients in the Tahanan.

In Manila I had felt the greatest synchronicity between the order and myself. I did the work I loved, and had companionship, support, and times of quiet. Nonetheless, it remained difficult to contribute ideas, and I felt inadequately trained to care for such sick people. All these things were on my mind as I set off for tertianship in India, where the order had begun.

CHAPTER SEVEN

Rickshaws and Reality

Missionaries of Charity leaving for dispensary, 1981.
(Photographer: Pat Livermore)

There was a rich man who used to dress in purple and fine linen, and feasted magnificently every day. And at his gate there lay a poor man called Lazarus, covered with sores, who longed to fill himself with the scraps that fell from the rich man's table (Luke 16:19–21).

On the flight to Calcutta Naomi and I had a chance to talk and catch up with each other. Although we had both lived in Manila, we had been in separate houses and seldom met. We had some difficulty clearing customs, as the officer was suspicious of two white "Indian" sisters carrying chalices. These had been donated by Filipinos for the chapels of the new MC houses that Mother was opening in India.

Clutching our belongings, we looked expectantly for a welcoming party in white and blue, but there was none, only heat, strangers, and stray famished-looking cattle. Details of our flight had either not arrived or had been overlooked. We rang the Mother House and, after a long wait spent fending off beggar children and taxi drivers, were collected and taken to the Missionary of Charity house at Dum Dum, near the airport. It was already dark.

The next day we drove into Calcutta, a pungent city of peeling paint, honking horns, and clinging clothes. The city rushed at me with its crowds of people in colorful saris, *dhotis,* and Western dress, many carrying parcels on their heads. Electric streetcars, trucks, bikes, and men pulling rickshaws or carts all jostled for position in the noise, heat, and smog.

Naomi and I were among the first of the new tertian group to arrive at the three-story, white, cement student house at 90 Park Street, which was a short walk from the Mother House, where the novices were trained. The senior tertians were away on their home visit prior to final vows, and the juniors had not yet arrived from the mission houses.

The front walls of the Park Street house abutted the street, and a small internal courtyard held a water tank and washing place. The flat roof was strung with clotheslines and inhabited by ubiquitous black crows. From this vantage point I watched as thin, sinewy rickshaw *walas* (men) worked as human horses up and down Park Street, straining in the oppressive heat and humidity to pull their passengers in a little buggy. Their fingers clicked a small bell against the poles of the rickshaw warning people to get out of their way so that they wouldn't lose momentum. Other men ran with high, heavy loads balanced on their heads or strained in front of carts piled with sacks of coal and other commodities. The rickety electric streetcars rattled along Park Street so tightly packed with human cargo that passengers had trouble emerging from the crush to alight at their stop. Buses also lurched along at worrying angles that became more acute as they rounded corners. Their passengers were perched precariously on the roof and hanging out of every doorway, holding on tightly to avoid falling. Soon I too would venture out onto these streets and fight my way onto and out of the streetcars like a local.

A mosque occupied the corner across the road from us. In winter we rose before the mullahs, whereas in summer they were up first, summoning the faithful to prayer at dawn. Our 4:40 rising time remained unchanged in all seasons. Families displaced from their villages by unknown calamities lived on the pavement outside our convent, separated from us by the front wall. They bathed on the streets under the gaudy Bengali billboards that advertised luxuries they could never afford. Women cooked whatever they could scrounge in curved metal pots on mud *chulas* (stoves). Squatting on their haunches they stoked the fire with the debris and dung that their children had scavenged from piles of rubbish nearby. Others lined up at hand pumps to fill their water containers. At night they slept in the open, shrouded in coarse sacks or whatever other covering they could find.

Dotted around the city, the Missionaries of Charity had several large training houses. Nearly three hundred sisters, mainly novices, lived in the Mother House on Lower Circular Road. A short walk away was the Shishu Bhavan community, the children's home. Another at Prem Dan, closer to our house at Park Street, had started life as a chemical factory and was pervaded by strong smells from a nearby tannery. In 1975 the British-based ICI (Imperial Chemical Industries), one of the world's largest paint and chemical manufacturers, had donated their plant to Mother Teresa, who turned it into a home for physically and mentally handicapped children.

While Naomi and I waited for the rest of the group to arrive, we spent our time cleaning. Even though I was used to the tropics, Calcutta seemed hotter than Port Moresby or Manila. Because we cinctured our habits with a rope into which we tucked our sari and a cross, I quickly developed prickly heat around my waist and found it hard to tolerate the usual MC penitential practice of wearing a spiky wire chain around my waist during Morning Prayer.

Sister Naomi and I wanted to see the Mother House, so one of the sisters walked with us down to the four-story building, which we recognized from photographs, with its statue of Our Lady gazing down from the external wall to the chaotic street below. Below her was the sign "Missionaries of Charity." We went up a side lane to the main door, to which was affixed a plain wooden cross, and pulled the visitors' bell to signal our arrival. "Mother Teresa out," proclaimed a sliding sign on the wall, but we already knew she was still overseas. A sister arrived and showed us into the internal courtyard used as a gathering place. In one corner was a grotto, and on the other side a hand pump and water holding tanks. Steps to the side of the tanks led up to Mother's small room on the first floor.

"Where are you from, Sisters?" the portress asked.

"We're Australians, newly arrived from the Philippines for tertianship," Naomi replied. "We haven't been to the Mother House before."

"Welcome!" she exclaimed. "I'll show you to the chapel, and then call Sister Agnes. She'll be pleased to know you've arrived safely." As we followed her up the stairs, we came face to face with a life-size crucifix hanging on the landing wall, with the familiar words I THIRST printed at its side. An open walkway to the chapel looked down on the washing place below. We entered the chapel, a long hall-like room with the fourteen Stations of the Cross hung around the walls, and knelt on mats at the back facing the altar and tabernacle. Joining the few sisters who were already kneeling quietly in prayer, we felt content to be in the Mother House at last. Then Sister Agnes invited us to afternoon tea in the professed refectory, where we met Sister Melissa, an Australian Loreto sister who had transferred over to Mother's order.

A few days later Naomi and I went in a large military truck to the train station to meet sixty sisters and new aspirants coming up from Kerala in the south. The train was three hours late, so we waited on the platform, which hummed with music and life. Porters gracefully carried huge loads on their heads, using a cord to keep the load balanced. The hawkers sold tea in little pottery cups. Beggar children scurried around, while their parents, who had made the platform their temporary home, went about their domestic chores. When the train arrived the crowd was tremendous, but we easily identified the battalion of blue-and-white saris advancing toward us. They clambered aboard the truck and we set off for the Mother House and Park Street.

There were about eighty of us in the Park Street house, divided into four communities: two lots each of junior and senior trainees, each with their own refectory. Our group started together because the second tertian mistress was late coming from Tanzania.

Tertianship lasted a year, and there was an intake every six months. Sister Naomi and I were the only non-Indians in our group, but we were in separate communities. The other sisters were from all over India, but mainly from the states of Kerala and Bihar. Sister Annette, who had been a year ahead of us in the novitiate, was with the senior tertians, but when we first arrived she was away visiting one of the mission houses while her group sisters were on their home visit. After about a week Sister Laboni arrived from Papua New Guinea full of news, and Sister Elina came from Australia with letters from Sister Regina and the sisters there. A few weeks after we had started our training, Mother announced that six sisters from our group would go to Rome to train with the eleven tertians there.

We followed the usual timetable, rising at 4:40. A few of us slept on the floor at the side of the chapel because there weren't enough beds or dormitory spaces upstairs. I didn't mind, as it was cooler than in the stifling dormitory. The red oil-burning sanctuary lamp flickered softly, casting shadows on the walls, and sometimes there was a bit of a breeze. We tidied our bedding and carried it upstairs before the bell rang for Morning Prayer.

When a sister was assigned to be the caller that week, she had to ring the rising bell and light the *chula,* a very fickle cylindrical coal fire occupying the cavity of a concrete block in the kitchen. She did this before Morning Prayer to ensure that there was boiling water for the breakfast cup of tea an hour and a half later. Once the five bells for prayer rang there was no opportunity to go back to check on the fire, and when it was my turn my worst nightmare was that the coal wouldn't light and that eighty sisters would not have their morning "cuppa." The only more serious scenario was alarm clock failure.

After breakfast we washed our clothes quickly in buckets, using water drawn from the big cement tanks. Then we hurried up the three flights of stairs to hang them out on lines strung across the flat roof. We received one cake of washing soap per week and a cake of bathing soap a month. The squat toilets in Park Street had the bowl built into the ground and they were flushed using a tin of water from holding tanks at the side. If bathing cubicles were scarce, we used the toilets to take our bucket bath. It was a catastrophe if the month's supply of soap slipped from your hand to disappear irretrievably down the toilet hole.

After the washing was hung out we cut vegetables for lunch and were ready for work by 7:40 a.m. We worked for half a day and returned for lunch. Each afternoon after rest we formed a human chain, passing buckets of water silently from one person to the other, up the stairs to fill the tanks on the three floors for bathing and the upstairs toilets. Classes, study, and further prayer filled the afternoon.

I was very disappointed when I was sent to do office work at the Mother House rather than work in the children's home or the home for the dying. This was more distressing because some sisters coveted such work and seemed jealous that I was assigned to do it, creating rumors that my tertian mistress was treating me as a favorite. The mistress then seemed to try to prove them wrong by being harsh with me.

At the Mother House I worked on a register of the sisters, keeping track of their religious name, surname, number, present mission house, and personal details such as whether they had their high school diploma. Many didn't, although in a lot of other orders it was mandatory for entry into religious life. At that time there were 1,762 MC sisters worldwide, 629 finally professed and 733 junior professed, and four hundred sisters in the various stages of training from thirty countries, including eighteen ethnic Indian groups. They lived in 107 houses in India and 71 houses abroad.

I also dealt with foreign parcels of food, medicine, clothes, and other donations, recording what had arrived and from where and sending our benefactors letters of thanks. I helped prepare hundreds of copies of compilations of *Mother's Letters* which were sent to communities world- wide. We printed them on salvaged paper, blank on one side, used on the other, which the sisters had collected from the Turf Club and business houses and then sorted into reams. Another of my assigned tasks was cataloguing the hundreds of books in the Mother House library, from which sisters selected their spiritual reading. Supposed to contain only religious books, the library also owned a copy of the *Dictionary of Biology* and *Pride and Prejudice,* which were shelved under the heading "Spiritual Life." *Jane Eyre* was found under "Our Lady," and a novel about Napoleon called *Holy Week* under "Liturgy."

After a while I escaped from the paperwork, but I was then moved around to many different jobs, like a pawn on a chessboard, changing work so often that I felt I didn't belong anywhere. Whenever I'd overcome that newcomer feeling and had started to settle into a work routine, I was moved again. There seemed to be no purpose to my frequent reassignments, though I rationalized that it might be to show me different kinds of work. Most assignments in Calcutta were for three months, but I was moved more often than that, almost randomly.

For a few weeks I was assigned to the tuberculosis center and dispensary near Shishu Bhavan, where people clutching ration cards lined up for injections, medicines, and milk. Unable to speak the language, I could do little but dole out rations and smile; the regular sisters gave out the medicines and injections. The people often joined their hands in front of their face and bowed in a gesture of wordless salute, "Namasté." Then I was sent to teach English to the typing class at the Prem Dan Center, which had a community of fifty junior postulants and twenty professed living on the grounds, caring for the children and providing schooling and vocational training for girls from the surrounding area. The place was scattered with piles of coconut husks that men from the nearby slum areas used to make rope.

Another of my assignments was at the Sealdah Railway Station Clinic, around which a throng of humanity strained and struggled for survival. Men pulled rickshaws and pedaled bicycles with carts attached carrying every imaginable kind of produce. Hawkers sold fruit from piles heaped on the footpath; meat hung unrefrigerated in butcher shops, where the owners chased off flies by waving a stick to which shredded plastic was attached. Here in the dripping humidity we had a dispensary, a long narrow feeding center for toddlers, and a ration distribution center. We bathed the street children and gave them milk and protein biscuits, after which the Bengali-speaking sisters taught reading and writing.

Through the metal grille of the dispensary I could see the crush of desperate people waiting to be seen. Many of the women were Muslim and wore long black robes and head coverings so that only their eyes were visible, which must have been stifling in the heat. They typically brought many children with them and looked exhausted. I felt frustrated that, due to the language barrier, I couldn't speak to them and find out more about them. I mostly helped by dressing wounds and feeding and bathing the children.

Every Sunday I was sent to a Protestant boarding school, a large colonial building with spacious gardens enclosed behind a high wall, to teach catechism to the Catholic girls who attended. Although well off, some had emotional difficulties and family troubles. Going there on the streetcar, my companion sister and I passed beggar children picking through the garbage mounds while their parents cooked on the curbside and washed in water from the fire hydrants. Once again I felt frustrated at not working directly with the poor on the streets, which I thought was my mission, rather than teaching catechism to the middle class.

As we walked to the school, crossing a park near the stately Victoria Memorial, I reflected on what a place of contrasts Calcutta was. I had told the boarding school girls about the poor children just outside their doors, and one day one of the students, the most difficult, sneaked out a banana from her breakfast and waited for me at the school gate in order to give the fruit to a naked toddler from the streets. She had made a connection to a child on the other side of the gate. Perhaps I had fulfilled a bit of my mission to serve the poor after all, in a less direct way than I would have envisioned.

Finally I was sent to Kalighat, the famous Home for the Dying that Malcolm Muggeridge had featured in his film. Mother Teresa called it Nirmal Hriday, the Place of the Pure Heart. Until she took it over the building had been a disused pilgrims' rest house within the Hindu temple complex of the black goddess of death, Kali. It was a large structure with arched windows embossed with decorations in the building's cement façade, and its flat roof was embellished with onion-shaped domes at each corner, which formed an incongruous background to the drying washing. Merchants' stalls with overhanging awnings surrounded the building, obscuring its entrance and its ornate architecture. The drying place provided a vantage point from which to view the frenetic mix of pilgrims, cars, bicycles, rickshaws, livestock, and hawkers below.

Inside Nirmal Hriday, the sick lay on low, stretcher-like beds arranged in rows. Many had haunted, pleading eyes and limbs like sticks. The sisters worked only in the women's ward; the MC Brothers cared for the men. Like the people I had nursed in Manila, the patients suffered from TB, malnutrition, cancer, and dysentery, but I did not feel one with the place as I had there. I felt a stranger and an outsider. Nirmal Hriday did not feel friendly and cheerful like the Tahanan in Manila but seemed harsher, more brutal, a contrast to what I had imagined it would be.

The no-nonsense sister in charge was Sister Luke, a thin Indian nurse originally from Singapore. Battling to do what she could with so many desperate people, she had stuck it out for years, where a lesser person wouldn't have persevered. It must have been difficult having so many new sisters rotating through the place and volunteers changing all the time. She had only one permanent professed with her who knew the patients and routine and a few permanent local staff who acted as night watchmen and helped during the day. I found the local staff quite rough and hostile, perhaps because the constant stream of the curious and the photo takers was difficult to tolerate.

Before some patients arrived at Nirmal Hriday rats had gnawed at them as they lay semiconscious on the streets. Others arrived with matted hair infested with lice, maggots, or ants, in soiled clothes, with festering wounds and taut, dry skin. We washed them, removed the maggots with dilute hydrogen peroxide and tweezers, and gave the patients something to drink and eat. It is easy to criticize the basic care that characterized Kalighat, but the sisters were constantly washing and cleaning and their ministrations were certainly better than leaving the destitute to die discarded on the pavement, where people walked past without even sparing a second glance. Many actions of love and compassion were performed within that building.

Nonetheless, I clearly remember my strong negative reaction to the place, even though I still don't fully understand it. In Nirmal Hriday I felt sad and bewildered. There was so much talk of love and compassion, but I often found it a harsh place in a hard city. The emaciated sick were carried awkwardly by a sister or worker hanging onto splayed limbs. New arrivals were put in the washing place and bathed in public on a tiled platform or the cement floor; their clothes were discarded and their hair cut to control lice. They often cried out as cold water was splashed over them. Someone with a camera might even walk in to photograph them. We had no wheelchairs, but did use basic medicines, antibiotics, and intravenous drips, often topped up with vitamin B complex injections and IV glucose.

I helped feed, wash, and clean patients, changed soiled beds, and mopped up messes. I couldn't get used to the way patients were given food and liquids lying down, and I tried to prop mine up.

As I washed the dead body of one woman, a sheet of her skin slid off in my hand. Another patient died in my arms; I hadn't realized that she was dying. She was fixated on something up on the ceiling, so I looked up to see what it was and she went limp. I helped wrap her in a white sheet and laid her on the shelves in the morgue to be buried in accordance with the customs of her religion. A black morgue truck removed the bodies, the Hindus to be cremated, the Muslims buried.

About half the patients recovered and had to leave to make way for others but often they had nowhere to go. It was heartbreaking and a betrayal of the love bestowed on them to force them back out onto the street. Those who had nothing or no one to go back to often bounced back to Kalighat after some months, as sick and emaciated as ever. I thought there must have been a way to move them to one of the other houses for some rehabilitation. In the Home for the Dying the possibility of the patients recovering and living had not been thought through well.

In Manila we had known everyone's name and could communicate with them. I struggled to learn words in Bengali and Hindi. One day I saw a patient wailing, hanging onto one of the sisters' feet, and she roughly pushed him off and shouted at him that he had to go. Overwhelmed at the sight, I just walked out onto the street, walking round and round, crying, broken and confused. I wondered what the point of it all was.

While working in Kalighat I became sick one day with stomach pains, diarrhea, and fever. I kept working until the van brought us home at

lunchtime and then was doubled up in the bathroom at Park Street. I
thought I would pass out there on the floor. No one seemed to notice
I was missing and, although I recovered after two or three days while
continuing with my normal duties, I still felt weak. Many of the other
sisters were also sick. For a while Naomi's face was as red as a stop light
and she stayed in bed, then on her first day back at work she fell over in
the washing place, twisting and spraining her knee so badly that we had
to carry her inside. Another sister had typhoid, others malaria, and once
many of us had food poisoning after eating donated canned meat. Rarely,
however, did anyone stop working to go to bed.

On a break in our routine, about twenty of us sisters and volunteers took five hundred Kalighat street children for an outing. It was a
riot! There was total pandemonium as volunteers and sisters showered
all those children beforehand in the washing place at the Home for the
Dying, using tins and water from the holding tanks. Then the girls were

Sister Tobit at the Kalighat Children's Picnic, 1980.
(Photographer: unknown French volunteer)

dressed in new clothes, their hair plaited and tied with ribbons. The boys looked smart with oiled hair and a new shirt and shorts. All boarded Assembly of God buses for a trip to a school near the airport for lunch and some games. When we tried to serve the food the children mobbed us, having learned that their survival depended on their ability to fight or push. All five hundred wanted to eat first, fearing that otherwise they would miss out. We adults got home in a state of nervous exhaustion.

I looked forward to attending a weeklong, intensive leprosy course at Titigah, a famous center, but I was able to go for only one day as I contracted malaria. It wasn't the cerebral malaria I had had in Papua New Guinea but the milder, *vivax* form. Brother George, a Missionary of Charity brother, had built the Titigah complex from nothing, the lepers and he clearing and filling a long narrow strip of land along the railway track that passengers had formerly used as a toilet area, reclaiming the land and erecting a bamboo and barbed-wire fence around it. The railway authorities came to pull down the fence, but Brother told them that, if they took away their sanctuary, the lepers would move onto the railway platform. Finally the officials relented and allowed them to keep the land along both sides of the railway track, where they built workshops and installed weaving machines, which the men operated skillfully, while their wives wound the yarn onto spools. Despite disfiguring deformities of their hands, they worked with dexterity and made thousands of white-and-blue MC saris. Many of the lepers had disfigured faces or had lost digits, hands, feet, and limbs. They made shoes out of old tires to protect their unfeeling feet, as their nerves had died. A fishpond, gardens, pigs, and chickens provided food, and they made their own furniture in the carpentry shop. Wards for the sick ones were located on the opposite side of the railway track and were staffed by former patients who did the nursing and physiotherapy and changed dressings.

My mail from home often didn't reach me. We suspected that people in the postal service opened letters going to Mother Teresa's sisters to see if they contained money, and when they found nothing tore off the stamps to sell and trashed the letter. Prepaid airmail was safer, but sometimes we didn't receive even these. Unbeknown to me, my brother Tony, who was a chief petty officer in the Australian Navy, suffered carbon monoxide poisoning in a submarine accident, and Mum had an operation in Canberra Hospital. I received a letter from her, written in red ink, with only four lines, scrawled crookedly across the page telling me she was okay. I was far from reassured about Tony or Mom and became anxious she would die while I was so far away from home. I wrote to her:

> To tell you the truth I am having some difficulties here, but they are quite hard to explain. It's difficult to be always living with people of another culture especially in such a big group as things can be misunderstood. I'm finding it more and more difficult to obey especially when it concerns other people and I am told to treat them or see them treated in a way I can't understand. This has always been going on. I have one idea of what love and service is, and my superior has another. In religious life sometimes, things are distorted and a tidy shelf and having afternoon tea (community duties) are considered more important than human beings. People are living and sleeping all along the street and sometimes they have such a desperate look. The sisters here are used to it and respect and courtesy for the poor isn't common. It's only given to the top ones. Anyway, I'll be ok. I never tell you things like this but I've always been struggling even in Manila. It is hard for someone outside to understand what it's like. I shouldn't have said anything as you are sick but I can't tear it up. Get well soon.

I attributed the fact that I was struggling so much to the lack of continuity in the work. We didn't get to know the poor people well. It is hard to see so many people without homes, on the street, so many neglected little children, and to be so helpless. And the crowds of desperate people all pushing and trying to get their share made it harder to give to each person respectful service. Nevertheless, our way of dealing with people disturbed me. Our rhetoric and our practice were contradictory. In the face of this contradiction, I found it more and more difficult to obey, to relinquish my own judgment. I was told this was because of my pride.

I came into conflict several times with those in charge of me. One feast day, the two junior communities were having afternoon tea together in the downstairs refectory. I noticed that a man was lying on the footpath outside the window, thin with stick-like limbs, covered in rags, obviously suffering from dysentery. Flies and mess were all around him. Uncomfortable with the contrast between life within and outside that wall, I asked if we could help the man, bringing down on myself angry scolding concerning my pride and self-importance. I was told that Park Street was a training house, and that if we started to respond to the poor, people would come to the gate expecting help. I couldn't see an alternative, as the emaciated man would have died unattended outside our window if we hadn't acted. Eventually he was taken to Kalighat.

One stormy night I went up onto the Park Street roof in the dark to be alone. In a doorway across the street I saw a gaunt man illuminated by lightning as he sheltered, ragged, sitting on his haunches. The sight of that man haunted me. I had vowed to serve people like him, and also vowed to obey my superiors. There shouldn't have been a conflict.

Whenever Mother was in Calcutta we walked to the Mother House to receive her instructions several times a week. I took notes of our meetings and typed them up so that they could be photocopied and read by other sisters. On one occasion we were returning, two by two, saying the Rosary, after listening to Mother's instructions about the sacredness of the poor. My partner and I were in the middle of the group, but we separated from them when we saw a man lying near the cemetery. Parched and emaciated, he couldn't stand and had only a bit of dirty rag wrapped around him that was falling off. When we asked him if he would come with us, he started crying and touched our feet with his hands. I pulled back, having seen people touch Mother's feet, and thinking, *Who am I for this man to touch my feet like that?* We hurried back to the Mother House to arrange his transport to Kalighat, but as a result we were late returning home to Park Street.

When we arrived, everyone else was doing spiritual reading, so we were in trouble. We explained to the tertian mistress what had happened, but she would not listen to our excuses. "Why are you the only ones who can't be here on time? Do you have such a need for a grand entrance? Do you think you are so much more charitable than everyone else? I don't

know how the poor of Calcutta ever survived before you came along."
The only answer could be "Thank you, Sister."

But I wrote in my notebook, "Don't ignore the poor just to keep out
of trouble." I was corrected for lack of humility, for conceit and pride,
for being opinionated and judgmental, but I feel that my true spiritual
struggle was to defeat cowardice. It was so much easier to be a yes-person,
especially in training, when we sisters were corrected harshly and continuously.

Every week I confessed many things, among them, "I don't have much
moral courage and this could lead me to a serious betrayal of Christ. I
don't have the courage to endure anger and disapproval and the ridicule
of others. I give up trying to help the poor people." But I wrote in my
notebook:

1. When I see any need, I will do my best to respond and not make
   the excuse that I can't do anything.
2. I will obtain any necessary permissions, stay within time limits,
   and face any scolding.
3. I will get to know the beggars, the garbage pickers, the squatters,
   and the street children and not be disturbed by the accusations.

Mass distributions of food to the poor were often not an expression
of love. The anonymous poor stood in the heat in long lines. Desperately
poor people are difficult to manage in crowds, and the sisters were rough
with them. Yet Mother taught, "The more disfigured or deformed the
image of God in the person, the greater will be our faith and loving
devotion in seeking the face of Jesus and lovingly ministering to him."

I thought we should respond with more respect, but when I voiced
my concerns I was told not to judge. As a result, I asked myself, *Am I
deluded?* I felt a kind of anguish, wanting to live my dream of helping, yet
waking up in a nightmare. I had a different opinion from my superiors
about how to respond to the poor. The fact that I had an opinion was
the real problem

Sister Naomi and I had been reported by an unknown fellow tertian
for walking together on one occasion. The informant must have thought

this was the sign of a "particular friendship" and that we had sought each other out because we were from the same country. A few days later I was accused by the tertian mistress of breaking a sewing machine that I hadn't touched. I became very angry even though it was a small incident, and, instead of silently accepting the rebuke, my pent-up frustrations were unleashed and I exploded in the hallway on the stairs near the kitchen: "I didn't touch that machine. Who said I did? Love is forever preached at us here, but where is the love? If a sister hits one of the poor, I'm told not to judge her, but it seems perfectly fine to judge me. Does anyone come running to you every time two sisters from Kerala or Bihar walk together? Yet because two Australians walk to the Mother House together, it's some sort of crime."

"Tobit, go to the chapel and calm down. Get some self-control and then I will see you in my room," my tertian mistress commanded.

I sat in the chapel wanting to punch something. Mother taught us that humiliations and failures were "chances," "gifts" that help us become holy and help us know our own nothingness.

After a while I went to the tertian mistress's office, knelt, touched my head to the floor, and spoke my fault for my anger. Embarrassed that I had lost my temper, I was still angry at the system that controlled me.

The motto of the order was *Ek dil, prem pur,* "One heart full of love," but often this was not the reality. In an order that symbolized love and compassion, there was an institutionalized harshness. Many of the sisters were deeply sensitive, gentle people, but some were unhappy, living a way of life not suited to them. The faces of some of the more senior women portrayed anger or depression; I thought some may have been—or become—psychologically disturbed. I heard of an incident where a sister had some decorative plants in pots on the roof of one of the houses in Calcutta. Mother demanded that the pots be taken down and broken up, which emotionally shattered the sister.

Every Friday we made the Stations of the Cross, praying and genuflecting at fourteen depictions of Christ on His way to Calvary. As we meditated on the sufferings of Christ, we were to learn from Him to accept humiliation without complaint. There are many different versions of these meditations; one, of which Mother was fond, was a set of fourteen questions for each Station of the Cross. For example:

"They torture you with insulting words and you set yourself only to love them all the more, and I?" In other words, when I, a sister, am insulted, what do I do? Do I just accept it as Christ would have done, or do I defend myself? Mother Teresa's view of suffering and obedience resulted from the way she immersed herself in the Passion of Christ, which to her was not a past event, but a living reality. Christ still cried, "I thirst," and Mother believed His thirst was quenched by the love and suffering of His spouses, of us, the Missionaries of Charity. Jesus had accepted the Father's will, had submitted to a humiliating death without hatred. In the Resurrection, Christ absorbed evil and turned it to good. By loving His enemies, He won for all humanity the chance to live forever.

Our entire life as an MC was to be one of reparation. In a way Mother thought the purpose of our lives was to suffer and become "victims of His love" in order to share His redemptive work. To Mother, our submission was not servitude, but a way of restoring a primal order. Mother said this often enough, but the concepts seemed so alien to my way of thinking that I was slow to understand them. I understood that suffering was an unavoidable part of life, but I believed that it should be relieved as much as possible. Mother, however, deliberately chose what was hard and penitential, which explained why she valued corporal penance and the silent acceptance of humiliation. I thought goodness was better defined as a courageous, even rebellious love. Surrendering executive control of the self, accepting orders without question, can lead good people to do evil in the name of God. One biblical text she encouraged us to study in order to submit was from St. Peter's epistle:

> Slaves, you should obey your masters respectfully, not only those
> who are kind and reasonable but also those who are difficult. You
> see there is merit if in awareness of God you put up with the pain
> of undeserved punishment; but what glory is there in putting up
> with a beating after you have done something wrong? The merit
> in the sight of God is in putting up with it patiently when you are

doing your duty. This in fact is what you were called to do because Christ suffered for you. . . . He was insulted and did not retaliate with insults; when he was suffering he made no threats but put his trust in the upright judge (1 Peter 2:18–23).

Mother Teresa had good support for her ideas in the New Testament, and at this point in my life it was unthinkable for me to consider that this book was in error. Yet her paradigm, her logic of faith, was very different from mine, and this inevitably led me to inner conflict and misunderstandings.

Mother was born in Albania just before World War I. After the premature death of her father, her once-prosperous family struggled. When she joined the Loreto order she was sent to Calcutta, where she lived during World War II and the subsequent bloody partitioning of India. She had witnessed famine and wars on several continents, had seen people washed away in floods and tidal waves, yet her faith was thought to be unshakable. As she tried to make sense of the world's agony, she concluded that any suffering, when united to Christ's passion, was a force for good. She taught that accepting hardship in union with Christ was a chance not to be wasted, the jewel of the spiritual life. Mother often said, "Let me be cut to pieces, yet let each piece belong to Him."

In 1969 Mother founded an organization called the Sick and Suffering Co-Workers as a way for people all over the world to share in her work even though they were too ill or elderly to work directly with her. This group had grown out of Mother's friendship with Jacqueline de Decker, a Belgian woman she had met in 1948, who had wanted to join the order in India but was unable to do so due to ill health. Mother thought that any suffering united to Christ's passion shared his redemptive power. Jacqueline became Mother's sick and suffering coworker offering her prayers, suffering, and practical help for Mother's intentions. During the 1970s each sister was assigned a sick and suffering coworker who prayed and offered their sufferings for the sister's benefit; the two also exchanged letters. A Hungarian woman, Sarolta Erdelyi, had the challenging job of praying for me. In Mother's eyes, this organization harnessed pain and illness as a spiritual resource.

Each Tuesday we recited the Litany of Humility, praying to be delivered from the desire to be loved and from the fear of being humiliated, despised, wronged, and ridiculed. I had trouble accepting that humiliation served any purpose. Far from being a spiritual tool, I thought that humiliation was destructive. Today I believe this even more strongly.

"Love one another" was on the wall of every Missionary of Charity refectory, but the way a superior spoke and corrected a sister created a culture toxic to the human spirit. I didn't find the heat, the work, and the environment hard to bear but the contradiction between the ideal and the reality generated turmoil in me.

In spite of this I tried to conform myself to the order's way of life. I fought tiredness and pain in my arms as I tried to say the Paters (ten Our Fathers) at night, kneeling with outstretched arms near my bed. As Mother stipulated, I offered these prayers to obtain perseverance in my vocation as an MC. The love of God was meant to fulfill all my needs, but to me Jesus was a blank darkness. I kept struggling to force myself into the MC mold.

Mother often quoted the Old Testament, especially "Obedience is better than sacrifice" (1 Samuel 15:22) to explain that it was more pleasing to God to surrender one's own plans than to choose to do something difficult. Yet to me this biblical passage demonstrated the dangers of mindless subservience. The "divine command" that Saul disobeyed was an order to kill everything in the captured territories, "man and woman, babe and suckling, ox and sheep, camel and donkey" (1 Samuel 15:3). Saul had spared some animals temporarily. He said that this was because he wanted to offer them as sacrifice. But God insisted through the prophet Samuel that He wanted absolute obedience, not sacrifice. Today, just as in biblical times, mindless, literal obedience to ancient religious commands presents a dangerous threat to the life and well-being of others.

A sister was to show "loving trust in the superior" and to become like an inanimate object. In support of this demand, Mother used an example taken from the writings of her patron saint, Thérèse of Lisieux, who taught that we were to be like a ball in the child Jesus' hands; He could play with his toy, destroy it, or discard it as He saw fit. Mother believed that because God was in control, we were "to accept whatever

He gives and give whatever He takes with a smile." She addressed us as "my dearest children," but I saw that no one is meant to stay a child forever.

I didn't fit within the Society. My way of thinking was different and I was not comfortable with the way we dealt with people, not only in India but also in other countries. But I had lost confidence in myself and couldn't decide if my own thoughts were valid or if my criticisms of the order were the empty reactions of an inexperienced person in an unfamiliar situation. My reason was paralyzed and had no contact with an unbiased outside opinion. I felt dull and empty and became devoid of emotion. My idealism and enthusiasm had dried up and in their place I felt the apathy of depression, not the peace of detachment.

Tertianship was meant to be a time of renewal, a time to deepen my commitment to my vocation. Yet I couldn't put aside my realization that, just as the Society expected the sisters to conform unthinkingly to its schedule and routines, it also expected the poor to conform: to have a fever on the right day, to die during office hours and not interrupt meals, prayers, or spiritual reading. But if someone approached me to say "I am hungry" or "My child is burning with fever," I wanted to be free to respond to him or her, not to face the prospect of being refused permission to assist them.

Young and impulsive, I had joined the order because a film about Mother had inspired me to work with the poor. I had not understood the implications of my decision, nor thought it through properly. Once in the Society I was not able to break free. Having fulfilled my long-cherished goal of working in Calcutta, I no longer felt attracted to the MCs' work or their way of life. My superiors in India called me "deformed" and "uncontrollable," yet I thought I was voiceless and too compliant. They told me:

"You are easily tricked."

"You have no experience of these people."

"You think you are so much better than everyone else. You will see what will happen."

However, Mother had often said something like, "It's better to make a mistake in kindness than to achieve wonders through lack of kindness."

I decided to leave the Society and asked to see Mother Teresa to advise her of my decision. I entered the room, touched my head to the ground, and, kneeling, "spoke my faults." Then, still kneeling, I said, "Mother, I can't stay in the Society, I don't fit. My way of thinking and responding clashes with the attitude of others. I am scolded if I respond in the way I think I should. I can't understand how some sisters are so angry or the way they treat the poor, even hit them. We have become like an institution here. Here we can't even carry boxes, like we do everywhere else, but have servants to do that. I don't think I should make my vows. I want to go home. I don't feel this way of working is for me. There is a longing in me that is not satisfied. This is not the way I want to live."

She was not sympathetic. "It is a temptation, Sister. You look into Mother's eyes. I tell you, Sister, and I would not tell you a lie, you have a vocation and a very beautiful vocation to be a Missionary of Charity. I forbid you to let these thoughts come again. If thoughts like this come, say, 'Mother has forbidden me to think like this.' It will be a source of pride for you. You will think, 'My superior is angry, I am never angry.' But you might do something just as displeasing to God that no one can see. Your face before God might be just as terrible as her angry face. Do not judge. You do not know how much she has struggled. One sister came here and lost her temper and then later she came crying with sorrow saying, 'Mother at least ten times today I kept my temper.' If you think like this, you must go to confession and say 'I was disobedient and judgmental'; otherwise, these thoughts will simply break you. They will come between you and the love of God and you will end up leaving.

"It is up to you to get the street people. Don't let them miss out. Follow the Rule. Fight for it, but be careful not to let these thoughts come. Make reparation for thinking like this. Take the discipline harder and make real reparation. Pray to Our Lady. Ask her to give you a heart so beautiful, so pure, so immaculate, a heart full of love and humility. You can become very holy where you are, but you must break off these thoughts. It is the devil coming to you as an angel of light. 'How can you say to your brother, "Let me take that speck out of your eye," while a plank remains in your own? You hypocrite! Remove the plank from your own eye first and then you will see clearly to take the speck from your brother's eye' [Matthew 7:4–5]." Mother then told me the story of a woman who had said she would rather have seen her daughter leave the convent in a coffin than to break her vows.

I should have stood up and said, "Mother, I intend to leave. I don't intend to hit myself or make further confessions. I don't intend to wallow in further self-examination and self-doubt. Please arrange for me to go home." However, I stayed on my knees until dismissed.

Mother had told me she had no doubts. She spoke with dogmatic certainty and assurance. She seemed to have no empathy with those who struggled to believe, and didn't admit to struggles with her beliefs. I was, however, plagued by questions which I thought were temptations against the faith and so I took the advice of the poet Tagore to wait out these feelings of darkness and nothingness in stillness and silence.

If thou speakest not I will fill my heart with thy silence and endure it. I will keep still and wait like the night . . .

The morning will surely come, the darkness will vanish, and thy voice pour down in golden streams breaking through the sky (Gitanjali XIX).

The dawn, however, seemed a long way off.

I live in the hope of meeting with him; but this meeting is not yet (Gitanjali XIII).

Whenever Mother was in Calcutta we continued to walk to the Mother House to listen to her instructions and I took notes. Mother described us MCs as sweepings—*kachara samage* (anglicized Bengali expression) and said that because of this God could work great things through us. She went on to say we must never become "tip-top" or experts. We must not be ashamed of our low educational standards. The apostles were fishermen, the experts, and during the whole night they caught nothing. Then the carpenter told them to throw in the net and though everything was against it, they caught plenty. This may be the underlying reason why I was sent so inadequately prepared for my work in PNG and Manila.

Mother wanted us to embrace poverty as she did because it bore witness to the true face of Jesus, poor, humble, and a friend of sinners, the weak and despised. We needed, she said, to deliberately choose to live a life of hardship, privation, insecurity, and empty-handedness in imitation of Jesus and in solidarity with the poor. We should be happy to be treated as one of the poor; ready to be ill-treated, insulted, refused, put to all kinds of inconvenience and falsely blamed. She said we must not seek to defend ourselves but leave it to the Lord to do it.

In the weeks leading up to Christmas Mother spoke to us again of the humility of Christ: "Christmas time shows us how small God is, how He lived that total surrender. We sing such beautiful hymns but it must have been terrible for Mary and Joseph to have their first child in that cold. This is what we must learn, Sisters, to be that child. It is for us Missionaries of Charity to be like that child in complete surrender, trust, and joy. Christmas shows us how much heaven appreciates humility, surrender, poverty. God Himself, who made you and me, became poor and humble."

When I went to see Mother about leaving the order I also spoke to her about the fact that we had a Christmas party for our wealthier catechism children but not for the garbage pickers and street children. I don't know if there was any connection, but afterward I learned that we were to give a party for the first time in Park Street on Christmas afternoon for the street children. I knew little about it and was not involved in preparing for it.

On Christmas Eve we attended midnight Mass in the Mother House chapel. About four hundred sisters sang; it was beautiful and uplifting. Afterward Mother gave us all her blessing by laying her right hand on each sister's bowed head. Like children, we all received a packet of sweets, and then around 2 a.m. walked, singing, back along the road to Park Street. On the pavement outside our house a whole group of street children lay sleeping on the pavement, waiting for the Christmas party the next day. I gave my sweets to one of them, who nearly pulled off my hand in his eagerness to get it.

On Christmas morning I was among a few sisters sent with a French volunteer who was also a musician to sing at the Christmas Mass at Fort William, a military chapel where one of the sisters had a Sunday school. The chaplain there was the cardinal's secretary, so after Mass we also visited the cardinal, who offered us Christmas cake and wine. I think we did eat some cake, in spite of the order's rules not to eat outside the convent. After all this was the cardinal. Then, at about 9 a.m., we left the comfortable drawing room to serve rice and curry to about a thousand poor people at Shishu Bhavan; most of them had brought their own dish, but some had to eat off banana leaves or plastic sheets.

On our return to Park Street we found that only five sisters were trying to work with the several hundred unruly street children in the washing place. The whole operation was hopelessly understaffed and disorganized and so we started to help. We let in a few children at a time and gave each child some clothes, cake, sweets, and a balloon. We finished at 5 p.m., after about eight hours; everyone was frazzled and exhausted. I felt certain that my tertian mistress blamed me for coming up with such a stupid idea.

On their way to becoming a part of a new foundation in Pakistan, Sister Hua and two newly professed Filipina sisters whom I'd taught, Rosario and Francia, came to Calcutta. We had a great reunion, and they told us of Pope John Paul II's visit to the Philippines. He had driven down Tayuman Street in his Popemobile and our children and the stronger patients had waited on the pavement to greet him; Sister Aloysius, the Manila superior, had put a garland around his neck. I received news of the other sisters and patients and of the new children's home being built near the Tahanan. The sisters told me that there were so many sick and malnourished children from the Tondo area that the sisters in Binondo could no longer cope with the number of admissions, so it was decided to build a home for children in Tondo as well. I also learned that Sister Eva, the first Filipina MC, had left, as had another Australian sister who had been sent to Bourke.

Prior to our vows, Mother gave us more intense instruction: "The making of vows is like the Crucifixion. That is why we renew our vows on the Cross. By poverty our right hand is nailed—it cannot freely give; by chastity the left hand closest to the heart is nailed—it cannot take the love of anyone but only Jesus. By obedience the right foot is nailed—it cannot freely step where it wishes. By our vow of humility, of service, of burning love, the fourth vow—our left foot is nailed and must always follow the right in humility."

Mother was clear; the fourth vow of service to the poor was regulated by obedience, and the left foot had to follow the right. Service had to be rendered through obedience.

Thirty-four of us were to make final vows on May 24, 1981, in the Church of St. Thomas, the doubting apostle, and eighty-one sisters were to make their first vows the night before.

Mum had decided to come to Calcutta to see me take my vows, which was financially difficult for her. It became even harder when a taxi driver robbed her in Bombay and left her in the dark some distance from the International Airport. I was on retreat when she arrived and couldn't meet her at Calcutta Airport, so she was taken to the house nearby. She was treated unkindly by some of the permanent live-in workers. I got her booked into the YWCA, where some of the coworkers and volunteers stayed, and was able to spend a little time with her the day before my final vows. She was very happy to see me, but traumatized by her experiences, she had formed a negative view of India and Calcutta. I was relieved that at least she was safe and not physically injured during the robbery.

Sister Naomi's parents missed her profession altogether because, at the last minute, Mother rescheduled the ceremony from May 24 to May 14. They had prebooked their travel, planning to visit Rome first, and so although they met up with Naomi in Calcutta, they missed the ceremony. Mother needed to be in Rome by the 24th as fourteen sisters there were making their final vows; inexplicably this scheduling conflict was not foreseen. Seemingly random changes in plans were common within the order and were to be accepted not as poor planning but as manifestations of God's will no matter the inconvenience or hardship they caused others.

Early in the morning, while it was still dark, we walked to the Church of St. Thomas in pairs, saying the Rosary and stepping over and around the still sleeping pavement dwellers. The Profession Mass started at 6 a.m. and Mum and other visitors were picked up from the YWCA in time for the ceremony. We had all written out our vows according to the prescribed formula the day before. At the top of the page we drew a cross with the words "I thirst" under it, because our vows were to help quench this spiritual thirst. Just before the offertory we stood in a semicircle around the altar, in front of a large cross. Mother stood with us as the priest called each of us by name. When it was my turn, I heard, "Sister Tobit." I bowed, stepped forward, and said, "Lord, you have called me." Once everyone's name had been called we read our vows together and went up two by two to sign our vow paper on the altar. We each then gave our signed sheet to Mother.

After our vows we went back to the Mother House to celebrate. The washing place had been decorated with streamers made of shredded paper covering string and interspersed with circles of yellow cardboard, on which was drawn a cross with rays emanating from it. Mother and many of the professed and the novices gathered to welcome us. They sang, clapped, and put garlands around our necks. We then had a special breakfast to recognize the importance of the day to us all.

Mum stayed as a tourist for a few more days, and some of the sisters went with us on a trip to Bandel, a church and shrine to Our Lady, at Hooghly, about an hour's train ride from Howrah Station in Calcutta. Greener and less polluted than Calcutta, it was enjoyable for me, but Mum was made uncomfortable by two women whose faces were disfigured by leprosy and who were begging on the train. At Park Street the sisters dressed Mum up in a red embroidered sari we had bought from the markets and told her she looked like Mrs. Gandhi. These few pleasant experiences didn't change Mum's mind about India, however. On her return to Australia she acted as a courier, taking mail and undeveloped photographic film home for a fellow Australian she'd met in the YWCA, even calling the woman's mother to advise that, if she were ever asked to visit Calcutta, she was to say a definite no.

From Calcutta I received the good news that I was to be sent back to Manila. Mother came up to the Dum Dum house close to the airport with a group of us who were leaving around the same time for various parts of the world. She was on her way to Rome for the professions, and then on to Brazil. Before she left, she gave us a long instruction exhorting us to remember the delicate love of Jesus and the terrible sin of Judas at the table with Him. Mother said that when Judas kissed Jesus, He did not withdraw, even though He knew that kiss would mean the Crucifixion. She commented that if we could remember this, our communities would be wonderful. I thought it would just result in the crucifixion of the gentlest sisters as it did with Christ. However, Mother went on to speak of the love of Jesus for the one who betrayed Him. Misunderstandings will happen, she said, and there will always be someone to carry tales; but Jesus is there to show us how to love. She reminded us that when the man slapped Jesus he didn't fight back and obeyed his own teaching to "Turn the other cheek." She said that we often resent it when someone hurts us—we give back—that is where we must see Jesus. Love begins and ends there. Either we put love into action and serve, or we put hatred into action and destroy. The Crown of Thorns, she said, teaches us the silence of love. Let us have the humility to accept the Cross without pride.

One of Mother's on-going themes was Christ's acceptance and submission and she elaborated on this again as we were about to depart for our mission houses: Jesus, she said, didn't avoid. In the garden He said, "I am He." The passion of Jesus is a lesson in love. When they said "Come down!" He could have come down. She encouraged us not to try to escape humiliation, but to grab the chance to be like Him, to allow Him to live His passion in us. To her, a carrier of love was a carrier of the Cross. She said we should ask sincerely from the depths of our heart: "Let me share your loneliness, your being unloved, your being uncared for." Do something today, she told us, to share in the Passion: just to smile, to be in time to say, "May I?", to give up an unhealthy friendship. Let us double our penance to obtain that one grace, to share in the Passion of Jesus in our lives. We are losing our grip on sacrifice. On the Cross, Jesus has shown us the deepest poverty: complete surrender and abandonment to His Father.

I had surrendered, I had made my vows, and now I was going back to serve in the one place in which I had felt happy and secure in my purpose.

CHAPTER EIGHT

Return to Manila:
Novice Mistress

Child at a Missionary of Charity feeding center.
(Photographer: C. Livermore)

*B*ack in Manila in early June 1981, I arrived to a great welcome. The sisters clustered around the airport doors and greeted me joyfully as I emerged with my boxes into the throng of porters and cabbies. I was touched and happy to be with them again and in a familiar place. In Tondo a blaring horn announced our arrival. The novices ran out, singing and clapping, and later the long-stay patients and people from the barrios also welcomed me back warmly.

While I was away, many more sisters had arrived, including Japanese, Taiwanese, and Korean trainees. Some had a very difficult time, especially those who couldn't speak English. To change country, culture, weather, lifestyle, and language all at once was overwhelming. To make it even harder, one or two were recent converts to Catholicism.

More buildings now crowded the compound. A new storeroom had been built next to the Tahanan and, adjoining that, a children's home, in which we cared for toddlers with malnutrition and other illnesses. In front of the children's home was a clinic where people from the surrounding districts came for medicine. A small house for visiting volunteers and guests had also been built.

When I arrived, Sister Gabrielle, who had become the regional superior for Asia, was in Japan opening the new house in Tokyo, but she was to return in a few weeks. Mother had assigned Naomi to Tokyo, but she was still waiting in Calcutta for her visa. It was a joke around the Mother House that sisters should stay out of Mother's line of vision if they didn't want to be sent to whatever house she was thinking of at the time. Apparently, Naomi had nearly ended up in several other countries before she reached Japan.

I was assigned to be Sister Gabrielle's assistant and was responsible for the novices when she was away. I worked in the Tahanan with the second-years in the mornings and also on the professed day off and was to teach the novices and postulants in the afternoon. On the weekends I visited Barrio Magdaragat.

For a few months a German medical student named Matilda worked with us, staying in the visitors' cottage and helping out with the children. A very ill, dehydrated child arrived late in the afternoon on the professed sisters' day off, so Matilda put in an IV line and nasogastric feeding tube and gave him fluids and antibiotics. I nursed him as he labored to breathe, his sunken eyes rolled upward so that only the whites showed. I thought he would die. Matilda and his parents stayed with him, as I was obliged to go to prayer and my evening meal. Afterward I escaped from recreation to see how he was. Matilda said he was a bit better, but he was feverish and panting, his eyes still lifeless and sunken. The skin covering his thin ribs was being sucked in with each breath. His family had gone home. It was night and I went out into the dark of the compound, which was the only way to be alone. The neighboring school choir was practicing Handel's "Halleluiah" chorus. The music was beautiful: "The king of all the earth . . ." I cried out to the darkness, "Why?" When I went back inside the child was improving. I thought God had worked a miracle through Matilda to bring him back from the brink.

When Christmas came, with its usual frenetic activity, we had our Christmas party in the Tondo compound, and this time the children played a *piñata,* a game in which a mud pot full of sweets and small prizes is suspended on a rope slung over a pole. The leader of each of the children's teams was blindfolded and took a turn trying to hit and break the pot to allow the sweets and toys to rain down for his team.

At the same time as the joyful party, a woman who had come to us late with advanced TB died. The father had already passed away, and we had to call her two boys from the festivities to break the news to them that their mother was dead. We accompanied them to the veranda of the Tahanan outside the women's ward, where she lay lifeless. The older son broke down, tearing at the window's wire mesh, crying and screaming. The younger boy didn't understand. In the background, amid the sobs of the bereaved children, others were singing Christmas carols.

I often came face to face with death, yet never got used to its finality or its effects on the living. One night a young man named Francisco died, his eyes fixed in a frightened stare. His pregnant wife collapsed over him, sobbing because he would never see his unborn child. The next day, seeing his shoes next to his bed, it seemed unreal that he had gone forever and would never wear them again. I saw little ones die and felt untrained and inadequate. Some of the boys' eyes seemed so large and innocent, yet they looked like old men at the age of four.

Sister Gabrielle left us to return to Calcutta, as she had been elected to the Council, a body of sisters who advised Mother. Our new regional superior was Sister Dolores, whom I had known in Melbourne and with whom I had an uneasy relationship.

Full of questions myself, by the beginning of 1982 I had become the first-year novice mistress, supervising the novices, who remained inside the house and only went out to work twice a week. They did the cooking, which included making several hundred *chapattis*, the Indian pancake-like bread we ate for breakfast. We rolled them out and cooked them in a heavy pan on an open fire. Apart from the kitchen, a first-year novice's major activities were prayer and study, but we also cared for two pigs, some chickens, and the vegetable garden, sorted medicine, relieved the professed on their day off, and did the weekly marketing.

Our garden produced beans, okra, corn, eggplants, and pumpkins, but I could not get potatoes to grow. I dreamed of growing tea bushes to have a proper "cuppa," as I don't think I have ever tasted anything I disliked more than the soybean coffee served as a tea substitute in Manila. As I forced it down, I remembered sitting in the sun on the front veranda in Moss Vale with Peggy, my blue cocker spaniel, by my side, reading the Sunday papers, my hands wrapped around a hot mug of sweet tea.

The novice mistresses answered to the regional superior and the Mother House in Calcutta for the running of the novitiate, but places such as the Tahanan and children's home were under the authority of the professed superior in Tondo. I reported to one of the councillors in Calcutta, who gave the overseas novitiates guidance, and I mailed her regular updates on the novices' progress and suitability. One young Filipina was a particular problem because she was psychologically disturbed and of below-average intelligence. Having written to the councillor about her, I received a reply saying that God used humble, less-gifted people and could achieve more through them than those who relied on their intelligence. Nonetheless, the situation became more difficult when the young novice became depressed, cried a lot, and said repeatedly that she wanted to die. She couldn't sleep and took clothes from under my bed to wash in the middle of the night. One morning she put yogurt instead of powdered milk into the tea for the whole community, and as mistress I faced rebukes from Sister Dolores that I was not training the novice correctly. Eventually I obtained permission for her to see a psychiatrist, who put her on medication, but a multitude of things made it clear it wouldn't be in the best interests of the Society or herself for her to remain in the novitiate. She seemed to have developed a preoccupation with me and shadowed me until I was finally allowed to arrange for her to return to her family.

In late August I was exhausted. There was a lot of cooking to be done for the Society's feast day on August 22, but I had to lie down. The superior of the professed, Sister Valerie, found out I was on my bed without permission and came to see what was wrong. She believed my problem was psychological and that I was depressed, but I had never felt like this before and had always been able to work hard no matter how sad I became. This felt physical to me, not psychological.

I didn't understand what was happening. In my notebook I wrote several self-admonitions urging me to overcome the pervasive fatigue and to suppress the surges of anger I felt when unexpected demands were made on me. "Even in the early morning I feel very tired, exhausted. I am weak and could easily lose patience. Help me to love, to accept, to not become angry. Help me to overcome the desire to run away from the novices and MC life. Help me to be patient with them, as you are with me." I saw a doctor, who didn't think much was wrong with me but started me on isoniazid tablets, which are a treatment for tuberculosis. I am not sure if the doctor thought I had caught or was in danger of catching TB from the patients, but the pills did not help, and I continued to be overwhelmingly weary. After about a week my urine went black. Sister Reka, the good-natured New Zealander who was still in Manila, had some dealings with the doctors at the Santo Thomas Hospital and had use of the van for business such as dispensary work and picking up parcels from the wharf. I collected some urine and asked her to help me. "Reka, my urine's gone like black tea. It can't all be in my mind. Take this and see if you can find out what's wrong with me."

Somehow she arranged for me to be sent to Santo Thomas for tests. It was a long way and my companion and I had to change jeepneys several times. The doctor took blood tests and checked me over and we started for home again. I had just arrived when a phone call came from Santo Thomas. I was ordered to bed until the van could take me back to the hospital.

I had a severe form of hepatitis and became jaundiced soon after admission. Being a non-Filipina *madre* who wore a funny scarf on her head, I was an object of curiosity in the ward. The other patients asked me why I didn't take off my "hat," but I imagine an almost-bald *madre* would have been even more of a curiosity. Since I was at a teaching hospital, full of medical students, they had great fun with my surname—"Livermore's liver collapsed!"—and asked me if I drank alcohol.

My serology was negative for hepatitis A and B and Santo Thomas did not yet have the ability to test for hepatitis E, a form discovered in the early 1980s and found largely in Asia. Like hepatitis A, it is transmitted by drinking water contaminated by sewage because of flooding during the monsoons. Hepatitis E mainly affects young people, who experience jaundice, fatigue, abdominal pain, loss of appetite, nausea and vomiting, and dark tea-colored urine. The doctors discharged me after about five days. I felt well but wasn't allowed back to work until my liver function tests were normal, so I was confined to a bed in the upstairs dormitory of the professed house because of an unfounded fear of contagion. Simple hand washing on my part was all that was needed to prevent cross-infection. I thought it ironic that when I felt exhausted I was in trouble for lying down, but when I felt well again I was forced to rest. I wanted to just pace myself, taking part in regular activities when I thought I could. As it was, I ate alone and had nothing to do. I felt quite depressed. I read spiritual books and continued to criticize and exhort myself to have the courage to speak the truth and the humility to bear dishonor. I wrote in my notebook, "You must be true to whatever you feel is right but you must stay in the Society." And I wrote out this prayer:

> Father, teach me your will. Let me know what to do. Show me the path that leads to you. Lord, I cannot see you, show yourself to me. Jesus, I cannot hear you, speak to me. All around is dark and doubt, redeem me. You are always by my side though the darkness hides you. Heal our weakness, pardon us.

After about three weeks I returned to work in the novitiate, teaching the young women how to become MCs even while I struggled to remain one. I don't think they detected my ambivalence. We had a reasonably happy life when just left to get on with our work, but I noticed that I had started to expect people to do exactly what I said and had to resist allowing the novices to do things for me that I should do myself, such as my washing. Those who have been superiors for a long time must find it difficult to avoid arrogance since all the other sisters speak and keep silent at their word. Everyone stands when a superior enters a room; what they say must be obeyed immediately; everything they say must be accepted; they cannot be argued with or contradicted; and some didn't do menial things such as washing and cleaning.

On Thursdays, when the professed had their day off, Sister Barbara, the second-year mistress, usually went with some of her novices to the children's home in Binondo. I stayed in Tondo to be with the novices in the children's home and the Tahanan. Other novices went to the markets in the van to buy or beg for our weekly supplies for both the sisters and the patients.

If Sister Barbara were needed elsewhere, I helped out at the Binondo children's home. On several occasions we had no water there due to a broken pipe, so we had to cart it in from the fire station in a jeepney in order to do the washing and bathe the children. One day I took an hour to cut a five-year-old's hair, which was stuck to her head from infected sores and lice.

I often worried that we didn't know enough about treating the patients' conditions at the Tahanan and the children's home. The number of patients varied between eighty and one hundred in the Tahanan, and, because the cots and beds were close together, there were problems with cross-infections. While Sister Gabrielle, who was medically trained, was living in Tondo she helped us understand the medicines and taught us various procedures, but when she returned to Calcutta we had only an occasional volunteer doctor's visit to rely on. At times we made serious mistakes with medicines and injections.

I wrote of my worries to Sister Gabrielle in Calcutta and received a confusing response. She said that she had also had these concerns when she first worked in Manila, and that she had raised these points with Mother, who was not at all perturbed by the lack of training and the substandard medical care in our centers. But Sister Gabrielle then said that she had changed her mind. She asked me, "What do you want? Do you want a hospital taken over by the clever ones of this world, where love and care are discarded?" I didn't agree that increasing our knowledge necessarily meant that we no longer loved our patients. Her reply seemed so contradictory, even conflicted, and I wondered if it were because she too was perplexed. Perhaps her irritation with me was because I was voicing concerns that she herself had suppressed and didn't want to confront again.

To reply to her rhetorical question: what I wanted was to know what I was doing and to know that we were not harming those whom we cared for and comforted. I wanted us all to know the difference between various medications, such as chloramphenicol, an antibiotic, and chloroquine, an antimalarial. A sister had recently mixed up these drugs due to their similar names, and although there were no serious consequences on that occasion, it concerned me. I wanted the sisters to know the major side effects of some of the tuberculosis drugs; for instance, that deafness can occur even from the correct dose of strepto-mycin, and isoniazid for tuberculosis can cause liver damage and should be stopped if a tuberculosis patient becomes jaundiced. I wanted those giving injections to know what they were injecting, and the purpose and strength of the drug. I also wanted us to take measures to keep contagion to a minimum, in other words, to keep those with active TB away from those without it, to isolate cases of gastroenteritis, measles, and other infectious diseases. With a little knowledge and communication, we could love and care for our patients in a simple way but also give them safe medical treatment.

I had great admiration for Sister Gabrielle and trusted her judgment, so her confusing response was difficult for me to accept. She had taught the novices all she could while she was in Manila to allow them to care for the patients safely, so I knew she understood the dilemma. What she said didn't ring true with the person I knew she was. I still don't understand it.

. . .

Shortly after I wrote to Sister Gabrielle a new local rule was made in Tondo declaring that no new admissions were permitted in the children's home or the Tahanan on Thursdays, while the novices were relieving the professed on their day off. One Thursday, however, a woman cradling a thin, ill child in her arms rushed with her husband toward the gate of our compound in search of help. Roused by the banging, one of the novices, Sister Trinity, let them in. The young boy stared impassively up at her with sunken eyes, so she knew that he was in real trouble and couldn't wait until the next day for help. She approached Sister Valerie: "Sister, I know it's Thursday, but a very sick child has come to the gate . . ."

"How many times do you novices have to be told not to disturb the sisters on their day of recollection?"

"Yes, Sister," Trinity replied.

The novice came to me in the Tahanan, where I was washing the body of a man who had just died of throat cancer, and asked, "Sister, can you come over? I don't know what to do. A very sick boy, about two years old, has come with his parents to the gate. He's feverish and breathing fast. I'm afraid he might die if we send him away. I tried to ask the professed, but they could not be disturbed because it's Thursday. The family is waiting near the dispensary."

"Okay, I won't be long," I told her, thinking this was to be just a routine admission.

I covered the man's body, washed my hands, and walked the fifty yards or so to meet the boy's parents. Many other people were also in the compound, lined up for the dispensary. The child was listless, his hot, loose skin hanging off his stick-like limbs. "Sister," his father pleaded, "we have no money for medicine. The hospital refused to treat him. Please help us." In Manila at the time, if hospital staff thought a patient's chance of survival was low, they refused admission, especially if the people were indigent and unable to pay for treatment.

"Yes, of course. We will do our best, but your son looks very ill. What is his name?"

"His name is Alex," he said, as tears filled his eyes. "We have tried to get help for him, but he's just getting worse."

The sun was scorching, so we moved into the shade near the children's home. It was then that Sister Valerie stormed out of the convent toward us. Our conversation was in English and so was incomprehensible to the child's parents.

"What are you doing here, Tobit? You are forever interfering in affairs that are none of your business. Return to the Tahanan."

"Sister, it is my duty to help the novices. They cannot take full responsibility for the work and, as you have said, the professed are not to be disturbed."

"Return to the Tahanan!" she repeated the command, her voice louder.

"What about this child?"

"There are no admissions today. I have said that repeatedly. Why can't you just accept that we can't help everyone?"

"This child needs someone's help and the hospital won't accept him. We have room. It will not disturb the sisters. The novices and I will do everything for him until tomorrow."

"It's not your concern. You neglect your own work and meddle in things that have nothing to do with you. The child cannot come in today."

Here we go again, I thought. My heart started to thump. Next will come, "You are proud, self-righteous, conceited . . ." I wondered why it had to be so hard. Was I really conceited and self-righteous? I didn't know anymore.

"Sister, the family has come asking for help. It's not right to send him away."

"So only you know what is right? You are too proud to obey. What are you teaching the novices? If you go back to the Tahanan, I will see to this child today, but otherwise no one should come on Thursdays."

I returned to my corpse, retaining a façade of normality, speaking to no one of the storm within me. I called the morgue van and started washing the patients' clothes and linen with the novices. Many of the patients were incontinent, but Mother considered a washing machine contrary to poverty. As usual, we said the Rosary aloud while doing the laundry, using brushes to remove the solid waste. I recited the words of the prayer, but my mind was elsewhere. *Sometimes a poor person is sacred*, I thought, *Christ in His distressing disguise. At other times, he is just another powerless person we can treat as we please.*

One of the novices, a nurse, started Alex's treatment. When I visited him later in the day he was responding to fluids and antibiotics.

The conflict between the ideal and the reality, between my assessment of a situation and that of my superior, pierced through my life like a thorn.

I wrote directly to Mother. I had written to her when I was in India, asking about this conflict between compassion and obedience, but had received no answer. This time I recounted the story of the sick child and then continued:

Often on a Thursday a very sick child will come seeking admission. I am rebuked when I try to help. At least three times, even though you would think it impossible, the children lived. Once a very senior sister told me: "You have no faith. Why do you bother so much to save their lives? They are slum children. If they grow up, they may lead wicked lives. As long as they are baptised it is better that they die." Jesus saved lives and had compassion. He didn't say, "It's best that they die and go to heaven."

So often it happens, Mother, that there is a conflict between charity and obedience. It really tears me in half. We are taught so often and teach the novices, "It is Christ in the disguise of the poor," and then we are told to send Him away.

Sister Gabrielle answered my letter to Mother. I had said that I thought we needed to make exceptions to the rules, and that even Jesus did this by curing on the Sabbath. She answered by saying that the devil also quoted scripture, so I should not be too sure of my ground. Then she asked, "How compassionate is God?" Did I think God was compassionate only when he did something for those who suffered physically? She spoke of Mary standing at the foot of the Cross, accepting as God's will the death of her son, Jesus. She concluded by saying that next time I saw a dying child or a suffering mother and my hands were tied by obedience

I should not stop saying my "yes"; in other words, I was to say yes to my superior and no to the person in need.

I felt violated that a private letter to Mother had been read and answered by someone else, but again I found Sister Gabrielle's reply impossible to understand. It threw me into turmoil. The aberrant logic of belief coupled with the responsibility of authority and enforcing rules can lead people to strange conclusions. The reply wasn't consistent with what I knew Sister Gabrielle would have done if she had been with us in Manila, because she was a woman of compassion.

Some of the superiors in the MCs were thrown into positions of power with little education or preparation, yet they were responsible for hundreds of people and many resources. Because Mother believed that God used the weak to confound the strong and intelligent, the Society acted almost as if preparing someone for a managerial role betrayed a lack of faith. The Society showed the same lack of logic by expecting God to make up for ignorance and lack of training in the medical work.

This incident was pivotal for me. I couldn't say "Fiat" to the unnecessary death of a child. If everything had been done that could be done, and the child died, yes, I could acquiesce to God's will. But I didn't believe that obedience needed to make responding to "Christ in the distressing disguise" so difficult. In my earlier conflicts, I had wanted to stay in the order and learn how to resolve the contradictions of obedience and compassion. After this incident, I saw that these paradoxes wouldn't be resolved because the order didn't see them in the same way. In my notebook I wrote rather melodramatically of my position, "You must speak the truth. You must walk on the edge of the cliff. You must pray and do penance or you will fall." And "I have been trying to follow You and it seems to me that I am further away from You than ever, on the edge of a precipice, which I could easily fall over. I become so angry with the Society. I want to leave and make my own life but maybe by doing that I will break the golden thread of your Providence."

I was not the only person having difficulty. One of the professed took the more dramatic step of just running away one night. We didn't realize what had happened and spent hours looking for her, fearing for her safety. Several other sisters also left the order. We didn't say good-bye, and they were never spoken of. I often thought about them and wondered whether they were able to fit back into their own culture, find love, and have a family, or whether they lived as displaced persons.

On another occasion, the sister who was then in charge of the Tahanan sent three of the male tuberculosis patients away from the ward because relatives had been taking food to them during the night. They had nowhere to go and no means of transport and so they stood outside the Tahanan, thin, sick, and pale in the heat without food or drink. I approached the sister to ask what had happened but was told it was none of my business. In the late afternoon I could stand it no longer, and I gave them something to eat and drink from the kitchen.

Then the criticisms started again: Did I think I was the only person who knew how to be compassionate? Do I have to interfere in affairs that are not my business?

I believe that if you see another person suffering, it becomes your business right then and there. You can't just turn away and pretend that you don't see.

A month or so after these incidents it became clear that I was going to be removed from my position as mistress of the first-year novices. Without discussing it with me, my bedroll was moved from the novices' dormitory and taken to the professed house. Later in the day the superior told me that another sister would soon arrive from India to replace me as mistress. This happened only a few weeks prior to the profession retreat, when the novices would complete their first year, but I was not allowed to continue until the normal changeover. Some days later I received a letter from Calcutta giving me the "good news" that I would no longer be in charge of the first-years: "According to how God will give you the strength, you can share in the teaching. At least the burden of the responsibility will not be on your frail shoulders any longer. At least for the time being."

I was twenty-eight; my shoulders were not frail. Forbidden from further teaching, I felt discarded and excluded. No reason was given, nothing explained. When the new novice mistress arrived from India I tried to hand over to her in an orderly, informative way, but she was dismissive and didn't want to hear from me. In my own mind I attributed the dismissal to the conflict over the child's admission to the children's home on a Thursday and my questioning letters. I had defied a superior and so probably had been deemed unfit to teach novices.

I was sent to Cebu, an island about three hundred seventy-five miles southeast of Manila, traveling by sea as companion to another sister who had been transferred from Binondo, reassigned because she had had difficulty with her superior, an angry person. We carried with us a large amount of cargo to help the sisters at our new centers with their work, and were berthed in the crowded, dormitory-like hull of the ship. We mostly stayed with our boxes, but whenever either of us ventured afield for reasons of personal necessity, our male fellow passengers stared and whistled at us. I suppose we were an odd sight: two nuns, refugees from authority, one a Filipina and the other an Aussie, dressed in Indian saris, sleeping with boxes in the cargo hull of a Filipino ship. They may also have sensed our air of failure and rejection. When the boat docked at Cebu City, the provincial capital, we carried all the boxes up to the wharf (frail shoulders notwithstanding).

I stayed with the community in Cebu for almost three weeks, accompanying the sisters as they visited various squatter areas on bicycles. We lived very close to where the sixteenth-century Portuguese explorer Magellan had come ashore, though the cross that marked the landing site was in the city. Whoever named the poor fishing village on the edge of Cebu City Alaska had a sense of humor, as it was hot as an oven. Most of our neighbors earned their living from the dried-fish business and from collecting shells, selling wood, or collecting and selling recyclables such as beer cans. Much of the transport was by horse-drawn carriage, which was much cheaper in Cebu than in Manila. I went to the markets and helped with the children, who were very cute, though some of the new admissions were swollen from malnutrition. There was also a lot of tuberculosis in Cebu. The sisters were trying to get land for a *tahanan* but were opposed by the local officials, who denied that there were any poor or abandoned people in Cebu, even though at least ten homeless, tubercular, and crippled people slept under the awnings at the side of the local church each night.

The return trip to Manila was a much more pleasant voyage. Six of us sisters were the only passengers in the cabins of a cargo ship. I watched the sunrise from the ship's bridge. We passed many beautiful little islands and could see fishing villages surrounded by coconut palms dotted along the shoreline. A pod of dolphins jumped in front of the ship's hull as if they were racing us.

Mother came for the professions in December 1982. During the retreat I worked in the Tahanan, excluded from the meetings of the novice mistresses and senior sisters even though I had been with the novices all year. Mother wanted us to say a daily prayer to St. Michael the Archangel, who is usually depicted as winged and with a pitchfork, standing on the devil's head. I felt guilty that I didn't believe in St. Michael or the devil, who seemed to be one of my chief advisers. My sense of humor was turning dark and cynical. I had tried with all my strength to do what I thought was good and yet felt like a failure and an outcast.

Now seventy-two, Mother Teresa suffered recurrent malaria, which strained her heart, causing her to be sometimes flushed and short of breath, along with giving her swollen feet. One night after prayer I called her to the professed house so that she could take an overseas phone call. I waited for her while she spoke on the phone and then accompanied her back to the novitiate dormitory, where she sat on her bed, under the mosquito net, too short of breath to lie flat. I remained standing there until she waved me away, whispering that she was all right.

At breakfast Mother was poured some tea. At the same time the salt was passed down the table in a rather large glass. Mother took two teaspoons and put it in the tea. The server came and whispered to me, "Does Mother like salt in her tea?" She didn't say anything to Mother, thinking she must have been doing penance. When Mother drank the tea, she coughed and went red with laughter, realizing her mistake. Such a penance wouldn't have helped her heart failure.

All the sisters went to see Mother privately to renew our general permissions. As the time for my appointment approached I became anxious because of the letters I had written to Calcutta and because I felt I'd failed as a novice mistress. After kneeling in front of her and touching my head to the floor, I "spoke my faults," still kneeling. I talked to Mother of my doubts and disagreements with my superiors. Mother told me to take whatever

He gives, give whatever He takes, knowing or not knowing, included or excluded, liked or not, with a big smile. Mother had to come here. It was very difficult, but as I am coming and doing this, I must enjoy it. Always smile. Even if Jesus is treating Mother badly it's a private matter between Him and me. No one must know; it's a family affair. If I frown and look sad, everyone will say, "Poor thing, poor thing." [She used the Bengali, *bechara, bechara.*] That's all you want. If your heart is right, pure, and you see someone at the gate, you can go to your superior repeatedly like the woman in the Gospel. If she is angry, that is hers, not yours. If it comes to it, tell Sister, "I am going to give the children something," but in all other things obey. You're too preoccupied with yourself. So preoccupied that you are separated from Jesus. You have no time to pray. You must smile. You belong to Jesus, you are His property. He must be able to use you.

Sister, I forbid you to think like this again, to be busy with the faults of others. If you do it deliberately, you must confess it. You must not judge—that someone is doing something wrong you can see, but why you don't know. I save myself that way. You, by judging, may commit a graver sin than the one they commit. You may say, "She knows nothing of the fourth vow, she has broken the vow"; that is a judgment. You must pray with attention. In the work you cannot always be thinking "God, God, God"; but you make the intention: "Jesus, let it be all for you." However, when you pray, intention is not enough. All your attention must be there. You must really pray. Be humble, Sister, and God will be able to use you. Whatever happened, however it happened, God allowed it to make you humble. If you refuse to be humbled, if you are angry and bitter, God will pass you by and give up trying to humble you.

Mother gave me a note asking me to be humble and completely forget myself so that I gave only Jesus to others. That was the last time I saw her.

That night I went out in the dark and prayed: "God, I hope you exist because I really do not want to live like this for nothing. If you have no objections, I want to leave." Although I never thought of harming myself, I didn't care if I lived or died.

CHAPTER NINE

Banished

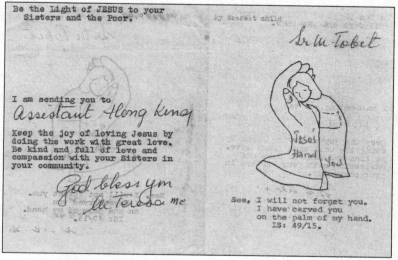

Be the Light of JESUS to your
Sisters and the Poor.

I am sending you to
Assistant Hong Kong

Keep the joy of loving Jesus by
doing the work with great love.
Be kind and full of love and
compassion with your Sisters in
your community.

God bless you
Mc Teresa me

See, I will not forget you.
I have carved you
on the palm of my hand.
IS: 49/15.

Mother Teresa's letter sending Sister Tobit to Hong Kong, 1982.

Five of us—our superior, Sister Dolores, Sisters Ling, Timothy, Paix, and I—left Manila to start a new house in Hong Kong on December 4, 1982. Mother Teresa had also decided that Sister Dolores would remain the regional superior. It was unclear what sort of work we would do there, but the Missionaries of Charity already had a house in Macau and we could stay there until we organized the new house in Hong Kong.

At Chep Lap Kok Airport immigration officials took away Sister Timothy. She was ethnic Chinese, and there was some irregularity in her travel documents. For several hours we waited at the airport, fearing

that the authorities had sent her back to Manila. No one could tell us
where she was. "Just wait there!" they told us. Eventually we learned that
officials had escorted her to the Macau ferry terminal, so we hurried
across town to rejoin her. Fortunately, Sister Ling was from Hong Kong
and knew her way around.

We set out together on the ferry crowded with other passengers
who, unlike us, were traveling to try their luck at the Macau Casino.
Everywhere we went, curious eyes kept us under surveillance. We said
our customary prayers on the deck of the ferry as we sailed past junks,
sampans, and little islands. I marveled that the junks looked just like
those depicted on the stamps I had collected as a child.

The sisters in Macau worked in a home for the elderly and sick started
by a Jesuit priest and also visited a depressed seaside area where some of
the houses were on stilts, as in Papua New Guinea. They also cared for
preschool children, and they were glad of our help with the Christmas
party and distribution of baskets.

Soon after we arrived we made a seven-day silent retreat, so I escaped
as much as I could to the roof of the house. Having given everything I
had to the Tahanan, the novices, and Barrio Magdaragat, and having
learned Tagalog, the language of Manila, I now was faced with the nearly
impossible task of mastering the characters and multitonal language of
Cantonese. Trying to overcome my disappointment at my banishment
from a community I had loved and hoping to find a way forward, I filled
up a little notebook with biblical quotations concerning love, prayer, and
the response to suffering. On the first page I wrote, "To escape criticism,
do nothing, say nothing, be nothing," as well as a quote from Mother:
"Let the MCs not be afraid to be humble, small, and helpless, to prove
their love for God."

The way I had been removed from the novitiate gnawed at me. I
was in disgrace but had not been accused of anything specific except a
nebulous pride. I told myself that anger was the rejection of the Cross
and that I must keep calm and not speak when decisions made no sense.
I repeated to myself one of Mother's mantras, "If God allows it, I must
also accept it," as I tried to believe that I had been sent to Hong Kong for
some purpose.

Once we finished our retreat Sister Dolores and I went back and forth by ferry from Macau to Hong Kong to get the new house ready. Some American Maryknoll sisters in Kowloon invited us to stay with them for one or two days, whenever we needed to. Their religious life was strikingly different from the MCs', and they were forthright and confident in their opinions. They didn't wear habits, lived more freely, without a rigid schedule, and told me I was too subservient, not exactly consistent with my MC reputation.

Rentals in Hong Kong were expensive, but a wealthy banker had donated an apartment to Bishop Wu for our use. Sister Dolores and I visited the apartment and arranged with the bishop's office for some changes and repairs to be made. We stayed in Macau for about a month that winter. I remember it being very cold in the dark of early morning as I washed my clothes in the bucket, my fingers so numb that I couldn't grasp the pegs properly. During meditation we heard crowds of people walking up the hill to the lighthouse, where they did their early morning tai chi.

Macau consists of three small islands joined by bridges. Portuguese-style churches, forts, and buildings grace the center of town. We went for our Christmas picnic to Coloane Island, where St. Francis Xavier died trying to get to Canton, and attended Mass in a church built in his honor. The happy old priest, Father Mario, had known Father Kolbe, who had given up his life in Auschwitz in place of the married Polish sergeant. "Here you are," he said as he handed me a small silver object. "A whistle to wake God up if he's asleep in the boat and doesn't answer you." I thought that might come in handy.

In early January we moved into an apartment in Kowloon. Sister Timothy stayed in Macau as she couldn't get a visa for Hong Kong, and an Indian sister, Diane, took her place. Our apartment was on the second floor, just upstairs from a noodle shop and overlooking an open street market that sold snakes, frogs, turtles, fur coats, and every other type of food and clothing imaginable. The barrow owners continuously called out the prices of their produce. We waited until the prices were cheaper in the late afternoon and then went down to buy our fruit and vegetables. Begging for food was out of the question: It would have been incomprehensible to the people in the Hong Kong markets. One of my first jobs was to learn the Chinese characters for numbers so I could read prices and avoid being cheated when I went to the market.

One of the sisters in our community, Ling, had been born in Hong Kong and was a great person to be with, quiet and spiritual. I had known her in both Melbourne and Manila. Her command of Cantonese was essential as we tried to discern what our work was to be, since at first we really didn't know what we should be doing. Sisters Paix and Diane met with the many Filipina maids working in Hong Kong and started a ministry among them. Sister Ling and I began by visiting our neighbors. Most of the surrounding apartments were deserted during work hours except for two infirm old women, who were confined to an upstairs room. When we first knocked on their door they were a bit suspicious, but when Sister Ling explained that we lived downstairs and wanted to meet our neighbors, they invited us into their incense-filled, cramped apartment. After that I was a spectator to many animated Cantonese conversations, and we often helped them with errands and cooking. Neither was well enough to go downstairs and so they were virtually trapped on the second floor.

Bishop Wu organized permits for us to visit the Vietnamese refugee camp at Chimawan on Lantau Island, which was about an hour by boat from Hong Kong. The immigration officials ran it like a prison. Surrounded by high fences and barbed wire, the overcrowded compound had a very young population, most of whom had escaped South Vietnam by boat. The boat people had suffered horribly at sea, many of them preyed upon by pirates who robbed them of what little they had and who raped and killed others. The people told of the joy and hope that they experienced on seeing a ship after months at sea with children on board and water and food running out—and of the unbelievable disappointment when ship after ship passed them by, leaving them to die. In the dormitories families slept on square platforms built on top of each other in bunk-like arrangements.

In the camp we found much uncertainty and little hope, though the people were resilient and had organized schools for their children with virtually no resources. I spoke to a young girl who was full of life and enthusiasm and had learned to speak reasonable English in three months. France, Australia, and England had accepted some of the refugees, but it was becoming harder to get visas. Before July 1982 the country of the vessel that rescued the refugees had accepted them, but after that date Thailand, Singapore, and Malaysia refused them permission to go ashore.

We also visited the Jubilee Camp in Shamshuipo, in Kowloon, a free camp for refugees who had come to Hong Kong early enough to get ID cards. There, thirty-five unaccompanied children were cared for by the other residents in what seemed a haphazard way. We made inquiries about what they needed in the way of clothes and how they could be enrolled in school. One of the youngest, Chien, who was only five and seemed vulnerable and alone, came running to us every time we visited.

Sister Ling and I also started to visit elderly street people who camped under the highway. Every night they climbed up to a cavity beneath the road, where they slept. We took soup and bread to them twice a week, which was a bit tricky on the buses. Several began waiting for us and, when they saw us coming from a distance, called out for us to hurry up. A ninety-year-old woman living under the highway wore her entire wardrobe all the time, like a big, round mobile bundle of secondhand clothes, including two blankets that she wrapped around her shoulders. One man living in the park told Sister Ling, "I lost my job as a delivery driver about three months ago because I'm losing my sight. I can see shadows, so I don't qualify for the blind pension, and because I am sixty-seven I am too young for the old-age pension."

"What about your family?" Sister Ling asked.

"They are all dead—they died in China," he replied.

Soon after we arrived we celebrated Chinese New Year, which started on February 9 and continued for ten days. Red streamers, signs, and greetings filled the streets. The market was packed with people buying dahlias, camellias, cherry blossoms, and *kalamansi*, trees full of small orange fruit. Under Sister Ling's direction we prepared special food for the old people under the highway.

The Maryknolls with whom Sister Dolores and I had stayed ran a hospital in Hong Kong and put us in contact with their home-nursing service. We went with them on their rounds when they changed dressings, bathed the disabled, and administered medication. If the people requested it, we visited them again and did errands for those who were confined to their apartment with no family support.

One woman had suffered a stroke and lost the use of the right side of her body. She struggled to care for her middle-aged, severely retarded daughter, so we helped her around the home and with the shopping. We did similar jobs for a ninety-four-year-old grandmother living alone. "I need to go to the bank," she announced suddenly one day.

"You're very weak. I don't think you can walk that far," Sister Ling reasoned with her. "We'll call a taxi."

"No, I want to walk," she insisted. Halfway through the market she was having difficulty.

"We think you should go back."

"No. I must get to the bank," she replied doggedly.

We tried to hail a taxi but none would stop for us. Then we decided to carry her in a fireman's lift, but had to stop a couple of times for a rest. Several of the market people gathered around to give us advice. Finally a police sergeant came to see what was causing the disturbance and piggy-backed the old lady to the bank with the two of us running behind him with his hat. The teller phoned for a taxi for the journey home, which was much less dramatic.

A diabetic man who lived in a tin hut in a squatter area called Diamond Hill couldn't walk well because of leg ulcers and lay all day on piles of old mattresses. We finally got his permission to clean the place, throwing out a dozen old rotting mattresses and installing a bed. After that, Meals on Wheels brought him food during the week, and we visited him on the weekends; more of his friends also visited him once they no longer had to climb over all that rat-infested foam rubber.

Sister Dolores received a phone call from Calcutta late one day saying that six novices on their way to Manila from Calcutta were stopping over in Hong Kong and would arrive in a few hours. We rushed out to buy some mattresses for them to sleep on before the stores closed, met the flight, and brought them home, but we had hardly enough floor space to accommodate them. At the airport the next morning we hurriedly wrote letters to the sisters in Manila before the novices took off again.

At our apartment Sister Dolores handed out the letters we had received, including one to me from Sister Gabrielle, who told me she was surprised I hadn't yet gone on my home visit, which was due prior to final vows and which had been approved for me to take before going to Hong Kong. I hadn't even known there was a possibility of going home to Australia. She also told me that they were missing me "terribly" in Manila. "The usual story," she said. "We only count our diamonds when we lose them." I was happy that some in Manila missed and valued me, as I certainly missed them but didn't feel much like a diamond.

The Church in Hong Kong contained the remnants of the Mainland Chinese Catholic Church, but few of those who had escaped the Communists were still alive in the 1980s. We met Bishop Dominic Tang, who had recently been released by the Communist government in China after having been imprisoned for twenty-two years. He had been the bishop of Canton and therefore considered a collaborator with the imperialists in the Vatican. "For a whole year I didn't speak," he told us. "And when I finally did, my voice sounded strange and wobbly. I was alone without solitude. My warders kept me under surveillance, and if I looked like I was praying or if I stood up to look out of my small window, they shouted at me." Despite all this, he had light in his eyes and face and now seemed to be deeply at peace.

"How did you get released?" I asked.

"I'm eighty now and have cancer, so I suppose they thought I was no longer much of a threat. I gave the bishop here a big surprise: everyone thought I was dead."

Life inside the convent was a strain. Sometimes Sister Dolores kept us home from our work to rub pots, which were never clean enough for her. We had to grind spices and make pastry for the complicated Indian dishes she liked to make, yet I had trouble getting permission to buy food for the diabetic on Diamond Hill or the people under the highway. Sometimes we couldn't keep our word to the people we helped because Sister had something else for us to do and she would not allow our usual visiting time. As in Melbourne, the people would wait for us and think we had forgotten them.

Because she was the regional superior, Sister Dolores went to visit the sisters in Japan and Korea. While she was away I was the next in charge. Sister Ling patiently tried to teach us Cantonese, and we made some funny mistakes as we tried to say the words at the right pitch. A priest who came to say Mass asked if he could help us. "Do you have enough books?" he asked.

"We have one good book. It has the Chinese characters and the anglicized spelling and meaning, but Sister Dolores keeps it with her most of the time. If you could copy some chapters for us it would be a big help," I replied.

"I'd be glad to," he said.

"That would be great. Then we could carry it on the buses and learn it in any spare moment."

When Sister Dolores returned, however, she was upset that I had done this in her absence. Another high-level decision I made that disturbed her was to make a ragbag to put near the back washing place to hold scraps of old cloth to use as dish cleaners. Often correcting us sisters in front of the whole community, pointing out various faults and character weaknesses she had noticed, she was even more critical in private. These episodes roused in me a growing anger, which I tried to quell. I wrote in my notebook:

> Keep peace with sister; don't be disturbed by her words or anger. Don't excuse. What she says does not matter except when she is an instrument of God's will by obedience. Nothing is an accident. She is here to help you grow in faith, humility, and self-control. The anger and bitterness must have a reason. Help me that it does not break me or my love for her.

In Manila Mother had asked me to be a cause of unity, and I had controlled what I said and had tried to absorb the anger. Nonetheless, other members of the community also found Sister Dolores difficult and tried to speak to me about it. One sister became angry when, remembering Mother's admonition, I cut short a discussion about Sister Dolores's way of behaving. Reactions against her were caused by her own actions, not mine. Nonetheless, she accused me of speaking against her in the community and turning others against her, which was untrue.

A superior didn't need to have any grounds or evidence for her accusations, and I was not permitted to verbally defend myself. If negative reports were sent to Calcutta the sister was given no means of redress, and she often did not even know the subject of the accusations. Mother constantly said that we should accept false accusations and not defend ourselves, as Jesus had. I reread in my notebook the instructions she had given us while in tertianship: "'I have not done it.' Thank God, you haven't done it. Grab it (the chance to make a sacrifice). Offer it to Jesus. Let Him take your good name." And again, "The destruction of the whole world started with, 'I will not serve.' Non-acceptance of humiliations destroys our community. . . . The only word you should utter is 'Thank you.'" Mother was referring to Lucifer's declaration, *Non serviam*, "I will not serve," which, although not in the Bible, is part of Christian mythology.

In her General Letter of April 28, 1983, Mother announced the opening of the Hong Kong house to the rest of the Society and asked us to live a life of greater love by freeing our hearts from uncharitable thoughts and our tongue from hurtful words of criticism and grumbling. She wanted no outbursts of anger and temper.

Mother's letter included a ten-point plan to increase the love within the Society, which included copying out into our prayer book the passage from St. Paul to the Corinthians (1 Corinthians 13:4–7) also quoted in our Constitution: "Love is always patient and kind. . . ." We were to examine our conscience daily on how we loved each other and the poor and to confess any failures. Charity was to be the theme of our monthly day of recollection and our spiritual reading. We were to hit ourselves with the discipline an extra ten times each day, except for Sundays, and to make extra reparation if we found any specific failures. We were to control our tongues; if anyone committed a sin against charity she was to ask pardon of the community before the evening prayer. We were to repeat a small prayer often during the day, asking God to increase our love for each other.

Mother proposed a way of increasing charity, which asked us to further subjugate, examine, and punish ourselves, as if physical pain could distract us from the psychological pain present in many houses. When a person is happy, she can reach out in compassion to others, but feelings of low self-worth, powerlessness, and loneliness generate simmering hostility and depression. I had prayed, read, tried to control my anger, and practiced self-denial, but these practices didn't make me a better person. The relentless regimentation and anti-intellectual attitudes enhanced our sensitivity and encouraged emotional immaturity.

A product of her history, Mother Teresa worked with the insights she had acquired from her culture and training. She didn't allow the grays of life to distort her vision or divert her strong resolve. If a thought undermined her convictions, she blocked it as a temptation. God either willed an event or allowed it to happen, and Divine Authority passed down the religious chain of command to the superior, whose will became God's will—even if the superior's stewardship was harsh or uninformed. Mother reasoned that Pontius Pilate had authority over Jesus only because God had given it to him, and even though Christ was crucified, God's redemptive plan was fulfilled. Therefore, suffering "under obedience" allowed a sister to share in Christ's passion.

I had been made the bursar in Hong Kong and given the job of doing the accounts. A question arose about giving a large amount of money to a middle-class Bengali woman who had once been in the orphanage in Calcutta. I was asked for my opinion as I needed to be aware of the gift when I balanced the accounts. I said I didn't think it appropriate. I was transferred to Bourke, Australia, shortly after this. I later learned that another professed sister had left the Society in Bourke and I was being sent to replace her. No explanation for my transfer was given. I had been in Hong Kong about six months.

The random changes in assignments meant we were constantly having to learn new languages and adapt to different cultures and work. We sisters could not research or take responsibility for our own visa applications as adult travelers usually do. We were sent on a tourist visa even if those in charge knew we needed a residential visa. God and the bishop were meant to pull strings at the other end to make everything legal. We had come to Hong Kong on a tourist visa, so we had a lot of trouble getting an identity card and the correct visa to remain there, because those formalities should have been completed before we arrived. Shortly after my long-term visa was granted, I was reassigned, and the whole process needed to be completed for another sister.

In less than ten years I had lived in five countries and partially learned half a dozen languages. Now I was on my way again.

Chapter Ten

The Back of Beyond

Sister Tobit's passport stamp on return to Australia.

he work in the Tahanan in Manila and in Barrio Magdaragat had made my life tolerable and given me a purpose. I had been happy doing the practical work there but had difficulty talking to others about my beliefs and disliked teaching catechism. I didn't know what I could do in Australia, and felt that it was going to be hard for me to remain a Missionary of Charity there. I was at a point where it was a daily struggle to remain in the Society, and I often wanted to leave. But I felt it was wrong to break my final vows to God and so I continued to obey my orders.

Because my transfer was sudden my family didn't know I was coming.

Home at last, I scanned the waiting crowd at Mascot Airport in Sydney with an air of resignation, knowing that no one would be there to meet me. On the airport commuter bus I couldn't slip into the comfortable anonymity of a local. Strangers stared at me in my tea-towel garb as if I was a foreigner. After the packed Kowloon market streets, Sydney seemed so empty that I thought there must have been a strike on. The bus took me to the Elizabeth Street side of Central Railway Station instead of the more familiar country platform side. "This is your stop, love," the bus driver prompted me.

Because I had not been home before my final vows I was allowed a two-week visit to my family prior to reporting to Bourke. I had trouble working the new public phones but managed to ring Mum from Central Railway Station. "Who is this, calling me Mum?" she asked, puzzled. Then she realized it was me and became very excited. She called my sister, Judy, home from work at Chevalier, a Catholic high school, and together they drove the twenty-five miles or so up the line to Picton to meet my train. At Central I went to the correct platform but got on an early train that terminated at another suburban station. As I waited on the platform for the country train to arrive, a woman commented, "It's strange, I've never seen anyone dressed like you before, and today I've seen you here and also someone dressed like you in Central. Do you belong to the Hare Krishna?"

"No. I'm a sister with Mother Teresa," I replied.

"That's wonderful," she said. "I thought Mother Teresa worked only in India."

"No, we are all over the world."

I finally boarded the correct country train and savored the familiar sights of my homeland, imagining what it was going to be like when I got off the train in Moss Vale. Mum and Judy reached Picton just as the train pulled in and rushed up the platform searching for me, while I sat in my carriage oblivious to the whole drama. Then I saw the two of them running frantically toward me. Judy was so tall, a grown woman now. When I had first left home she was only ten years old. Mum looked the same as ever. I jumped up and got my things. They had asked the guard to hold the train until they found me; he thought they were both mad. I hugged Mum and Judy. We were all in tears. I could hardly believe I was home.

It was great to be with my family again, but the sari kept me "in role." I had to stay faithful to my prayers, which took up about three hours a day. I couldn't slip into civilian clothes with my very short hair, and I was a bit of a novelty around the quiet country town in my distinctive habit. I was asked to speak at my primary school and at the Catholic high school, and was even featured in the local newspaper. I didn't tell Mum much of what was going on within me as we were not meant to talk with outsiders concerning private matters within the community. It was bad timing that I went home then, because the town might have forgotten that I had joined Mother Teresa.

My two-week holiday was quickly over and I drove with Mum to Bourke. The scrub stopped abruptly as we neared the flat, dusty town built on the banks of the Darling River. Locals called our road the Crystal Highway because the broken glass from beer and wine bottles was ground into the dirt, giving the impression of a glittering road. Five of us, two Indians, two Australians, and a Filipina, lived in a masonite house on the outskirts of town near the Aboriginal reserve, a collection of tin huts and lean-tos. Many Aboriginal people had moved into regular houses, but several hundred people still lived on the reserve as squatters in poor conditions. Our large house was partitioned into two sections: the sisters' quarters and an area reserved for the work. Sister Patience, who had been with me in the novitiate, was the superior and was very happy to see me. I knew the three other sisters there as well, having taught them in Manila.

Bourke was a culture shock. Many of the Aboriginal people seemed completely lost, often fighting and drinking, their children growing up hard and uncontrollable. Sister Patience was often in tears, not knowing what to do. After twelve years of service there, nothing had changed, although the Church had taught people how to play bingo, which occupied a lot of time, as did cards.

Through an adult literacy program I worked with Aboriginal women to help them learn to read and write and also taught catechism classes at Engonia, about sixty miles from Bourke. The trip was enjoyable after the rains, when yellow and purple wildflowers bloomed along the road. The children in my class were sinewy balls of energy who loved to run, sing, and draw, but hated sitting still for too long.

People from our parish helped us sisters by leaving oranges, cakes, and clothing for our extended family. We often had knocks on the door when someone needed a lift to hospital or had run out of sugar or flour. Every morning Aboriginal children came to the preschool run by Sister Clara, the Filipina sister, and Sister Shaddai, an Australian. They bathed and fed the children, played and sang with them.

In the morning I looked after about nine elderly men, both Aboriginal and white, in a large, corrugated-iron, shed-like house. Several had been stockmen and were tall and wiry with the bandy-legged gait of horsemen. I did their washing, bathed some of them, cooked and cleaned. I also went out visiting families and shopping. Some of the Aboriginal women had grown up in the Cootamundra Girls' Home after being separated from their family due to a government policy based on race. Many said they were not neglected or abused in their family homes, but had been removed from their Aboriginal mother because their father was white.

In the afternoon forty to fifty elementary school children came to our place so that we could help them with their schoolwork and play games with them. Some were hard cases, hitting the other children and calling us "fuckin' bitches." A few, especially the young boys, were glue sniffers and always in trouble for theft and fighting. The courts sentenced them to custodial detention, and they came back angry and hardened, with no dreams. My vocabulary increased, as I learned what a "fuckin' cunt" was. One child put a machete into our water tank and another robbed us while we were all at Mass. Others improved at school with a bit of tutoring.

Children in the outback were handicapped by neglect and abuse long before they were old enough to decide what was right or wrong, by which time their patterns of behavior were already established. The whites and Aboriginals didn't start life with equal opportunities. Many people on the reserve were demoralized and had lost their "dreaming," that hopeful vision of the future that called them forward.

Destructive forces of differing intensity were present in many lives in Bourke. Alcoholism led to fighting and illness. Women and children occasionally stayed with us in the preschool area when it was dangerous for them at home. We had to lock our doors against the threats and obscenities yelled at us from the outside. One man, a shearer, took a swing at his wife and hit the infant she was holding in her arms. He may have been on edge because there was a lot of tension in the town between Australian and New Zealand shearers, ostensibly over shearing comb size but it was really a turf war over job security that boiled over into scuffles and arson. There was also ill feeling in the town between Aboriginals and whites. Soon after I got to Bourke the Darling River flooded. A rock-melon farmer's whole crop was ruined because of the rain. Even though there were many unemployed Aboriginal people in town he couldn't get any of them to help him pick his fruit quickly and it became mildewed, sparking in him feelings of anger and hostility.

Some houses built for the Aboriginal people were ruined through overcrowding and fights within the house that caused broken windows and paneling. The white people, especially those struggling in poor housing, became angry at what they saw as neglect and destruction. I thought there might be a way to manage the housing differently so that the Aboriginal people themselves designed, built, and managed the houses, but I was in the middle of a cultural divide, copping hostility from both sides.

Our normal approach to the social problems certainly wasn't working. Life was much more complex than the free will "Thou shalt not" model. In Hong Kong refugees used to put plastic flowers together for money, and I wondered if we could find a simple industry so people could earn money. I also thought we might get a community vegetable garden going.

I tried to settle down, but it became clear that working as in MC in Australia was going to be impossible for me. I had been struggling for years, but now I was home it was clear I was in the wrong place. Back in my own country and culture, the clash of my own values with the MC way of life was even starker. When I was working in Manila the struggle of the people on the garbage mountain distracted me from my own inner turmoil; helping them gave my life some purpose. In Bourke the mismatch was clearer. I was asked to call Aboriginal children for Mass on Sundays, which I now can see was a form of harassment, banging on their doors every Sunday morning. I was sent to beg for meat at a local butcher, as if we had no money, rather than just buying it.

I wrote of my bewilderment again to Sister Gabrielle, who didn't know how to respond. She tried to console me by saying that, if the Crucifixion of Jesus could be part of God's plan, so could all these minor setbacks we all suffered. She said she didn't know the reasons for my transfer to Bourke or what had been discussed in Hong Kong and Manila, and that forces within the Society could more readily destroy it than attacks from outside. She tried to encourage me: "Keep your vision clear and antennae intact." Her reply allowed me to see that she understood what I was experiencing and didn't think it was entirely my fault. Until I received this letter any approach to my seniors concerning my problems within the Society usually resulted in a lecture on my own pride and lack of faith and humility.

In August 1983, two months after my return to Australia, I could no longer suppress my desire to leave the Society, and one night I talked to Sister Patience when we went up to check on the men. I'd already begun growing my hair in preparation for my departure. She pleaded with me to try again and arranged for me to see a priest, who tried to convince me that my desire to leave was the result of an evil spirit. I didn't believe in evil spirits, so he asked me, "What would you do if you left? Where would you stay?" I had known what I would say for months, years even. I told him that I would look for an apartment or room in Sydney, that I planned to study nursing or medicine, and I intended to apply for Austudy, a scheme to help adult Australians get a degree.

He lectured me: "You should bring yourself to nothing; you must lose your life, according to the Gospel logic, in order to find it again. Your idea to study medicine is unrealistic, and just a hidden form of pride, to show you can accomplish something, but frankly I think it is an impossible dream. You are reacting against your sense of failure within the Society, but don't forget God uses the weak to confound the strong."

Sister Margaret, my regional superior who had also been my superior in Kerema, came up to visit from Melbourne and wrote a report to Calcutta. She convinced me to stay a while longer, so I cut my hair again. But it was futile. I couldn't stay. I had thought through things as I worked in the vegetable garden; I knew I needed to leave.

I went to the doctor because a pain in my neck and left shoulder made it difficult to turn my head enough to reverse the van. I had had trouble with it since Manila, when I had carried many sacks of corn meal on that shoulder, probably a wear-and-tear injury. The doctor asked me straight, "Are you happy?"

"No, I'm not. I don't think I can live as a sister much longer."

Strangely, he responded by giving me sleeping tablets, which made it impossible to wake up at 4:40. I told Sister Patience, "Sister, I don't want to take the tablets the doctor prescribed."

"You must, Tobit."

"They're not medicines for my shoulder. They're sedatives because the doctor thinks I'm uptight and carrying the tension in my shoulder. Sister, I just can't wake up in the morning with these tablets and they're doing nothing for my shoulder."

"Go back to the doctor, then, but you must keep taking them till he says otherwise."

I traipsed back to the doctor. "If you think the pain in my shoulder and neck is just psychological or that there is nothing you can do, just tell me that. I can't take the tablets you prescribed. It makes it too hard for me to wake up at 4:40 in the morning."

"Why didn't you just stop them?" he asked, puzzled.

"Because I live under a superior who controls all aspects of my life. She knew you prescribed tablets because she bought them for me. She insisted I take them until you said to stop."

I returned home. "Sister, the doctor said to stop the tablets."

My uncle Toby and childhood friend Paul, both Franciscan priests, came to see me in late September and we had a few hours to walk along the river levee and up to the reserve. I cooked fish and chips for my visitors up at the men's place, and talked about my struggles to find an answer for the young people's despair, but not of my own turmoil.

My letters home were superficial. For a while I maintained the impression of normality, but this façade was soon to break down. Mother Teresa wrote to me unexpectedly in October 1983, saying she would visit soon. She asked me again for total surrender of my life and plans and urged me to love until it hurt. Mother suggested in her letter that people we served were being difficult and this caused my discontent. But I knew that it wasn't the people, but the way of life that was impossible for me.

Sister Gabrielle wrote to me, "There is one thing . . . which I cannot understand from you—when God gives you the REAL THING, the Cross, why is it you cannot accept?" She spoke of the dark night of the soul, as taught by St. John of the Cross, and she felt that I too had to pass through this time of crisis to be purified by God, and that it would be a tragedy to give up at a time when God was calling me to a deeper level of being. This idea was insidious, because it flattered me. But I knew I wasn't becoming better or holier, I was just cracking up.

My superior, Sister Patience, knew I was shaky. When she became sick and had to be admitted to the hospital I took over her duties and continued with my own. I often did business in town, and Sister Patience didn't notice the cost of a stamp to India, which I duly entered in the account book, but this time I did not ask permission to write to Mother, lest the pressure to stay start again. I had given in too many times before.

In November, close to my twenty-ninth birthday, I wrote, asking for a dispensation from my vows. The reasons couldn't have been clearer. I was not leaving the order because of the occasional personality clash with a superior or because I was unhappy in Bourke, but because of the oppressive pattern of strictures and behavior within the Society. I felt the order, whose raison d'être was to show compassion, chronically failed to do so, both to its own members and to the poor. I had been taught that a suffering human being was sacred, the embodiment of Christ Himself. Nevertheless, I was expected to ignore the pleading of a man whose friend lay dead among metho bottles, to send dying children away, to ignore a man dying in the street with dysentery, and to shut up and submit no matter what I was told to do or how stupid the order was. The Society demanded that I have no mind of my own and censored everything I read, a form of brainwashing that had almost turned me into an automaton. It asked me to surrender my judgment and the ability to discern. And it told me not to judge another and not to speak or intervene if something cruel or unjust was occurring. It did all this in God's name. He was supposed to be pulling the strings behind the scenes to make everything turn out okay.

I was quite frightened that panic might swamp me once I posted the letter, but that didn't happen.

When Sister Patience returned from hospital I went to see her and told her, "Sister, I have written to Mother to ask for a dispensation. I can't go on living like this."

My superior was devastated. "I was so happy when I heard you were coming," she said. "Everyone said you'd be a good sister here and help us, and now I'm very disappointed. I will have to let the other sisters know." I had had no trouble in the community at Bourke, and it saddened me to realize that Sister Patience might be blamed by sisters in Calcutta for my decision to leave. I didn't realize even then that I had been sent to Bourke to replace another sister who had left the order and that five or six others had left the Society from Bourke.

I wrote to Mum telling her I wanted to leave, and she rang me as soon as she got my letter and was supportive. She would drive up and get me as soon as Mother wrote allowing me to leave. My brother Rod also rang and offered me a room in his house in Newtown if I wanted to stay in Sydney after I left. I wrote to Mum, "Really I don't know what will happen to me, I don't know what the future will be like or where I have gone wrong. Sister Regina wrote to Sister Patience saying that I am seeing everything negatively because I had been hurt so much. They never seem to see any point in what I say. I hope this is what God wants me to do—in that case He will bless me and still be with me."

I tried to work as usual while waiting for Mother's reply, but it was very difficult. Sister Patience stopped eating for two days and didn't come to prayer. It was ironic that it was my place to lead the community in her absence. I thought of just walking away. Sister Rachael, one of the sisters from Ranchi in India, was crying all the time; she had been a novice with me in Manila and felt I was letting her down. While I was still in Bourke she wrote me a note telling me that my plan was hurting her very much. I wished it were over.

In the New Year, 1984, for the first time since I had joined the Society, I was left alone in the house for a few days. I looked after the old men while Sister Patience took the other three to Dubbo for dental and specialist appointments. When I collected the mail there was a letter from Mother addressed to me. I thought I would have to wait until the end of January to receive a reply because that was when Sister Margaret was due back from India, but Mother had written to me on December 14, 1983, and I received her letter on January 6, 1984. It was exactly eleven years since I had joined the Society.

Outside on the Crystal Highway, I was alone when I read the letter that set me free. I read it quickly and was elated. I was free to go. I was so relieved that Mother didn't tell me to wait, to pray, to do penance, or to otherwise delay the inevitable. If she had, I had already decided that I would walk away. I had reminded Mother in my letter that I had spoken to her in Calcutta before my final vows, asking to leave, but in her letter she seemed to have overlooked this and asked why I hadn't discussed these matters with her before my final profession. She felt the devil was trying to deceive me by coming to me as an "angel of light," and suggested prayer and penance as a way to recognize his tricks. Nevertheless, she reluctantly conceded that canon law did allow me a year of absence from the Society, during which she said I could return to my mother. Even though I was nearly thirty, she seemed to think I had to be in someone's care.

When the sisters came back I told them I would leave in a few days. The parish priest, Father Ebert, helped me by arranging for some clothes for me from a local shop and giving me five hundred dollars, which I was later able to return to him. When he advised me to register for the dole as soon as I left, I was dismayed that he thought I would have trouble finding work because I had no skills or qualifications.

The day of my departure came. The sisters asked Mum not to come to Bourke to pick me up lest someone see me in civilian clothes, so she was meeting me in Dubbo, where my uncle John now lived. The community was in tears as I left with Sister Patience to meet her there. All felt that I was betraying my vows.

In Dubbo I changed out of the habit and sari that I had worn for eleven years, gave it back to my superior, and put on a skirt and blouse. My hair was very short, and it felt strange to walk without the sari around me. Sister Patience was very distressed, and I worried about her driving back to Bourke alone. It had been a traumatic day for me. Uncle John's solution was for us all to go out for a stiff drink and a meal. I had never drunk alcohol and couldn't just shrug off the past eleven years like a bad dream. I wanted to stay home, but we did go out for an awkward, self-conscious meal.

Mum and I drove to Sydney the next day, where Rodney made me welcome at his house in Newtown, a fairly avant-garde inner suburb of Sydney near the university. I didn't want to go home to Moss Vale because I was embarrassed that I had been there in my habit only six months before, a member of the order of a "living saint."

Most people were dubious about my prospects for studying medicine, and it was too late for me to apply for the 1984 intake at Sydney University. Still determined to try, I enrolled in a correspondence course in high school chemistry and physics, hoping to improve my chances of being accepted into medicine in 1985.

Rod showed me around cosmopolitan Newtown, where people dressed eccentrically and wore their hair in a multitude of weird styles. Amid the funky haircuts of the inner city, uneven crew-cut didn't look unusual. I acquired a wardrobe by visiting several shops that sold cheap secondhand clothes and within a week had a job as an assistant at a nursing home on the night shift. I had told the matron the truth about where I was from, and even though I had no qualifications or references, I did have a letter from the parish priest of Bourke corroborating my story and vouching for my character. Similar to the work I had done in the Tahanan, I helped the registered nurse with the showering, dressing, and toileting of the residents; made beds; and served breakfast. It was probably too soon for me to start work, but I didn't want to go on the dole and so used Father Ebert's money to buy uniforms and a bicycle to get from Newtown to Redfern, where the home was. Unfortunately, the beginning of my night shift coincided with the closing time of the area bars, and I often had to avoid drunken people who lunged out at me from the sidewalk. I tested the brakes of a few cars with my avoidance maneuvers.

Sister Patience had also kindly given me three hundred dollars, and she wrote to me saying that they all missed me and that the house felt empty without me. Another sister wrote, "Nowadays, I am sad. Something is lost. Even all the vegetables and flowers in the garden are asking for you." She pleaded with me to come back soon.

I knew I wouldn't be back. Relieved to be free of such tight regulation and control, I felt almost euphoric at times, although on other occasions feelings of emptiness and loneliness came over me. It was as if the past eleven years of my life had just disappeared. I was at the beginning again. It was hard to talk to anyone about what had happened during my time in the order, as it was such a different sort of experience. After the first few months, however, I had very little contact with the sisters, and although I missed my friends in the Society and the patients and others with whom I'd worked—they had given me a sense of purpose, and that had made me happy—I never thought of going back. My inner anger rose and fell like a water table. I had given all I could but felt a sense of failure and reproached myself for being weak in character and taking too long to find my own voice.

I had not joined a suspect cult but a Catholic religious order, founded by a nun who had been judged a living saint by the Church that had guided me since childhood. Society in general admired her, and she had been awarded the Nobel Peace Prize in 1979. Mother was trustworthy, and I had followed her in the same way that an athlete obeys the orders of a demanding but talented coach, believing that she would guide me spiritually and help me liberate at least some people from the slavery of extreme poverty. I left existentially lost and disillusioned. I was, however, glad to be free of the tension, anger, and hurt that pervaded some houses, and I wondered how I had put up with it all for so long. From the outside, it seemed like nonsense.

My tertian mistress wrote that the fact that I had been thinking of leaving in tertianship but had stayed was a sign that Jesus wanted me to be a Missionary of Charity. She said God could fulfill His will using Pilate, Herod, or a Pharisee, if only I would lay down my life as Jesus did.

She said that God was asking me to lay down my plans of becoming a doctor to be a simple handmaid of the Lord. She asked would I say "Yes, Lord."

They were all missing the point. I was not leaving to become a doctor, but if I left I had to do something, and medicine had always been my dream. I wrote to Mother on March 13, 1984.

> How are you, Mother? As you know, I left Bourke with your
> permission on January 9th, and you have given me until April 9th
> to come to a decision concerning my vows. It is already very clear
> to me that I should go ahead with my petition for a dispensation,
> as it seems impossible for me to continue to live the life of an MC.
> I have struggled for many years, and have only tried to persevere
> in this life because I thought leaving the Society would cut me
> off from God's will for my life. In my work and studies, I have,
> however, found a new joy and peace. Mother, please tell me how
> to go about obtaining a dispensation.

Our letters crossed. Mother wrote that she was sure that the devil, "the father of lies," was trying his best to destroy my vocation, and that my decision had been made out of pride. She asked me how it would profit me to gain all possible degrees but lose my vocation to be "the spouse of Jesus crucified." She pleaded with me to come back, and that if I did she would send me to Africa, where the suffering of the people would help me come back to God.

The Biafran famine had prompted me to join the MCs in 1972, and in 1984 tens of thousands were dying in the Ethiopian famine. I saw the sisters on television working in the midst of the suffering and thought I should be with them but I knew I couldn't return, and instead gave most of my wages to the Freedom from Hunger appeal.

To be "the spouse of Jesus crucified" was not the life for me. I wanted to help bridge the gap between the rich and the poor and to decrease suffering and hardship in the world. I was happy to put up with inevitable difficulties, but not with artificial and unnecessary turmoil. The rigid structure of religious life, as we lived it, defied common sense and often clashed with the ideals of love and service we professed. Each sister was to obey like a soldier, without question. Some women trained under this system were like emotional time bombs, packed with suppressed anger, bitter and physically unwell. It seems a waste of a life so freely given if the person does not become happier and better for having lived this way.

I wrote back to Mother on March 23, confirming my decision to leave and making it clear that I was not asking for a dispensation to follow any particular profession but to be free of the tension and internal conflict caused by the way authority was exercised within the Missionaries of Charity.

Three times Mother sent me the same card, depicting Christ in his Passion, mutilated and crowned with thorns, and under it the message in her handwriting, "Be the One."

Mother asked me to accept suffering in imitation of Christ:

"Ill-treated and afflicted he never opened his mouth, like a lamb led to the slaughter house, like a sheep dumb before its shearers he never opened his mouth" (Isaiah 53:7). The irony was that much of the suffering within the MCs was home-grown and self-perpetuating. Young superiors copied their seniors in the way they inter-

One of three identical cards with the inscription "Be the One" sent by Mother Teresa to Sister Tobit when she left in 1984. (Artist unknown; distributed by Monastery of Our Lady of Mount Carmel, formerly in Brooklyn, NY, and distributed by the Scapular Society, USA.)

"I looked for one that would comfort Me, and I found none." Be the One

acted with their community. I couldn't understand why Mother didn't put more emphasis on speaking courteously to each other. Every person needs to express his or her own truth, not keep silent. It is not a worthy human ideal to be a victim. Humility is nothing more than living courteously, mindful of the other.

I wrote to the Pope in a form directed by Sister Frederick, the second in charge of the Society at the time, and received my dispensation later that year.

CHAPTER ELEVEN

Transitions: Emerging from Mother Teresa's Shadow

Colette with nephew Matthew Andrews, on her Graduation Day in Medicine, 1990. (Photographer: Judith Andrews, née Livermore)

When I left the Society my dreams and ideals were shaky, but still intact. I didn't tell my new acquaintances that I had been a sister with Mother Teresa, though eleven years was a long time to leave blank. My leaving was difficult to explain succinctly, and people in general treated me differently if they knew I had been a nun.

My friends in the Society wrote to me sometimes. I received a touching

letter from Sister Ling in Hong Kong, saying she understood the struggle
and misunderstanding I had been through; she thanked me and wished
me well. Another sister, an Australian, reminded me that I had helped her
through her first days in the Tahanan. She joked that I taught her how to
put on her sari and then she had to learn to do it again properly. When
she was sick and couldn't eat anything, I had brought her some vegemite
on toast, and she said her life had started again.

After a couple of months, I moved out of my brother's house to give
him back his space and privacy and stayed in a room at the nursing home.
I applied to be accepted into medicine in every faculty in Australia, and
for science and nursing degrees in Sydney. I completed a two-year correspondence course in high school physics and chemistry in one year,
thinking this would make my first year of university easier. I stopped
work in October and went home to live with Mum and registered to sit
the exams at the Moss Vale High School in November.

Back in my hometown I felt uncomfortable as little groups of people
looked askance at me in the street and talked among themselves. In my
local parish church I had a panic attack and had to leave Mass as I felt the
walls were closing in on me.

After my exams I worked as an aide in a nursing home in Bowral, near
Moss Vale, as I waited for acceptances to the universities to be published
in the newspaper. Miss Harper, the cocker spaniel breeder I had worked
for as a teenager, was now a resident there, and felt bereft without her
dogs, though sometimes her friends brought one in to visit.

Just before Christmas 1985 I received an application form from the
University of Queensland Student Union before any official offer of a
placement. Medicine was the only course I had applied for interstate, so
it could mean only one thing: that Queensland University was going to
give me the chance to study medicine. I received other offers for nursing
and science in New South Wales, but my heart was set on medicine. After
Christmas the official offer came. I was very excited and went by train to
Brisbane two weeks before the semester started. Uncle Toby put me up
temporarily in an apartment on the grounds of his friary and went with
me to find a cheap place to stay, a room in a boardinghouse.

About thirteen years older than most of my fellow students when I started university, I was asked if I was in the subquota, a form of entry for mature students. There were about fifteen other older students in the class of 220, but they were all postgraduates with degrees in biochemistry, pharmacy, microbiology, nursing, and similar subjects. When I applied I knew nothing of the subquota and so hadn't tried to get consideration as a mature-age student but as a regular undergraduate. The computer was not programmed to block me, and its error gained me entry into medicine on the merits of my thirteen-year-old high school tests, on which I had scored in the top percentile. Not until my second year did the dean realize that he had a thirty-year-old undergraduate in the course.

In medical school I had to learn to think again, to doubt, to analyze the evidence rather than to give unquestioning assent to what I was told. During the first year I was an outsider in a much younger group. Slowly I made friends with some classmates, and we had tutorials, electives, and holidays together and helped each other through the constant exams. My group included the chain-smoking, brilliant Kathy, a science graduate; Andrew *longus,* as we called him, a tall biochemist; Andrew *brevis,* also a science graduate; Robyn, a microbiologist; and Jean, Tuntuni, and George, all young undergraduates. On breaks we went to Stradbroke Island, Fraser Island, and O'Reilly's in the Gold Coast hinterland. I love the bush and had missed it terribly while in the Society.

In the first year I floundered in inorganic chemistry because I needed long-forgotten calculus to do some of the math. I managed to scrap a pass by doing reasonably well in the other calculations. During a spectrometry experiment I confided in an eighteen-year-old fellow student that I had used log tables at school to explain why I needed his help to use some of the functions on the scientific calculator. He was aghast. "How could you be old enough to go to school when they didn't use calculators, and still be admitted to medicine?" Once we started clinical subjects, such as anatomy, physiology, and psychology, I did well.

I pedaled to anatomy classes at St. Lucia each day on the bike track that snaked along the Brisbane River, human bones jutting out from my backpack. I was haunted by the story of the Calcutta rickshaw *wala* with tuberculosis in Lapierre's *City of Joy,* who sold his skeleton to a medical dealer to pay for his daughter's dowry and wedding feast. The man died soon after the celebration, and his body was duly collected so that medical students such as me could learn anatomy.

During parasitology I asked my lecturer about a "friend" who had contracted cerebral malaria in the Gulf province of Papua New Guinea. "Her tongue started to protrude and her back arched involuntarily even though she was conscious. What was happening to her? I haven't found it in any of the textbooks."

"The parasites were slugging her brainstem," he replied. "You'll find it in the *Complete Oxford Text Book of Medicine*. How is your friend now? A bit knocked off?" Parasitology was the first subject I did well in. I was personally familiar with many of the diseases, and the subject interested me. The high distinction gave me confidence and a bit of status and acceptance in the class. After that, I didn't look back or question my choice of career.

Although I enjoyed studying medicine, I had lost my youthful bravado. At school I seemed confident enough, but the Society had taught me to doubt myself. I dreamed of becoming a competent remote rural GP, able to operate, anesthetize, deliver babies, and deal with any emergency, but I was not able to become that person. I was anxious and hung back in tutorials, hoping the instructor wouldn't select me to perform procedures. I doubted I could do them. Afraid of harming the patient by my incompetence, I struggled to unlearn my religious training and my learned helplessness, but the self-doubt was tenacious. I felt guilty going out to meals with friends, thinking it a waste of money. I put up with not having things I needed. Once, trying to pin an essay together, I thought, *For heaven's sake, just go and buy a stapler!*

At the end of my first year I received a letter from Mother Teresa saying she wished me well and hoped I would be able to finish the full six years of my medical degree. She also said that she was sorry that she had hurt me by attributing my decision to leave the Society to pride. She felt at the time that I did have a vocation to be an MC and that I was throwing it away in an attempt to do my own will. I was happy to receive this letter, which was a step back from Mother's earlier stance. I was still very confused about how wrong things had gone. Mother was a good woman. She tried her best according to what she believed, and I had done my best. With such goodwill I had expected that my attempt to share with her a life of service would turn out well, but the inherited structures of an older form of Catholic religious life and our different worldviews preordained failure.

In my second year at uni I was offered the use of a little apartment at the back of a house on Fernberg Road owned by the O'Sullivan family in Milton, a suburb of Brisbane and a few miles from the university. At the time I was still attending Sunday Mass and had met the O'Sullivan family there. They were very kind to me, and we became close friends. Their garden was alive with birds and possums, a change from the boardinghouse.

My sister, Judy, saved up all through the year and gave me money for my medical books at Christmastime. I worked as a cleaner, a nurse's aide, and a kitchen dishwasher to supplement my government study allowance, as my textbooks and equipment were expensive. For the last two years of my study this became a loan that needed to be paid back after graduating. I was able to buy a car, an old Galant, for about a thousand dollars, which my friends called the Bogmobile because I had patched up the rusty bits with filler, colloquially called "bog" and made from Fiberglass.

For two of my student electives overseas I won scholarships to Western Samoa and the West Sepik province of Papua New Guinea, where medicine was at a much more basic level, without most of the tests and equipment we had to aid us in Australia.

In 1988 Brother Andrew came to Brisbane to give a talk at one of the Catholic schools of All Hallows. By this time he was no longer a Missionary of Charity brother. Having been the servant general of the order for twenty-one years, and having helped the brothers grow into a congregation of five hundred men working in thirty countries, in 1987 he resigned to give other brothers an opportunity to head the order. He remained an MC brother, and shortly after resigning his leadership role, he was summoned to America for a meeting. In a letter sent to the Catholic periodical *The Messenger* (January–February 1988) he recounted how at that meeting he was confronted with a list of times, over a twelve-year period, when he had drunk too much alcohol. His problem seemed to have started after the fall of Saigon, when his people had been thrown out onto the street and a young trainee in his care was shot. Most of the incidents he was now accused of had occurred many years before. His new superiors had made arrangements for him to go directly from that meeting to a rehabilitation center. Although he admitted that he had drunk too much on several occasions, shown bad example, and behaved foolishly, he didn't consider himself an alcoholic who needed to be packed off to a rehabilitation center without any discussion. No doubt, he felt ambushed. He refused to obey and so had to leave the order he had guided for over twenty years. Cut adrift, he set out, as he said, in a very small boat. Whatever the rights and wrongs of the case, the new superiors could have handled it differently.

As he spoke to the people assembled in the chapel, he looked weary and gaunt, with a gray beard and receding hairline. He continued to wear a polo shirt with a crucifix pinned on the left side, MC style. I listened to his talk, alert to any hints of his own disillusionment and struggle. There were none—only a call to simplicity, to break free from the preoccupations of materialism and modernity to be able to see the afflicted in our midst. A genuinely humble man, he was aware of his own weakness but conscious that frailty was a universal human condition. He talked of Mother with admiration and of the dedication of the MC brothers and sisters.

I was not prepared to listen to Andrew without challenging the Society's façade, however, and afterward I said to him, "You know it's not like that, Andrew. It's an ideal you're talking about, not the reality." I was still angry.

"I know what you mean. Human weakness is everywhere, but we need ideals to challenge us and call us forward. Without the inspiration of the saints among us, we may stay safe and comfortable behind our walls and gates. We are called to follow Christ with nothing." He spoke with resignation, not anger.

Slowly I was reintegrating into life in Australia. My family had welcomed me back, but some of our connections had frayed after my twelve-year absence. I had missed my brother Tony's wedding in 1983 but was able to celebrate with Judy and Rodney at their weddings in 1987 and 1989. Uncle Toby was the minister on all three occasions. Part of the family again, I was able to welcome the births of my eight nieces and nephews. Mum turned sixty in 1988 and celebrated with me up in Brisbane.

I had been working as a part-time cleaner for a librarian at the university, but I had to stop in my fifth year because my terms in surgery, obstetrics, and medicine were out of town. To survive financially, I signed up for a rural traineeship, and so needed to work in the country for at lease two years after graduation.

Finally, in December 1990, I graduated in medicine from the University of Queensland. Mum, Judy, and Matthew (my baby nephew) came for the ceremony. The O'Sullivan family, who had supported me all through the course, were also there.

The transition from student to doctor was sudden, and in January 1991, I commenced my internship at Toowoomba General Hospital in Queensland, in part to fulfill the terms of my rural traineeship. On one of my first nights in casualty I had to answer an emergency page to the obstetric ward to resuscitate an infant who looked dead but was able to be revived. I was also on duty when a serious motor vehicle accident came into Accident and Emergency. A man was taking his son's friend home on a Saturday afternoon when a semitrailer hit them on a roundabout. Both boys were about eight years old. One, wearing a Mambo T-shirt, couldn't be resuscitated; the other had serious head injuries. While a more senior doctor cared for the injured boy, I looked after the father.

"My son?" he pleaded, distraught.

"What is he wearing?" I asked gently.

"A Mambo T-shirt." I looked down, and the man understood and began sobbing. Death had shattered the security of his life.

"It's just a bloody Saturday afternoon. It's just a bloody Saturday afternoon," he repeated. He had mowed the lawn, then jumped into the car to drive his son's friend a few blocks to his home, and now his boy was dead. He couldn't believe his world had changed so rapidly on a "bloody Saturday afternoon."

After examining him I moved to the cubicle where the semitrailer driver was sitting alone. He too was an ordinary man, doing an ordinary day's work. He was physically uninjured, but in a split second many lives were damaged or destroyed.

During rounds on the surgical wards one day, an elderly man, Bob, called out repeatedly, "Holy Mother Mary!" My registrar thought Bob had become delusional, but I recognized him as one of the men I had looked after in Bourke about eight years before. He associated me with the Church, hence his religious exclamations, and I didn't enlighten the registrar about the cause of his outburst.

In 1992, seven years after leaving the order, I visited the Philippines again to see Sister Regina, with whom I stayed in touch and who arranged for me to stay in a house up the road from the convent in Naga City. The Filipina sisters making final vows no longer went to Calcutta for tertianship, as it was too difficult to get visas; instead, they completed their final year of training before final vows in the Philippines. Sisters Regina and Naomi were both teaching there. By coincidence, the group that had been first-years with me in Manila were on retreat prior to their final profession. They couldn't speak to me, but one sister, Christella, accidentally came into a room where I was waiting for Sister Regina, recognized me instantly, and jumped up and down excitedly, repeating "Sister! Sister!" I didn't know what to say to her.

I spent most of my time with Sister Regina, helping in the children's home for a few days. She took me to visit the beautiful Mayon volcano, which had erupted in the nineteenth century, killing many people, and showed me the stone ruins at its base. I didn't have the chance to speak much with Sister Naomi, who had been my friend for my eleven years as an MC. We had a conversation one evening, but we had both changed and seemed to have drifted apart even though I remembered her with great affection.

On the way home to Australia I revisited Tondo. Tayuman Street had become even more chaotic. The sisters had expanded and had another house across the road from the church. In a small parlor near the gate there were still some photos of me on the wall as part of a display to encourage vocations. At the Tahanan the workers welcomed me and still remembered our struggles together, though none of my old patients remained. Although I had lost fluency in Tagalog I could still understand what was being said around me. I had felt very at home in Manila as a sister; now, as a lone tourist, I felt like a scarred stranger.

After I finished my rural service in Queensland I moved down to the Central Coast of New South Wales, where my mother and sister and her family lived. I trained for a Diploma in Obstetrics at Gosford Hospital and started my general practice training. I tried to continue to believe in the Gospel, which had been my life's anchor, but the scandal of widespread pedophilia within the Church made me wonder what the point of our beliefs and ceremonies were if child abuse was the result.

My faith was also shaken by the suffering of my cancer patients. Despite advances in medicine and palliative care, some patients with invasive cancer were difficult to keep comfortable. Their nerves were invaded, their bones replaced by tumors, and their hollow organs blocked by the disease's relentless advance. Sometimes the only two options were sedation or pain, and the sufferer could only cry *Eli, Eli, lama sabachthani:* "My God, my God, why have you abandoned me?" (Matthew 27:46). In a way even Jesus had expressed doubts about God's love as He died on the Cross.

In our world, children die of starvation and nothing marks their passing. Irritated by the prayers of the faithful in church, I wondered what purpose they served. Surely God didn't need to be asked to save the life of a child or to send rain. Even Mother Teresa was puzzled by the pain that people suffered. After the tidal wave in Andhra Pradesh in 1977, when over ten thousand were killed and cholera broke out, Mother said something like, "God is trying to tell us something, but we can't understand what He's saying."

I sometimes received small notes from Mother, who no longer addressed me as "my child," but "Tobit, Dr. Colette Livermore."

Sister Deidre, who was professed with Sister Lara's group in 1976, visited me in Gosford in 1995, having left the order after more than twenty years. She had become anxious and had changed so much from the young, enthusiastic person I remembered. Of that group of four Australians who had joined in 1973 only Anthea remained.

I was paying off my house in Gosford, had good friends, and was close to my family, but still I didn't fit in. I was disappointed that I hadn't met someone to share my life. Interested in Aboriginal health after my experiences in Bourke, I often read articles outlining the problems of remote communities. Knowing there were no quick answers, I decided to move to the Northern Territory, where I found a job in Katherine Hospital.

I drove the twenty-five hundred miles from Gosford to Katherine. The sunflower fields of the Darling Downs gave way to the arid cattle country around the mining town of Mount Isa. It was the wet season, and I was lucky to get across the bridge at the Georgina River near Camoweel. I inched along the recently opened, single-lane ribbon of flood-affected tarmac for about a hundred yards and then drove along the highway that connected with the Track, the north-south, nearly two-thousand-mile highway connecting Adelaide and Darwin. At the eastern junction, called the Three Ways, I headed north about three hundred miles to Katherine. My life as an outback doctor was soon to begin.

CHAPTER TWELVE

Air Medical

Child fishing in Wulgar, Northern Territory, Australia, 1999.
(Photographer: C. Livermore)

The Northern Territory is a vast, ancient, stripped-down sort of place, with little time for the pretenses and cosmetic veneers of the South. Life there was both more relaxed and more intense. Sometimes the hospital staff gathered for evening drinks on the hospital lawn under the watchful gaze of the resident frilled-neck lizard, enjoying comradeship with people from many countries and states. In the Katherine Gorge the ancient river had carved out the red-ochre sandstone, leaving sheer cliffs on both banks. Here Livistonia palms manage to grow in the inhospitable rock, and the Jawoyn Aboriginal people use the rocky overhangs as art galleries. It was a favorite spot for dinners. There at sunset millions of flying foxes flew past, and magnificent lightning shows flashed as storm fronts collided on the horizon.

I started as a medical officer in the hospital, but after a few months transferred to the Air Medical Service, which covered a large area: down to Elliot in the south, north to Pine Creek, then out to the Queensland and Western Australian borders. Our work was twofold: conducting general practice clinics in remote communities and providing an emergency on-call advice and retrieval service for the area.

Every week or fortnight, depending on staffing levels, I traveled the 280 miles by mail plane to Kalkaringi-Daguragu, a remote Aboriginal settlement, for a routine clinic that lasted three days. Kezia, a vibrant Englishwoman of Jamaican descent with wild dreadlocks and a great smile, traveled with me because she covered Lajamanu, almost a hundred miles farther southwest.

It was in Kalkaringi that the struggle for Aboriginal land rights had begun, with the famous Wave Hill Station walk-off in 1966. Aboriginal stockmen, previously paid only in rations, demanded a wage and the return of their traditional lands. In 1973, the year I joined Mother Teresa's order, Prime Minister Gough Whitlam went out to Daguragu and, in a symbolic gesture, allowed the red desert sand to run from his clenched fist into the hands of Vincent Lingari, the leader of the Gurindji, thus restoring to the local people part of their ancestral lands.

"Hello! Who have we got here?" Nora, the clinic sister, asked in her broad Scottish brogue as she spied my new face alighting from the mail plane. Having served at Wave Hill Station and Kalkaringi for many years, she had seen numerous doctors come and go. Patients were already waiting at the clinic when we arrived: diabetics, dehydrated and out of control; limping stockmen; sick kids; women with wounds from assaults and domestic violence. Discharged patients and mothers with their newborns piled into the clinic troop carrier (called a troppie) for a lift into town. Nora knew where everyone lived.

At first I was awkward in the communities, learning another new culture and routine. The people avoided eye contact and I learned to lower my eyes and to speak while looking away. Sometimes a person's name was *kulum* and couldn't be uttered, because a person of the same name had died. Such a person had to be called another name for a certain time.

On the second day of my visit I crossed Wattie Creek to another clinic, at Daguragu. A Brahman bull and a donkey waited outside the bakery near the clinic for a feed of bread or buns.

The Aboriginal health workers, Double R (Robert Roy) and Helen, chased up skinny kids and others whom they knew needed attention and brought them to the clinic in the troppie. A resourceful and resilient lot, remote clinic staff are able to deal with snakes, floods, car accidents, brawls, and most other outback disasters. Together we did regular checks on the children, recorded their height and weight, and took hemoglobin (blood count), blood pressure, and urine tests. We checked their ears for perforations, their hearts for murmurs, and their skin for sores, and we followed up with them if they needed to see a specialist. A community computer database tracked the health of the children. I was bewildered to hear from nurses in the communities where I used to work that often during the recent government intervention in the Northern Territory to improve indigenous health the staff on the ground were not consulted and their experience and data was ignored. Disadvantage and ill health among Aboriginal Australians is a very complex problem. These dedicated staff, with limited resources, endure isolation and hardship for years to try to make a difference.

After work, if I finished before sunset I walked around the community armed with a stick and a rock to protect myself from the camp dogs that were always out for a good feed of *kartiya* (white person), and climbed a nearby hill to see the sun set over the grassland, with its low shrubs, small trees, and flocks of white parrots. I felt I belonged there, I think because it was similar to the hot, dry plains around Leeton. On Possum Hill a few miles from Kalkaringi, I could see for miles around. Our clinic mob would sometimes have a barbecue up on the ridge to watch the fireball sunsets. The sky was magnificent, a jet-black dome adorned with the diamond sash of the Milky Way. Shooting stars trailed across the heavens, while the Southern Cross, slung at an angle like a slouch hat, blazed through the night.

At the end of the three-day visit we returned by chartered aircraft to Katherine. Patients requiring nonurgent admission flew in with us. Depending on the roster, I was sometimes on-call as soon as I arrived back in and my beeper would go off as we taxied down the runway at the RAAF (Royal Australian Airforce) Base at Tindal which also served as the civilian airport. Sometimes it was necessary to meet the flight nurse at the airport and transfer straight to the aerial ambulance, or King Air, which was fitted with stretchers and resuscitation equipment. There were many evacuations from different communities and stations: unstable diabetics, children with pneumonia, casualties from car accidents or crocodile attacks, ringers (stockmen) with broken legs, cowboys hurt in rodeos, and women in labor. Sometimes we were diverted in midair and sent to another community to pick up more patients. In the wet season we flew through clouds pulsing with lightning and circled dark strips waiting to see if the community could get enough flares alight for us to land safely. My other regular community was Wulgar or Beswick as it was called by the first settlers, a small community of about four hundred people on the banks of the Waterhouse River, about sixty-five miles southeast of Katherine. Hundreds of feral donkeys grazed along the road to the community, and the surrounding country was beautiful with horseshoe-shaped ponds, called billabongs, covered in water lilies. A large lake near Wulgar was rimmed by red sandstone cliffs through which cut a small waterfall. It was a favorite spot for the community to relax and gather food. Little children fished along the melaleuca-lined banks with a line or stood in the traditional way, poised on one leg, spear in hand, ready to strike their quarry.

Wulgar was home to fine artists and men skilled in making and painting didgeridoos in the more pictorial X-ray style of the North, whereas the artist in the desert country near Kalkaringi used the dot-style of painting. Senior women taught the children how to weave dilly bags, traditional Aboriginal handspun bags, and mats. They prepared the pandanus fiber for both under a tree in the schoolyard and boiled different roots and bulbs for color.

Wulgar was a dry community, but a core group, made up mostly of men, waited at the cattle grid on the outskirts of town for the green cans of beer to come from Katherine by taxi. They drank for hours and then staggered back into town abusive and violent.

Many children had troubled home lives and missed a lot of school. At my school health screening I noticed that many children in the middle and upper primary grades couldn't read or write. Older children had left school at age thirteen to fifteen and were still illiterate, with no further educational options. With no bus service, Wulgar parents found it difficult to get their older children to the high school in Katherine.

The Territory is both beautiful and daunting. All around Katherine groups gathered to drink in parks or on the median strips. In our region violence, motor vehicle accidents, and attempted suicides were the result of too much grog, which the people used to numb life's frustrations. There were also rapes, assaults on young girls, and an outbreak of conjunctivitis, which we later found out originated from a sexually transmitted disease, gonorrhea.

I stayed in every community in the Katherine region and was often hyperalert and on edge from listening to fights in the surrounding houses. I wondered, *Is there any way to turn the situation around for the next generation?* Australians along the southern coastal fringe have little knowledge or understanding of the struggles of remote Australia, where the clash of two cultures is still an everyday experience. In only the last century the Aboriginal people lost a large percentage of their population from illness, as well as losing their traditional lands and food sources. They were killed by pastoralists as recently as the 1928 Conniston massacre, during the lives of this generation's parents and grandparents.

The majority of Aboriginal people do not drink alcohol, but for a sizable minority it is a serious problem. In Katherine a group of itinerants called "the long grass" drank heavily and lived outdoors. They could be seen sitting in the parks, drinking, shouting, littering, and generally getting the townsfolk angry. I treated some children for fetal alcohol syndrome, skinny kids who struggled at school, if they attended at all. From before birth these children had been affected by social problems not of their making, their mothers' alcohol consumption impairing the development of their bodies and brains. Tragically, they too are likely to end up drunk on the median strip in Katherine, censored by the general population, with skinny kids of their own.

The Missionaries of Charity looked after twenty to thirty elderly Aboriginal women in Katherine, some of whom were blind or crippled. If I wasn't working I helped every Sunday morning showering, cleaning, and serving lunch. Sister Leena had been a novice in Manila, but the other sisters, from Papua New Guinea, Australia, India, and the Philippines, were new to me. Some of the residents were great characters. One of them, Doris, was a stockwoman who had rounded up cattle on horseback as she balanced a baby in a *kawala* (bark cradle) in front of her. On Sunday afternoons many of the long grass came for soup and sandwiches at the sisters' center, where I helped with the serving and patched up their sores. The situation became uncontrollable with drinking and fighting inside their yard, so the sisters stopped it.

In April 1997 Sister Agnes, the first person to have joined Mother Teresa, died from cancer. Her death made me very sad, as she had been a gentle, quiet person whom I'd met several times. Sister Margaret, my superior in Kerema, also died of cancer. I wondered if there were a connection between cancer, gentleness, and being an MC.

Mother Teresa died while I was in Katherine, on September 5, 1997. I helped the sisters set up a TV in the women's home so they could see her military-escorted state funeral trundle through the streets of Calcutta, with the sisters following some distance back in a truck. It seemed incongruous that a humble woman who had won the Nobel Prize for Peace was carried through the streets on a gun carriage surrounded by soldiers. But her life was a paradox. I felt a sense of loss at her passing and wished we had been able to understand each other better.

While on the Central Coast I had drifted away from the Catholic Church, though I still went to Mass occasionally with Mum. In Katherine I became part of the Church again, but continued to vacillate on the vexing question of God. Unsure whether God existed, I thought that, without another dimension to life, it would be hard to preserve hope when faced with life's tragedies. I didn't know how the spirits of all those who had ever lived were held in a Christian, life-after-death scenario, but given the vastness of the cosmos I felt it was possible. Despite the institutional Church's strictures and behavior, the spirit of the local Catholic community in Katherine drew me back.

After two successive cyclones around the top end of northern Australia, the Katherine River was rising, and at 8 a.m. on Australia Day, Monday, January 26, 1998, it was at 45 feet—at the top of the bridge markers and threatening to break its banks. The river level fluctuates a lot in the wet season but usually flows at around 18 to 25 feet; when I returned to the bridge at 10:30 a.m. with some of the Aboriginal women from the MCs who wanted to see the river in flood, it was at 55 feet, a dangerously rapid rise. It was a holiday, and since I was not on call I was not wearing my beeper. Wondering if there were any warning bulletins, I rang Air Med.

"Where the hell are you?" my boss demanded. "We've been looking for you."

"I'm down at the Little Sisters," as the MCs were called.

"Well, tell them to get their people and themselves ready to leave. Pick up a four-wheel drive from the government compound and then come to Casualty. I want you to go to Tindal with the patients. We're evacuating."

We evacuated the hospital with the help of field ambulances and trucks from the air base. The usually invisible river was brimming at its banks as we passed through town. Although East Katherine is on higher ground and was not inundated, water was everywhere else. The flood-affected residents moved into schools, friends' houses, and sports centers on the dry side of town. We set up the hospital at the Tindal Air Base. Kezia went on a plane evacuating the sickest people from the hospital to Darwin, but had dramas of her own. Smoke had filled the plane's cabin, and in the monsoonal weather the pilot had to do an instrument landing. In that terrible week one of our patients had a heart attack on the tarmac, another plane had engine trouble, and we continually loaded planes in driving rain with little sleep.

The central part of Katherine Township was flooded. The second-story verandas of pubs became mooring places. Woolworth's, the post office, and the whole Main Street were submerged by floodwaters extending for miles on either side of the bridge. The Katherine Gorge ceased to be a gorge, with the river covering it up to sixty feet. Half of the town's homes and almost all the businesses were inundated, and crocodiles were sighted in the middle of town, attracted there by carrion.

Rocky Ridge, a nursing home on high ground opposite the hospital, had not been evacuated as it was thought to be out of reach of the rising water, but it had become a vulnerable island, and sewage was flowing back up the drainage pipes. A rescue mission was mounted and, one after the other, à la *M*A*S*H,* the helicopters came into Tindal base. The rotors whirred in the pouring rain as we helped the incontinent and frightened patients out of the cabin and carried them in a fireman's lift across the tarmac. Some yelled, and one old fellow attempted to deck me with a spare set of helicopter headphones. These patients went to Darwin the next day with their nurses, after bedding down in a large storeroom overnight.

The MCs hadn't acted straightaway when I advised them to evacuate because someone from the Church had told them it was safe to remain. They seemed to have been overlooked by the authorities, as all other nursing homes had been moved to Tindal, but as the water rose higher the police moved them and their wards into a corner of a gymnasium in East Katherine.

On Tuesday I received a hand-delivered note from Sister Leena asking for help. They needed clean sheets and a change of clothes for their women. I hadn't been into Katherine since the evacuation on Monday, but decided to try as some vehicles were getting through to East Katherine. The sisters had only the clothes they were wearing and very little linen for their charges. They hadn't slept at all the first night, as they were caring for twenty-three frail, elderly women who called out all night. There were hundreds of people in the gymnasium, and some were angry with the sisters because of the noise their patients made. Besides this, the sisters couldn't easily toilet the frail ones. I reached them on the Wednesday evening with some linen I had requisitioned from the base. On Thursday we moved them out to Tindal, and they were evacuated on a Hercules transport plane to the MC house in Darwin.

By Friday I was able to get into the town proper only to find mud and ruined homes. The stench was overpowering, but people hadn't lost their sense of humor. Someone had put up a sign in the main street showing a pelican wearing a slouch hat and holding a placard saying "Katherine, the Northern Territory's tidiest town." Someone else put a notice on a pile of ruined books: "Pulp fiction, some without covers, no exchange or refunds."

My apartment was putrid, and most of my books and personal possessions destroyed. A small turtle crawled over my vinyl record of *Jesus Christ Superstar*. My Nissan pick-up truck had been partially submerged, and I was without it for a few weeks until a mechanic was able to resurrect it. I had trench foot from wearing wet shoes. Everyone lined up for rations or ate cooked food from the fire station. Beginning on January 31 the Air Med pilots and planes were temporarily stationed in Darwin, and for a while the Katherine Air Med staff was not on call for emergencies so that we could attend to the affected clinics and our own affairs. I was able to stay in the pilot's house for a week until the hospital could provide another apartment.

I was the first to enter the sisters' house on Saturday, as they were all still in Darwin with the women from the home. The whole place was covered in thick, fetid mud. Beds and cupboards were upturned, food had rotted in the home's freezer, and the fences had been knocked down. It would be an overwhelming task to set it right again.

I worked for hours retrieving the sisters' few personal possessions and books and spread them out on the wire bed frames to dry. Some of their saris, which they had left on indoor lines strung across the dormitory, were now brown with caked-on mud. I took them to my temporary quarters to wash them and filled the yard there with laundry and drying books and papers. Even though they were in Darwin and couldn't attend to the house, I heard later that some sisters criticized me for interfering with their possessions. I just can't seem to win with the MCs. Later, on another occasion, while on remote call for Air Med, I looked after the elderly women in their home and lent them my ute to go on a picnic as their van had broken down. When they returned, one of the sisters told me the superior was upset because I had charged my mobile phone "without permission" from an electrical socket in the old people's kitchen. On both occasions, I had wanted to confront the sisters who had issues with me, but my informants pleaded with me not to. In the MC culture, petty things were still magnified and complaints made via a circuitous route so that they can't be redressed directly. Since I had my own work and sodden apartment to get back to, I didn't spend too much time ruminating on the complaints, happy that I was no longer in that sort of culture.

After the adrenaline rush was over, everyone was bone tired from the pervasive smell and persistent chaos at home and at work. I dumped most of what I owned on the lawn in front of my apartment. The army arrived with graders and rubbish trucks and took it all away. In the second week after the flood the river was down to an innocuous twelve feet. Our communities had struggled prior to the flood but would have even more difficulties now. The clinics at Wulgar, Mataranka, and Jilkmingan had all been inundated by floodwaters. Kezia and I went there to retrieve what records and medicines we could and to bag ruined drugs and files. Health posts that were not flooded were also affected because their clinics, mail, and supplies were delayed. We had a lot of catching up to do.

A year after the flood I resigned from Air Med and went to work at the Wurli-Wurlingjang Aboriginal Health Service in Katherine. My temperament was more suited to public health than emergency work, which I found stressful. I preferred the preventive and general practice side of medicine. There were three doctors on the staff, all women.

I worked with a young Kiwi doctor, Deidre, who thought a lot about spiritual matters. She was a Buddhist, and we discussed many things as we walked to the beautiful waterholes and cascades around the Katherine Gorge and Edith Falls. "It doesn't matter what you believe, as long as it helps you live a good life," Deidre proclaimed as she piggybacked her daughter, Rosemary, through the bush, on top of her backpack.

"It matters to me," I countered. "You can't hold to something just because it helps you. You have to be convinced that it's true."

"How does anyone know what's true? Your truth and my truth are different, but does that mean that one is less true than the other?"

"If everything is equally true, maybe that means all beliefs are equally mythical," I countered. "Does a personal presence, call it God or whatever you like, pervade the universe or not? Either God became incarnate in Jesus or he didn't. Either we live beyond the grave or we cease to exist. Truth isn't relative."

"I just don't think we can know for sure what's true. All we can do is lead the best life we can. If any teachings help us live well, that's fine," Deidre repeated. Once again I felt in turmoil. For many years I had suppressed the thought that He who was called Yahweh, "I AM," did not in fact exist. I wrote in my diary:

> *If there is no God, I am alone,*
> *There is no strength to aid my lack of strength*
> *There is no reason to love the unlovable, or to forgive the*
>   *unforgivable,*
> *No remedy against the poison of hate and bitterness,*
> *No hope for those whose lives begin and end in pain.*
> *If there is no Truth, we pray to emptiness.*
> *I am lost, if You are not.*

In September 1999 it felt as if Australia were at war as F-111 jets screeched overhead and Hercules transports lumbered by. East Timor had voted on August 30 to become an independent state, separate from Indonesia, which had invaded in 1975 after East Timor's colonial masters, the Portuguese, withdrew. When the result of the 1999 ballot was announced, the country erupted in a frenzy of destruction and violence. The Timorese pro-Jakarta militias, backed by the Indonesian Army, went on a rampage, using tankers of kerosene to torch schools, hospitals, and even churches crammed with people seeking sanctuary. In Katherine I listened to radio reports of mass killings. The capital, Dili, was ablaze, and corpses lay in the streets. The Australian INTERFET troops (International Force in East Timor) landed from the sea-cat *Jervis Bay* on September 20 and found a country of burned-out buildings and traumatized people.

The Timorese had endured four hundred years of Portuguese colonial rule, a transitional civil war in 1975, followed by twenty-five years of Indonesian domination. With the eruption of postreferendum violence, thousands were forced to flee to West Timor. Families separated; some stayed in Dili, while others escaped across the border, hoping at least a remnant would survive.

Katherine is an Air Force town, and so there was a lot of anxiety. Would there be an all-out war with Indonesia when our troops landed? As it turned out, there was little resistance. The Indonesians withdrew across the West Timor border, and the Australian command didn't attempt to surround the Indonesian forces or cut off access to their home territory. The TNI (the Indonesian Army) were allowed to leave the scene of death and devastation. Hundreds of refugees had escaped to camps in Darwin on the Air Force Hercules transports. The people of Katherine started to collect goods to send to East Timor and to the Timorese in the refugee camps in Darwin.

In early 2000 I received an email from a Darwin GP canvassing for volunteer doctors prepared to work in East Timor. His wife was an administrative officer with a Portuguese NGO known as OIKOS, which was based in Dili. Still under contract to Wurli-Wurlingjang, I said I would go to East Timor in June, when my contract expired. As the time came closer I moved out of my house and stayed with my friend Pat, who stored some of my things.

In May Brother Andrew came to Katherine to visit the sisters, looking even more gaunt than during his previous visit as he spoke in the church and joked with the Aboriginal people. His ideas had not changed. He distrusted the powerful and those who thought themselves just. Having thrown in his lot with the sinful and the weak, he lived with them on the edge of society. He had only recently come back from India, where he had celebrated Mass at Mother Teresa's tomb in the Mother House on the second anniversary of her death. His two months in Kolkata had drained the life out of him, as he struggled to overcome dysentery, humidity, and the crush of people.

"I've got a gnawing pain in my stomach," he told me. "It won't go away." He was leaving the next day so I couldn't arrange any medical examinations for him, but he promised to see a doctor in Melbourne. He was slow to fulfill his promise, but when he did, the diagnosis was stomach cancer.

I stopped work two weeks prior to my departure for East Timor and drove down to Yuendemu in the desert west of Alice Springs. I wanted to visit the Little Sisters of Jesus, whom I had met in Papua New Guinea and Redfern and who lived among the Warlpiri people. I listened to tape recordings of Tetun, the lingua franca of East Timor, for hundreds of miles along a red dust road to the community. When the road trains thundered by, the dust storm they created in their wake blinded me, and I had to stop driving until I could see again.

One of the sisters in Yuendemu, an American mathematician and poet, worked in the local preschool. "I don't know if it is the same here," I said as I walked with her to work, "but I just don't know how to re-spond to the violence and despair in some of the communities. I feel very powerless."

"The people are more powerless," she replied. "What we try to do is build bridges of friendship, but as for the big picture—it's difficult."

"Some communities have their own solutions but have no support," I continued. "Many of the women are very capable, but they have few resources. There's no alcohol rehabilitation center, even in a big town like Katherine. Often it's the old people holding families together."

"Yes, it's the same here," she agreed. "Grandparents often 'grow up' the kids. Many of the middle generation are lost to addiction."

On the way home I visited the MCs in Tennant Creek, who asked me to stay for the night. It was still a long way to Katherine and I was glad of the offer. I could hear the sisters laughing and joking in the refectory while I ate alone in the parlor. After Mass in the morning they invited me to eat breakfast with them. It was the first time since I had left, seventeen years before, that I had eaten with the sisters. One of them asked me,

"Sister, why did you leave us? Even now, you seem to be trying to do similar work. Why won't you come back?"

I briefly told her my side of the story, though I found it hard to do so succinctly. Her reply surprised me.

"A similar thing happened to me, and it upset me a lot. I was refused permission to admit a man suffering with tuberculosis. Then I asked to give him medicine and extra food to take at home, but the superior again said no, and I couldn't understand why. She said I should pray for him and told me I was not the only one God could use to help him."

Then some of the other sisters related similar stories. I felt relieved that they believed me and validated what I said, though they still were able to remain in the order. Each person finds his or her own way in the quest for meaning and the best way to live. It's a work in progress; we can only do our best with the insights we have at the time. I was moving on again, this time from Katherine to East Timor, where hatred had again made part of the world unlivable. We cannot seem to overcome the urge to destroy each other and the world around us. Our major religions don't seem to have saved us from that. My life was still more of a question than an answer.

CHAPTER THIRTEEN

East Timor:
A Land Laid Waste

Roadside examination, East Timor, 2002.
(Photographer: Julio dos Santos, infirmeru [nurse]).

J landed in Dili on June 22, 2000, on a Hercules military transport after a noisy, windowless flight. Most of the other passengers were military men decked out in a range of uniforms. There was an unenclosed toilet at the front of the plane with a curtain hooked up at the side, but a soldier used it as a footstool. A girl would have to be bursting to ask those size thirteens to move. Thankfully, it was a short flight.

Built on a narrow coastal plain, Dili was wedged between the mountainous backbone of the country and the sea. I was met at the airport by

Graham, the logistic officer from OIKOS, the Portuguese NGO I was to work for. As we hurtled along the coastal road we passed many ruined buildings. Children playing along the beach waved and called out to us. The majestic Atauro Island floated like a mauve double-peaked circus tent on the horizon, while on the eastern side of the bay a statue of Christ looked out to sea toward Indonesia. The seaside homes of the wealthy were in ruins, though the UN and foreign government missions were repairing some for their own use.

We pulled up at the OIKOS compound, where I was welcomed by Mica, a Portuguese doctor, who was working as an administrator. "Would you like to go to Aileu tomorrow?" she asked.

"Yes, as soon as possible," I replied.

"Dr. Hans has been up there for a few months," Mica said, "so you won't be on your own."

After lunch Graham showed me around Dili so I could get my bearings. We passed the Motael Church near the wharf. "This is where the funeral procession of a guy called Sebastião Gomes started," Graham said, gesturing at the white church. "He was a student shot by Indonesian soldiers. The procession started here and ended up down at the Santa Cruz Cemetery. That's when the soldiers started shooting."

"The Dili massacre?"

"Yes," he nodded.

"How many died?"

"It's hard to say—at least two hundred and fifty, and the same number again disappeared. Some say many bodies were dumped offshore. Hundreds more were wounded. I knew the chap who filmed it, Max Stahl. He buried the film near a headstone in the cemetery and then went back for it later. It was very dangerous."

"How did he get it out?" I asked.

"Well, the story goes that a Dutch activist smuggled it out in her bra. It certainly opened the eyes of the world to what was going on here."

He gave me a potted history of the country. After the Portuguese started losing control of their colonies following a military coup in Lisbon in 1974 there was a struggle among political forces and parties within East Timor. The Fretilin, a left-wing political party, and the Falintil, their military wing, gained ascendancy and declared East Timor independent in November 1975. In December 1975 Indonesia invaded East Timor, supported by the United States, which feared the Fretilin were pro-Communist. The Indonesian rule was brutal; at least 100,000 Timorese died either directly as casualties of war or from starvation due to crop and livestock destruction. The Falintil continued to wage a guerrilla war against Indonesia throughout the twenty-five years of occupation, while José Ramos-Horta kept the East Timorese cause alive at the UN. Xanana Gusmão took over as head of the Falintil after the Indonesians killed his predecessor, Nicolau Lobato. Imprisoned by the Indonesians in 1992, Gusmão was released in 1999 and in line to become the first president of the country. Because of its Portuguese colonial past, East Timor is mainly Catholic, though a traditional belief of a Father God of heaven and a Mother God of earth coexisted with Christian doctrines. There were also a few East Timorese Muslims. *Leste* means "east" in Portuguese, and *loro'sae*, literally "sunrise," is "east" in the Tetun language. Therefore, East Timor was also referred to as Timor Leste or Timor Loro'sae.

We drove past the impressive white Government Palace, which flew the flag of the United Nations and dominated the otherwise burnt out center of town. Nearby, moored just offshore, was the infamously expensive Olympia floating luxury hotel, the incongruous home of UN officials and other foreigners. Along the shoreline little stores of tin and rough-hewn wood sold food and Victoria Bitter beer. Farther along the beach fishermen peddled their catch hauled in from dugout canoes.

Dili was a burned-out shell of a city. If it were to have a mascot, it would be the ubiquitous fighting rooster, whose raucous call rang out day and night. The traffic was chaotic. Soldiers from numerous nations screeched around in UN four-wheel drives and white Indian Tatas, while the Timorese squeezed into small buses known as *microlets*. Sometimes both parents and three kids would pile onto one low-powered motorbike. Modern young girls in carefully faded, figure-hugging jeans mixed with traditionally dressed, gaunt women in ankle-length *lipas*, bright high-collared, long-sleeved blouses, and tightly wound headscarves. Huge black sows with udders brushing the ground waddled across the road, oblivious to cars, to forage in open drains and rubbish. Chickens and goats also meandered onto the road, and famished, apathetic dogs sat unperturbed in the middle of the traffic as vehicles detoured around them. Human road-wanderers were as bad as their animal counterparts. It's just as well the speed limit was only 20 mph.

In the center of Dili the *malae* (foreigners') shops and cafés were multiplying in order to service the UN staff and take their cash. On the periphery of the expatriate hangouts street urchins called out "Malae! Malae!" (Foreigner! Foreigner!) or "Hello Mister" whenever they sighted a non-Timorese of either sex. They sold pirated CDs, hand-woven cloth called *tais,* newspapers, and mobile phone cards. In Dili it was normal to feel hot, hassled, and a bit insecure. Children swarmed around cars as they parked and for a fee offered to provide "security" or a car wash, though they simply rearranged the dust on the vehicle and smeared its windscreen with dirty gutter water.

The next morning Graham drove me up to Aileu, about an hour from Dili along a forested winding road. As we climbed higher beautiful panoramic views of Atauro and the northern coastline unfolded before us. We passed thatched shops selling palm wine and bananas, a bus that lay on its side halfway down the embankment, and many gutted homes. On the side of the road children struggled up steep slopes carrying plastic containers of water or produce from their gardens. They called out excitedly to passing cars, the little ones jumping up and down on the spot, smiling broadly, and shouting "Hello Mister" or "Da," which means "good-bye."

Villagers cut wood from the steep hills, as they had no other source of building materials or cooking fuel. At the side of the road they sold small bundles of firewood and long poles used to build huts. As a result, the slopes were denuded. The initial deforestation had started with the bombings and defoliating agents used during the Indonesian invasion in 1975, but torrential rains had widened and deepened the eroded, ochre scars on the hillsides. We passed farmers hoeing their fields as they prepared to plant corn with the hoped-for rains. The mountain valleys were cultivated for rice; up in the hills villagers grew maize, tobacco, vegetables, and coffee.

"Shit!" yelled Graham, slamming on the brakes as he narrowly missed a *microlet* on a blind corner. "You'll get used to this if you live long enough," he exclaimed. "There are lots of accidents on this road. Thank God they don't drive fast, though some of the UN drivers are a nightmare." We inched past another section of the road, which had been partially washed away during the prior wet season. Finally we trundled down the hill past thatched huts, poinsettia trees, and coffee bushes, through the Falintil checkpoints and into Aileu. We pulled up at a small white house opposite the Aileu markets. The town had a population of about five thousand and serviced a district of forty thousand.

Dr. Hans had a visitor, Professor Max Kamien, from West Australia, whom I knew from his scholarly articles in medical magazines. Over local brewed coffee, Hans recounted how the pro-Indonesian militia had burned down the hospital and clinic in Aileu, along with most other buildings in the town, during the destruction that followed the Timorese vote for independence. Not many structures escaped the kerosene trucks and flame-throwers as the Indonesians withdrew. A woman was said to have been murdered in our house and the body put in the water tank. Hans told me we were running the clinic from a burned-out building next door to the former hospital, which OIKOS was repairing. There was no power or water in the clinic.

The health system worked through village-based clinics run by nurses. Our clinic had about ten nurses, but Hans said their medical knowledge and reliability were variable. We didn't keep patients overnight in Aileu, as we had no facilities, so the Bombeiros, a combined fire and ambulance service, took serious cases to the Red Cross Hospital in Dili, that is, if the ambulance was in working order. I gathered from his tone that it was often out of service.

The next day Hans showed me the clinic, which was just a dilapidated, roughly padlocked building with boarded-up windows. "Doctora Fong, Doctora Fong," Hans repeated by way of introduction as we toured the clinic. I thought he'd got my name wrong, though Fong resembled neither Colette nor Livermore. Then I realized *foun* was the Tetun word for "new."

The clinic had medicine cupboards with some basic dressings, syringes, IV fluids and needles, and oral and intravenous medicines; there were a few old beds but no sheets, pillows, chairs, tables, or shelving. It also lacked simple equipment, such as tape measures and scales to weigh the babies. I couldn't find a mop or a bucket, and without running water the standards of hygiene were poor, with dirty gentian violet-stained instruments left lying around. The two stalwart nurses of the Aileu Clinic, Americo and Rogerio, were welcoming, although their interactions with Dr. Hans seemed strained. They were very dedicated nurses, having risked their lives during the occupation to attend to the people and give them basic medical help.

"Where you from, Doctora?"

"From Australia."

"That's very good. You here long time?"

"I don't know. A couple of years, I hope."

"Years? Good, good, better than one month. Doctors go away very fast." I felt a bit apprehensive and wondered why that was so.

I did my first Saturday clinic alone, without nurses and struggling with the language because Hans had gone to Dili for the weekend. It was unclear if the nurses worked on Saturdays, which was an ongoing source of conflict with Hans.

I was glad that I had fought with the flight clerk to get my doctor's bag onto the Hercules, even though I had exceeded my baggage limit, as there was little other equipment in the clinic. I had armed myself with the UN protocol for treating various infectious diseases, in particular malaria. One little girl who came that first Saturday was about four but weighed less than an Australian one-year-old and was very anemic due to repeated bouts of the disease. Among a group of waiting patients I spied the familiar yellow T-shirt from the Clyde Fenton School in Katherine. A little chap with gastroenteritis wore it like a dress that reached below his knees. At least it proved that some of the things we had collected got through to the people.

That evening a boy came in unconscious with cerebral malaria. I treated his seizures and set off with him in the Bombeiros jeep ambulance. It was a terrible trip and I thought he would die on the way. In the foggy darkness on the winding road the lights of Dili were tantalizingly close as we zigzagged along the ridge. I suffered motion sickness because I was moving a lot trying to control the boy's fits and stop him inhaling vomit. I had no seat and was crouched beside him at the rear of the ambulance, as his father and uncle were on the one seat at his side. His intravenous line blocked just as we arrived in Dili, but he reached there alive, and I heard later that he had survived.

Shortly after I arrived Dr. Hans left for a holiday. For a while I felt a bit constrained from introducing anything new, as it was his show and I was expecting him back anytime. The weeks dragged into months, but he never returned. I heard he was working for Shell, but I never found out for sure.

In Aileu I had clinic four days a week and went with the mobile clinics to surrounding villages twice a week. After about a month the hospital was reopened, but water and power were very intermittent and we still had little in the way of beds or furniture. I saw about a hundred people a day with the help of the nurses. When we went on mobile clinics some of the staff remained in Aileu to run a clinic there. The main conditions we treated were chest infections, sores, parasites, malaria, gastroenteritis, and tuberculosis. I did a lot of antenatal and obstetric work and kept lists of patients with eye disease and orthopedic, heart, dental, and ear, nose, and throat problems so that when the teams of visiting doctors, dentists, and other health professionals came from Australia we would know which patients to contact.

I received a letter from Brother Andrew on July 8, 2000, in reply to one I had written to him some weeks after my arrival in Timor. Typically, he did not mention his illness, but said my descriptions of East Timor reminded him of Cambodia: "What you say about the impossible balance in the local economy when lots of expatriates are functioning in another financial set up is so true. . . . The aid-relief scene is not pretty on the frontiers." He went on to talk about our shared fallen humanity, one of his recurrent themes. No one, not Mother Teresa or the UN secretary-general, could escape our shared weakness. There was, he said, a bull-headedness in the saints and a bit of the saint in the crooks.

Andrew died about three months later, on the Feast of St. Francis of Assisi, cared for by the MC sisters in Melbourne. I liked Andrew. He wasn't a saint, but he was a man who did his best, sometimes smashing against the rock of the Church and his own lofty ideals. I missed him and felt sad he had ended up on the margins. But that is where he wanted to be: in the company of "the poorest, the lowliest and the lost."

Aileu, like most of East Timor, was mountainous and the roads were perilous, especially after heavy rain. Our four-wheel drive, laden with medicines and dressings, set out for different clinics and villages twice a week where often hundreds of people waited for us, though many of them were not very ill. A clinic had become such a rare event that villagers wanted to visit it when they could to get medicine in case they were sick in the future. It didn't seem to dawn on them that there were different medicines for different diseases and they couldn't be stored up and used later.

I started out in my rudimentary Tetun with "Ita boot moras saida?" (What ails you?) Some people had every possible symptom—headache, fever, backache, leg ache—so I started asking questions another way, to see if there was an acute problem. Gastroenteritis, pneumonia, skin diseases, and malaria were the most common illnesses, along with malnourished children and people with suspected tuberculosis. Quite often we brought those who were very ill back with us to treat them in town or to send them on to Dili. People would also wait for us on the side of the road to flag us down for a roadside consultation. When they knew we were in the area people called me to deliveries. Sometimes we passed houses with a white or black flag displayed on the roadside, alerting us that someone had died; a white flag meant a child had died, and a black flag signified an adult death. If we knew the house we went in to give our condolences.

The Maryknoll sisters—Dorothy, Nora, Susan, and Teresa—the same order I had known in Hong Kong, lived in part of the parish priest's house after the militia burned down their convent and clinic. Within the blackened shell of their former dwelling and workplace a broken plaque on the roofless wall said in Tetun, "Thank you to Miseror who helped us to build this place." Miseror, a Catholic German NGO, had been very helpful to the Maryknoll sisters as they had been to the MCs in Manila. Just prior to the destruction of 1999 they had built a rehabilitation center with the collected donations of many people, only to see it destroyed by the wanton actions of a few. Charred sewing machines and caliper boots, used for bracing the limbs of those with polio and other lower limb problems, were scattered on the floor.

The sisters became my friends and sometimes invited me to their house for pasta, meatloaf, and, on special occasions, roast chicken. It was a great change from the daily fare of suspect eggs, vegetables, and tuna that were easily available from the local markets across the road from my house. If a child had died or if I had had a bad day at the clinic because the nurses hadn't come to work, I wandered over to the sisters' house.

The Maryknolls had been reported dead during the militia's rampage in 1999, and I believe a Mass was said for them in Bandung, where they had worked in Indonesia. But though they had come close to death and had some frightening encounters as they made their escape to Dili along the militia-infested road, they reached Darwin, where they stayed as refugees for a few months, living with the OLSH sisters without having to go to the refugee camp.

In September 2000 East Timor remembered those killed the year before. Little piles of rocks decorated with red bougainvillea marked the place on the road where a loved one had died. At night hundreds of candles lit up the footpaths. Around this time the sisters invited me to go with them to Suai, in the far southwest of East Timor. I asked OIKOS for a few days off and set off with them on the long journey over the mountains and across the flat dry southern coastal plain. Bishop Belo presided over a ceremony to commemorate the first anniversary of the massacres there. The militia had killed many people, including three priests, and incinerated them in the church. Much to my surprise, I met up with Teresa Osland, who had worked with me in Beswick after the Katherine flood and was now an aid worker with Oxfam. Our arrangements for accommodation fell through, and we ended up camping in her house.

At the front of the church in Suai was a circle of stones, each bearing the name and sometimes a photo of one of the 170 or so people who had been bludgeoned or burned to death. The bereaved families prayed all night and brought up to the altar wreaths of flowers and burial *tais*, which would have been used to wrap the dead if they had been allowed a proper funeral. Relatives wailed and prayed around the circle of stones ablaze with hundreds of candles. The next day thousands attended a funeral Mass. Pallbearers carried a tabernacle-like structure, bearing the names of all the dead, in procession from the church where they had died to the outside altar.

After two days I returned to the clinic and was greatly helped when Sara, a young high school graduate, became my translator and Tetun teacher. She lived with me and helped me understand the culture. "What was Dili like last September?" I asked her.

"It was really horrible," she replied. "Full of burning. Nobody smiled. There was smoke, gunfire, explosions, and shouting. We couldn't sleep. People were running everywhere. Parents and children were divided from each other. I slept under the bed with my friends in the brothers' house [Christian Brothers]. The militia were threatening people with guns and forcing their way into houses. Some were TNI; some had the Indonesian flag wrapped around their heads. I saw the militia behind my house. They banged on the doors of my neighbors. They threw in kerosene, cut the electricity, and used grenades to destroy the houses. I felt my life was hopeless. The TNI were looking for my father to kill him because he wanted independence. We lived in a dangerous situation and felt close to death."

Sara was among a group who fled with Brother Dan from Australia and Father Peter from India. Twenty-three of them crammed into one four-wheel drive, braving the militia and TNI roadblocks. "We were very crowded in the car so that when we arrived in Kupang [in West Timor] at 3:15 in the morning, my legs were numb and I couldn't walk," she explained. "I had to hobble bent over like an old person into Father Peter's place."

They stayed in a convent for six weeks but had to move to a refugee camp in order to get papers to return to East Timor. All this time Sara didn't know if her family in Dili had survived. "We had a big struggle to get back to East Timor. Thousands of people were there. It was crowded as if in a market. We had to push to get the papers. We waited in the sun with no water. Brother Dan had given me 150,000 rupiah. I used it very carefully to buy some food and water for us. People just went to the toilet where they were and we couldn't sleep. We went to the toilet at night.

Sebastiano's [Sara's uncle] son was very sick with vomiting and diarrhea. The militia were there and attacked a bus going from the camp to the harbor. The people came back with wounds and couldn't get on the boat so I was afraid. It was really horrible. Many people died. I was very sad and cried all the time."

Sara was very nervous around armed soldiers and found it hard to pass the checkpoints. Two of her relatives had died in Dili and her grandfather was badly beaten. "How are you, now?" I asked.

"I'm okay. I sometimes feel scared. Sometimes I see the Falintil's faces and the guns and I suddenly get frightened. In Aileu, I'm trying to get used to the guns slowly. From this experience, I know what suffering is and I am inclined to reflect more on my life and my situation. Although it's a painful experience, I think I have learned a lot from it. I'm more serious. I know how people feel if they have no parents, and have to ask for food and clothes. When other people suffer, I can feel how they feel. Before, when I was growing up, I was safe. Everything was okay. If I wanted to eat, there was always rice."

Sara and I worked well together, and I became friends with her uncle, aunt, and family, who lived in Asirimou, a neighborhood of Aileu near the high school, but owned a stall in the markets in the center of town.

If I drove about twenty minutes up the mountain in line of sight with Dili, I could get a signal on my Australian mobile phone; otherwise, we had no phone service in Aileu except for the UN's satellite phones. At this time Telstra still provided phone service to East Timor. It was bizarre. I was perched on the side of a mountain, overlooking Dili, at times in the pouring rain, surrounded by curious village children and thatched huts, trying to buy an airline ticket or settle business in an Australian office. Once I was on hold so long that my battery ran out, so I had to drive down the mountain, wait for power to come on, recharge the battery, and have another attempt the next day.

I had decided not to renew my contract with OIKOS, who were soon to pull out of Aileu. Sara, my friend and translator, had won a scholarship to study teaching at the University of Newcastle and was soon to leave for Australia. The Maryknoll sisters said they would be happy if I worked with them and their staff at Uma Ita Nian (Our Home) Clinic, so I approached Palms, an Australian volunteer organization with links to the Catholic Church, to see if they would sponsor me. They agreed, so I returned to Australia to spend Christmas with the family and to attend the Palms orientation course in January 2001.

Their lecturer on Aboriginal issues seemed to have no experience of life in remote Aboriginal communities and just gave us tired platitudes. Another lecturer warned against "rescuing" and imposing "Western concepts" such as punctuality on other cultures. In East Timor I had struggled to have enough staff to go on the mobile clinics. Not imposing Western concepts of time and work attendance meant that people who had walked long distances could wait in vain for a mobile clinic to arrive. If staff didn't come, clinics didn't happen and people died of preventable illnesses.

I had sent my Nissan ute, packed with books, a pushbike, and kitchen utensils, over on the barge from Darwin to East Timor. I was to live in the teachers' quarters, which the sisters had rebuilt: two semidetached houses built of cement with a front room, two bedrooms, and a small kitchen. My house, like all the others, had a cement tank in the bathroom to hold water for all household purposes and a squat toilet. The water flowed intermittently, but my house had a much better water supply than the convent, which was on higher ground. In the dry season we carried containers of water from my house to the convent in the car as they frequently ran dry.

My years as an MC had made me an expert on the bucket bath, but the concept was not as clear to some of the new UN staff, who, instead of drawing water into a bucket and using a tin to throw water over themselves, jumped into the tank, contaminating all their water at once. I bought a gas cooker in Dili, and men from the sisters' carpenter's shop made me a bed and cupboards, so I was well set up.

When I first started to work with the sisters the clinic was still temporarily located in a damaged school building. We slowly restarted the various aspects of the clinic's work, which had operated successfully before 1999. The staff were easy to get along with and well motivated, so I found work much easier than the year before. In the clinic we saw all the routine ailments—chest and skin infections, TB, malaria, broken bones, and cuts—and conducted a prenatal clinic, giving women supplements, immunizations, and safe birthing kits. The sisters' clinic cared for all tuberculosis patients in the district as part of an East Timor–wide program funded by the Catholic aid organization Caritas. The sisters had developed a system in which health monitors supervised the six to eight months of TB treatment in the villages. Without these volunteers to directly observe the taking of the medication, all the patients would have been obliged to live in Aileu, as intermittent use of the drugs causes resistant, untreatable TB.

I was often called by people overnight and on weekends. The OIKOS clinic was taken over by the national health service, and after some time it was staffed by a Kenyan, then a Brazilian doctor, but there was no formal way of sharing the on-call, and the doctors were often away on weekends. One night I was in the back of a ute with Rosa, who was in critical condition, on a mercy dash to Dili, as the Bombeiros were again out of service. Her unborn infant was dead, trapped within her. I had started intravenous fluid as she was in shock with low blood pressure and no urine output. Her husband, Clementino, was vomiting over the side of the truck. I had covered her with a tarpaulin but she was still bitterly cold. I looked up at the majestic sky; the Southern Cross shone brilliantly, as it did in the outback. *Are You there?* I wondered? *Do You care about our desperate struggles to survive?*

Rosa was resuscitated and had a cesarean to deliver the dead baby as the very severe swelling made vaginal delivery impossible; she lived and later had a healthy baby.

Late in the morning on September 12 Sister Dorothy, a New Yorker, walked toward the clinic carrying her radio, her face set in sad bewilderment. We had just finished cleaning up after the morning consultations and food distribution and gathered around her and the crackling radio to learn that planes had flown into the World Trade Center and Pentagon; many were dead and no one was sure why. Sister Dorothy's brother had just retired as a captain in the New York Fire Department and she knew that some of his men would have been killed. A blanket of sadness came over the sisters, three of whom were American, and indeed over all of us.

A few days later I received a message through the UN to ring home. I drove up to the "telephone box" hill and rang Mum. My uncle Toby had died suddenly in Singapore and my family had been trying to reach me. Mum was broken-hearted as Toby was the youngest and fittest among the four siblings and had been very close to us.

Ansett Airlines had just collapsed and it was impossible to get a flight home. "I understand that you probably can't come, but if you can . . ." she pleaded. I really wanted to be with her because I had been absent when Gran died. "I'll try to come, Mum, but I'm not sure if I can get a flight."

I went to Dili, my passport at the ready. Seats were available on the flight to Darwin, but there were no flights from there to Sydney. I finally got a flight from Dili to Denpasar on Merpati Airlines, and then to Sydney on Garuda, but it was a bank holiday and I couldn't get enough money from the automatic teller to pay for the ticket. The travel agent, who knew the sisters, trusted me, and I just made the flight to Denpasar, where my ticket for the ongoing journey was to be waiting. When I arrived, though, the ticket wasn't there as the paperwork was slower than the flight. After a few stressful hours I was able to board the plane to Sydney.

At Kingsford Smith Airport the immigration officials complicated matters further by canceling my passport because it had been slightly damaged in the Katherine flood and the photo page was lifting at the side. Nothing had been said to me when I'd left the country earlier in the year, but now security was heightened. Sleepless and stressed, I made it home about an hour before the funeral.

Rod picked me up at the airport, and without me saying anything, said he would pay for my ticket home. We went straight to Mary Immaculate Church in Waverley, where Mum was married and Toby ordained. I hugged Mum, who seemed more vulnerable than I had ever seen her. Paul said the Mass along with several other Franciscan priests, and Judy's little girls took up the offertory procession. After the burial I stayed with Mum in her apartment and made several trips to Sydney to get a new passport. I saw for the first time the September 11 footage that had sickened everyone. It seemed surreal and unbelievable. I bought *Time* magazine and *Newsweek* and gathered any other news clippings I could to take back to the sisters.

Mum wanted me to stay home until Christmas because she would feel Toby's loss more at the time when he had always visited, but I was committed to return, and she seemed well, busy with her pottery, painting, grandchildren, and wide circle of friends. Occasionally she said things that puzzled me; for example, she had a "disabled" parking sticker she had used for years because of bad arthritis in her back, knees, and hips, but when I drove her down to the shops and went to park in a disabled spot she was adamant that only people in wheelchairs could use it. In addition, she couldn't learn to use email to keep in touch with me, despite Judy setting it up for her and showing her how to use it several times. However, she didn't appear confused or unwell.

I flew back to East Timor and into a drought. The atmosphere there was changing. The juxtaposition of UN wealth with such onerous poverty caused resentment and a sense of betrayal among the Timorese people as they look at the foreigners sipping their lattes in roped off cafes and spending more on a coffee and lunch than a Timorese family had to live on for a week. The ordinary people felt that outsiders were making a lot of money from the UN, while the Timorese missed out. The word *malae* came to sound like an insult. Mother Teresa had been wise to want us to be poor with the poor, to live as close to the people as possible. The highly paid UN staff had a reputation for inefficiency and waste.

In the second half of 2001 we moved from our burned-out school into the newly rebuilt clinic. The opening ceremony was on October 13, and Bishop Belo came for the blessing, as did representatives of Caritas Norway and Caritas New Zealand, the clinic's main donors. The staff made banners welcoming the dignitaries and erected a large decorative bamboo arch. Children from the school danced in traditional dress with swords, gongs, and drums, and a little girl solemnly recounted in Tetun the story of how the sisters—"Only women alone! And old! With white hair!"—had bravely returned after the 1999 destruction to rebuild their clinic and house. A vibrant and courageous lot, the sisters had stuck it out with East Timor through all the adversity.

• • •

Late in the year my friend Sister Pat and a sister from Our Lady of the Sacred Heart working in Katherine sent me two separate articles by Albert Huart and J. Neuner from the September–October 2001 edition of *Review for Religious*. The authors, both Jesuit priests who had given Mother Teresa spiritual direction, spoke of the private letters of conscience she had written in the 1950s and 1960s, telling of her feelings of loneliness and abandonment and of her struggle to resist thoughts that God did not exist. Mother had asked that her private letters be burned, and many were, but some survived. She wrote, "When I try to raise my thoughts to heaven there is such convicting emptiness. . . . I am told God loves me—and yet the reality [is] of darkness and coldness."

I felt strangely elated when I read these articles. Mother had always been so certain, even dogmatic when she spoke with me and had not admitted to any doubt, but these articles revealed that she had experienced "darkness, coldness and loneliness." Having detached herself from all human love, she had tried to give all of herself to each situation. These efforts left her bereft. She experienced a terrible emptiness and absence of God, which she feared would "unbalance" her. Her cheerfulness was "a cloak" to cover her "emptiness and misery." She held within herself a cavernous loneliness and was troubled when people said they were "drawn closer to God" seeing her strong faith. She wondered whether this was "deceiving people?" She wanted to "tell the truth—that I have no faith" but remained silent. She felt Jesus had left her alone to walk in the darkness.

In 1959 Mother wrote to her confessor, Father Picachy, later to become Cardinal Picachy of Calcutta, of her struggle. She had so many "unanswered questions" within her but she was "afraid to uncover them—because of the blasphemy." She prayed, "If there be God please forgive me."

Mother died a woman of faith. She feared God might not exist, but she blocked those thoughts, made confession, and did penance to rid herself of these disturbing ideas. Mother Teresa *had* to remain a believer; the alternative was unthinkable. It was the essence of herself and her work to profess faith in God and the Catholic Church. Her spiritual guide gave her the writings of the mystic St. John of the Cross to read, and Mother accepted that these feelings of abandonment were part of a purifying, spiritual trial to strip away her ego. I had read these works while I was in Calcutta in 1981 and copied sections into my notebook, such as the following: "To reach satisfaction in all, desire its possession in nothing. To come to the knowledge of all, desire the knowledge of nothing. To arrive at being all, desire to be nothing." The mantra of St. John of the Cross was *Nada*, "nothing," and that was what Mother found within herself.

In a similar way the young Thérèse of Lisieux, Mother Teresa's patron saint, had struggled before her premature death from tuberculosis. Both women attributed the absence of God not to natural questioning, but to this "dark night of the soul" during which the sufferer was to learn to love God not for consolation or a promised reward but for God's own sake. Reading the articles, I had the impression that Mother was overwrought, strained, and tormented, as if confined in a psychological pressure cooker. Some ordinary human comfort and recreation may have released the pressure, but she never allowed herself any respite.

In East Timor I felt an increasing distance from the Catholic Church. A statue of Our Lady of Fatima was flown by helicopter around the country in the buildup to independence, but such a mode of transport could never be mobilized to rescue a woman dying in childbirth in a remote village. Perhaps this was a government, not a church, decision but it seemed incongruous. I heard a wealthy Timorese cleric upbraid the congregation during a sermon for distributing communion from plastic containers, instead of having chalices and ciboriums. He felt Jesus, the One who emptied Himself to become a poor man, needed to be encased in gold. The weekly collection from the impoverished parish was less than ten dollars. Perhaps the priest could have donated a chalice, as the people certainly couldn't afford one. St. John Chrysostom taught, "He who said, 'This is my body,' said, 'You saw me hungry and gave me no food.' Honor him by sharing your property with the poor for what God needs is not golden chalices but golden souls."

Then I heard another priest give a "woman as temptress" sermon during which he reproached women who, he said, used their bodies to lead men astray. He made no counterpoint, no mention of violent or predatory male behavior. The week before this I had treated a fourteen-year-old girl who had been raped by six men, two of whom where her relatives. Then an edict came from the Church in Dili saying that foreign doctors should respect the Catholic beliefs of the country and not prescribe contraception. I had recently treated a young woman whom I thought was going to bleed to death in front of me. I worked desperately to stop the hemorrhaging, and she survived, but when it was all over I felt physically ill. The women trapped between the "conjugal rights" of their husband and the dangers of isolated, often unassisted childbirth needed some options.

I admired the work and attitude of the Maryknoll sisters but could no longer call myself a Catholic, though I still looked to the Gospels for inspiration and guidance. I stopped going to Mass, but thought God, in some form, might be possible.

After two years of preparation it was time for the interim UN government to hand over control of East Timor to the president, Xanana Gusmão, who had been elected in the pre-Independence poll and the Constitutional Assembly.

On May 20, 2002, people from the surrounding villages streamed into town, the men adorned with feathered headdresses and silver caribou horns, the women robed in colorful *tais*. They played gongs and drums as they danced and sang their way to the sports field, where the Independence Day ceremonies were to be held. In anticipation of the occasion, I bought a drum (*babadok*) from the market and had lessons from my child neighbor, Carlos, who thought me to be rhythmically challenged. The local women's cooperative decked me out in a *tais*, though I couldn't quite get the hang of the headscarf. On the eve of Independence there was a special Mass for the vigil of Pentecost Sunday, which was celebrated at the same time all over the mainly Catholic country. However, authorities in Dili dictated that the Mass be said in Portuguese instead of the usual Tetun, so the celebration was a bit of an anticlimax and the responses and singing were not as robust as usual. The priest, fluent in Tetun and

Indonesian, had problems reading the Gospel in Portuguese, and the people were unusually lifeless because, except for some older *senhoras* in the front row, no one understood the language. At the end of the Mass, the priest blessed the flag and presented it to Donna Maria Pas, the district administrator. Tears streamed down her face as she handed the red, black, and yellow flag of East Timor to Manaloi, the chief *katuas* (elder), to guard until midnight, when it was to be raised aloft.

"Viva Timor Loro'sae!" (Long live East Timor) proclaimed the priest.

"Viva!" shouted the congregation, as they cried and hugged each other. It was a poignant moment of hope after years of struggle and deprivation. The Maryknoll sisters were also in tears, as they had walked with the people during the years of fear and intimidation. Sister Susan, who had suffered a stroke the year before, had trouble keeping her balance as people pressed in to embrace her. Unfortunately, Sister Dorothy was away in the United States and missed the night of celebration, which continued until 11 p.m., when the official Independence ceremonies began.

The Portuguese peacekeepers performed a minor miracle, getting a satellite dish to relay a direct telecast from the Independence Day ceremonies at Tasi Tolu, literally "Three Seas," an area on the outskirts of Dili, to a screen on the Aileu soccer field. As we watched the live feed from the capital, the caribou horns sounded their long low note in Aileu and drummers announced the arrival of two hundred traditionally dressed local warriors who marched the new flag of Timor Loro'sae onto the soccer field. The Timorese police respectfully lowered the UN flag, and then, on the stroke of midnight, in unison with the ceremonies in Dili, the crowd and school choirs sang the new National Anthem of East Timor as the national flag was raised for the first time. It was a very emotional moment. The dancing and partying continued all night while warriors stood guard around the flagpole, symbolically securing their hard-won independence.

It didn't take long for the problems of the world's newest nation to manifest themselves, but at least for that night, the long years of struggle seemed worth it.

Portuguese was proclaimed the official language, though only a minority of mostly older people spoke it. There were problems with water, power, medical supplies, gangs of unemployed youth causing destruction in Dili, and disputes with Australia over oil and gas rights. Still, the people believed that being free from oppression was worth such trouble.

I continued to work at the clinic, seeing patients, organizing antenatal care, helping with the nutrition program for the TB patients and malnourished children, delivering babies, and conducting remote clinics. Once I received a frustratingly vague summons, delivered by a boy on a pushbike, to attend a sick child in a village on the outskirts of Aileu. It was about 2 in the afternoon, and I was about to walk home for lunch. The messenger didn't know the child's name or even have a vague idea of what was wrong, but he knew where he lived. It was raining torrentially, so I threw his bike in the back of the Nissan and we set out. He guided me to a very dark, earthen-floor hut in Bandadato, about a fifteen-minute drive away. A nine-year-old boy was in great pain and breathing quickly. He had no fever, but his abdomen was swollen, tense, and silent. Perhaps he had a twisted bowel. There was little air entry into his left lung. His diagnosis was unclear, but I was certain he needed surgery.

I addressed his parents and neighbors in the suffocating, crowded room, shouting to be heard above the rain. "To have any hope, Flaviano needs to go to Dili." Neither the boy nor his father wanted to go. Rita, the man's wife, had suffered a stroke giving birth to their last child, and they felt they couldn't leave her. I suggested to the neighbors that our health motivators—volunteers in the village who worked with the clinic—could help while they were away, but the onlookers demanded, "Just give the boy some medicine."

"See, the boy is screaming in pain," I pleaded. "There is something wrong inside, in his stomach. I have no medicine to help him. It is not something simple, like malaria."

"The boy does not want to go to Dili," the father said.

I reasoned with him. "You are the father. He will go, if you take him."

The child continued to cry out and groan in agony. I had no narcotic of any kind, and none could be imported. I could feel myself getting angry at the impossibility of the whole situation.

They finally agreed he could go with me to Dili. It took a long time, as they wanted to change the boy's clothes. I pleaded with them, "The clothes don't matter."

"We can't go to Dili in dirty clothes," the father insisted. Eventually he carried Flaviano out and nursed him on the backseat of my car. I had only driven three or four minutes through the downpour, hoping I wouldn't bog down on the muddy road, when the groaning stopped. I heard the gurgling of death. I stopped the car and looked around. The boy was dead, staring ahead, foaming at the mouth. Any attempt at resuscitation was futile. In retrospect I was glad a pain killing injection was not available as I may have been blamed for his death, however if I'd had it I would have tried to relieve his pain. We turned around. His slightly retarded sister ran out happily into the rain, laughing as she called out, "Flaviano is back. He wasn't long." Her father snapped back angrily, "Is la iha" (He has no breath).

The villagers came wailing, screaming, and crying. At times of death, the women of East Timor chant a story, telling of the person's life. In that dirge, a neighbor wailed, "The doctor said nothing is wrong, and now you are dead."

I hadn't said "Nothing is wrong," only that I couldn't do anything to help in that dark crowded hut.

I lived alone, some distance from the sisters' house. People came to my door constantly. I had many nights with little sleep. One Thursday I didn't go to the mobile clinic because I knew I needed a break. I planned to catch up on paperwork, reports to the World Health Organization and the World Food Program to keep our nutrition program going. I was talking to the TB coordinator at the door to my house. A group of women walking home from the church spotted me and a woman approached and asked me to see her sick mother. "Please go to the government clinic," I said. "We are not open today."

"My mother is too weak to walk."

"Call the Bombeiros. They will take her to the clinic."

"Fila, deit!" (I will just go home!)

I was angry. "Your mother is very ill, but now you won't call anyone else?"

Irritated, I went with her. We drove as far as we could, then set out on foot across the fields to a thatched hut. The woman's elderly mother had pneumonia. I started penicillin injections. In the house was a nine-year-old boy with cerebral palsy and severe contractures. As I left, they gave me a gift of two eggs and some bananas.

What is happening to me? I wondered. I felt I was right to try to take a day off to prevent burnout, but I also felt I should have responded to the needs of that woman without irritation. I couldn't see a solution. Even if I no longer believed in the Gospels, I had always believed that they contained a guide to living, a distilled form of human wisdom. Yet now I started to doubt even this. I couldn't live Mother Teresa's "totally surrendered life" or the Gospel counsels to "give to anyone who asks." I wondered if unconditional love and forgiveness were possible, or if it just crushed the individual who tried to live it and turned him or her into a doormat.

I was still operating under the MC principle that if life asked something of me, I had the strength and ability to deal with it. I had been taught to "ask for nothing and refuse nothing," to "take whatever He gives and give whatever He takes with a smile." These counsels were given in the context of a tightly controlled religious life. The assumed principle was that the strength of God was there. If I was not coping, I was doing something wrong. Although I had lost my faith, I was still operating under the assumptions of faith: "I have strength for every situation through him who empowers me" (Philemon 4:13).

St. Paul's great hymn to love says that all manner of heroic and self-giving actions are useless if not done with the courteous love that "endures long and is kind" (1 Corinthians 13:4). I had not found a way to protect myself from overwork.

In October 2002 Capt. Rodney Cocks, an Australian UN military officer stationed in Aileu, was on leave in Bali. He had just left Paddy's Bar to go to an Internet café when there was an explosion behind him and all the lights went out. Soon after, there was a second, stronger explosion. He raced back to the Sari Club, searching in the dark, smoky chaos for the companions he had just left, but came across a young Balinese woman. Although she was still alive, most of her body was burned. He stayed with her and found an ambulance to transport her to hospital to fight for a chance at life. Many charred corpses lay around him. Among them was one of the Portuguese peacekeepers from Aileu.

It was incomprehensible that these things could be done in God's name, but history is strewn with similar acts of religious violence. After hearing his story I thought, *Beliefs have consequences. One truth is not equal to the other. It is better to confine oneself to the knowable and provable than to risk making terrible mistakes in God's name.*

I had intended to return to East Timor in 2003 for another year, but Judy emailed me to say Mum was having a bad time. The doctor had asked her to surrender her driver's license because he believed she had Alzheimer's disease. She had lost her handbag, forgotten to turn off the stove, and couldn't remember how to get back from the shops, a trip she had made hundreds of times. I emailed Palms to say that I needed to be with my family for a while and so wasn't able to continue in East Timor.

I was to leave in a month and needed time to arrange for an adequate handover. I had a lovely dinner with the sisters, staff, and health motivators and said an emotional farewell to several families, but I didn't have time to see many others. It was tough to say good-bye to the sisters; in the three years I had been in East Timor they had become part of my family.

Once back in Australia I had to adjust again to normal life. It's easy to take for granted hot showers, refrigeration, water on tap, reliable electricity, and supermarkets laden with fresh food, but when I first came home they felt wonderful. My sister had settled on the Central Coast with her four children, and Mum owned a self-care unit in a retirement village at Bateau Bay in New South Wales. The complex had two levels of care, the independent living units and a hostel and nursing home section, where residents were provided with meals and whatever level of personal care was required. Because of her failing memory, Mum was finding it difficult to cook and shop, so she decided to move out of her unit and into the hostel and nursing home. Judy and I helped her move, struggling to condense her life into one small room. She had so much stuff to sort through: books, photo albums, pottery equipment, paints, art boards, a spinning wheel, fabric, and a sewing machine.

I wanted to travel with her through the last part of her life, as she had accompanied me through mine. I found a downstairs apartment in a house in Bateau Bay close to Mum's village and moved in there for a few months while I sorted out where I would work. My car and all I owned remained in East Timor, but I was able to use Mum's car since she was not allowed to drive.

I had read some material in East Timor about Christian meditation, a quiet form of prayer based on the repetition of a single phrase, which I had found helpful as an MC. While in Dili I had signed up by email to make a retreat at Ballarat led by the British Benedictine monk Lawrence Freeman. People of many different beliefs attended, so I thought I might find some answers there. In the silence of the retreat, however, my thoughts were in turmoil.

As I listened to Lawrence's reflections on the Gospel stories, I found they no longer helped. I just didn't believe anymore. In our time, if seafarers are out in a small boat in rough weather, they may call out to God but still capsize and drown. Dead little girls stay dead. In the Gospel Jesus often rebuked us for our lack of faith and fear. He followed up with a miracle to reinforce the lesson of faith, but today no miracles occur. I continued to argue back and forth with myself:

Of course these things did not happen; magical thinking is only for children. God is not a magician.

Fine, so why did the Gospel portray Him as one? If these lesser miracles are symbolic, did the Resurrection occur? If it didn't occur in some form, if there is no life after death, Christianity collapses.

I wondered again if there really was a reason to die in hope. What fragments of the Gospel were true, in the sense of really occurring or of being a reliable guide for life's journey?

I had seen how scripture was used to encourage people, especially women, to put up with treatment they shouldn't have to endure. They were counseled to carry their cross and offer up suffering, as if God willed us to put up with bullies in His name. Many Christians in the Philippines and East Timor still endured maltreatment in this way, hoping for a better life in the world to come. My faith was leaving me.

After returning home I went to see a doctor in Ourimbah with the East Timorese version of Delhi belly and aching joints. I came out with a job. It took a few months to regain my confidence working in general practice, as it was a big change from outback Australia or the Timorese hills. I thought first of Dengue fever when a patient came in complaining of pain behind the eyes, though sinusitis was more common on the Central Coast. I brushed up on menopause, antidepressants, and weight reduction and slowly readjusted to life in Australia.

I moved out of the apartment, and my sister and I bought a house together on a large block of land. I live downstairs and Judy and the children live upstairs. We set up a room for Mum to come home to on weekends, but after two years she couldn't get in and out of the car and the change in her environment produced too much anxiety. We have a big garden and the brush turkeys do a lot less damage than the Timorese water buffalo that used to ravage my attempts at gardening in Timor.

I lead a contented, full life, though I sometimes feel uncomfortable in unfamiliar social situations when the conversation swings to me: "And so enough about me, what about yourself? Do you have children?"

"No, I don't."

"But you're married?"

"No." Then follows an uncomfortable silence, or the person may even walk away. What else could there be to talk about?

I hear general practice caricatured as treating only coughs and colds, but it is not like that. It is full of quirky characters and people battling to survive physically and emotionally.

I have been back to East Timor to visit the clinic and the sisters. The plane trip from Darwin to East Timor takes only an hour and a half but brings a seismic shift in life's realities. The trip is much more comfortable now, in a commercial airline that serves drinks and chocolate bars rather than the lumbering Hercules. The Darwin newspaper still has the same headline about yet another crocodile attack, and the *Timor Post* tells of Timorese students going off to study medicine in Cuba. Nine Cuban doctors now work in our little district, though medical help is still hard to find.

When I visited, parents greeted me warmly and showed me their children, whom I had treated in the past, saying, "See, he is well now." Sara, my translator, graduated with a degree in arts and education from the University of Newcastle in April 2006 and soon after, she returned to a chaotic Dili to teach at St. Joseph's, her old school. Brother Dan, who ferried Sara and many others to safety in 1999 and assisted her to study in Australia, was badly injured in a motorbike accident and is no longer aware of his surroundings.

East Timor continues to be wracked by internal violence. There was so much hope when the Timorese flag was raised for the first time that night on the Aileu soccer field, but it takes more than speeches and fireworks to build a nation. I hope East Timor finds the leadership it deserves. People in power so often lose contact with the struggles of the poor. Those who perpetrated acts of violence against their neighbors have not been brought to justice, and unemployment and poverty continue to sow the seeds of despair. It is so easy to tear down and destroy, but to build and nurture a new country takes years. We tend to respond to the dramatic, to the crisis, but to ignore the silent deaths of those who die for lack of a road or water.

CHAPTER FOURTEEN

"I Will Give Saints to Mother Church"

*Saint Peter's Basilica, Rome, on the day of
Mother Teresa's beatification, October 19, 2003.
(Photographer: C. Livermore)*

I am not sure what prompted me to travel to Rome in October 2003 for Mother Teresa's beatification. For the first part of my trip I joined a tour group and then returned to Rome for a week on my own staying in a convent guesthouse I had found on the Internet.

I arrived a few days before the ceremony and in the ancient heart of the Eternal City I walked along the cobblestones through the Arch of

Titus into the Forum, where Lawrence had been burned at the stake for saying that the poor were the treasures of the Church. The Colosseum and the stark catacombs testify to a people who died with hope.

The *scavi,* the excavations deep under the Vatican, have revealed a small town with ancient streets and frescoes, preserved as they were when buried by the earthworks carried out by the fourth-century emperor Constantine, who built the first Basilica of St. Peter. Constantine misinterpreted the Cross, using it as a battle standard. Although well educated and fluent in several languages, perhaps the emperor hadn't read the Gospels. His Basilica buried a small city and a collection of bones belonging to a man called Peter, along with an unadorned ideal.

The Renaissance Basilica of St. Peter's, built above Constantine's structure, was indeed magnificent in marble, brass, and gold but seemed in stark contrast to the Gospel exhortations "Sell everything you own, and distribute the money to the poor . . . then come follow me" (Luke 18:23). I tried to rest at the base of a column, but an usher told me to get up. Christ said, "Come to me, I will give you rest" (Matthew 11:28). Perhaps, but not here. The Basilica was a tourist scrum, not a Holy Place. It was a wet day, so I got in line to escape up to the Dome of St. Peter's. As I climbed I was at eye level with the stained-glass window depicting the Holy Spirit. Little light was entering the darkened church.

I was up early on the day of the beatification and queued to get a good place in the square. When I arrived in Rome I had rung Sister Regina and planned to meet her straight after the beatification; however, she was in the front red section of the Square, along with the other MCs, and I was at the back near one of the fountains. There was an impenetrable sea of people and temporary steel barriers between us.

I walked around St. Peter's Square trying to find some of the sisters I knew, but they had all gone into the Paul VI auditorium for lunch, and colorful, solemn Swiss Guards secured the entrance. No one could go in without a pass. I stood outside the gate waiting to find someone who would take a message in to Sister Regina for me. Then my tertian mistress approached the gate from the other side. I called her by name, and she looked at me warily. I said, "Tobit."

The meeting was a bit awkward. "Hi, how are you?" I asked.

"Fine, I'm just leaving," she replied.

"Can you get me in?"

"Just take this ID, and they will let you in." It was her own ticket, bordered with blue, identifying me as an MC Sister from the Primavale community.

The Swiss Guard was not concerned that I didn't have a habit as long as I had that ID. I walked into the auditorium where hundreds of sisters of many nationalities crowded together. At first I didn't recognize anyone, but then I saw Sister Regina hurrying along an aisle with her characteristic energy. Before coming to Rome she had lived in a remote part of Tanzania, close to the Rwandan border. It had crushed her to see bloated bodies floating irretrievably down rivers and waterfalls after the tragic massacres. She had cared for people with advanced AIDS in mud huts built by the sisters and villagers. As I had hoped, I met up with many of the women I had known within the order, although I was disappointed that Gabrielle, Naomi, and Ling hadn't attended the beatification.

In the afternoon we saw the premiere of *Mother Teresa's Legacy,* a film by Ann and Jeanette Petrie. The film's showing was delayed by a Republican female politician whom an American archbishop introduced. She talked about President Bush's agenda for the world for over half an hour, saying little about Mother Teresa. Even Sister Regina was irritated. Once the film finally started, however, it was vintage Mother Teresa speaking directly to the camera, interspersed with footage from her life. She still had that something—the light in her eyes, her smile. A woman of action, she had responded to a suffering world one person at a time. For the first time, however, I detected a flash of ego as she argued her case and pointed out her order's achievements to male clergy who were obstructing her.

On October 21, 2003, two days after the beatification of Mother Teresa, John Paul II made several men, including the archbishop of Sydney, George Pell, cardinals. In the Vatican paper, *L'Osservatore Romano,* the pope called on these men to be bishops of the Beatitudes, the Gospel counsels that exalt the poor in spirit, the merciful, and the meek. In the same issue of the Vatican paper the pope exhorted Christians to dedicate themselves to the hungry of the world as they celebrated World Food Day on October 16, 2003. After the Mass which celebrated the elevation of the cardinals to their princely rank, many people milled around on the cobblestones just beyond the colonnades of St. Peter's Square. A late-model, chauffeur-driven Mercedes, carrying an aristocratic, scarlet-robed cardinal, sped away from the ceremonies, nearly scuttling some of the faithful. *Not very beatitude-like,* I thought. Some members of the church acted paradoxically honoring the ideal of Gospel poverty and service to the poor but acting in a way that seemed to contradict it.

From Rome I traveled to Assisi, the home of St. Francis, a childhood hero of mine, an ex-soldier who became a man of peace and a lover of nature. Even though the beautiful walled town was crowded with tourists, it retained its spirit. Our guesthouse was opposite the Basilica of St. Francis and overlooked the Umbrian Valley. The dome of the Basilica of St. Mary of the Angels shone below in the distance. It enclosed the tiny chapel of Portiuncula, where Francis had died. As bells rang out across the valley, the blazing sunset gave the cloisters in front of the Basilica of St. Francis a golden sheen. I rose at dawn and walked up to the Basilica along the cobblestones. The flowerbeds on the front lawn spelled out *PAX*—PEACE. There were no tourists at this time of day. I wandered around the huge church undisturbed, while the brown-robed, hooded friars chanted the morning office in a side chapel. I thought of my uncle Toby, and descended into the crypt where Francis was buried to sit quietly for a while, trying to break life's code, to make sense of the incomprehensible.

In the early morning sunshine, I climbed the narrow cobblestone streets. Potted geraniums, mosaics of the Virgin, and rainbow-colored peace flags decorated the façades of the houses. Beyond the arched gates of the town wall, autumn yellow trees lined the road to the olive grove that surrounds San Damiano, where Clare, who followed Francis, had her sparse convent. Later in the day I went farther up the mountain to the simple stone hermitage that encloses the cave where Francis had escaped to pray. The doves perched on the tiled roof made soft cooing noises. Below, the stream flowed under the arched stone bridge into a cool wooded area. The spirit of Francis still resonated with me.

In other cities, such as Venice, Siena, Ravenna, Florence, and Padua, I saw how the Church honors saintly people who during their lives renounced materialism, by encasing parts of their bodies in golden reliquaries and building basilicas around their tombs. It was so contradictory. When I returned to Rome and wandered around the Vatican souvenir shops, I noticed that Mother Teresa was also for sale. Statues and medals had been cast in her honor, and pieces of her habit placed in laminated cards were being distributed as relics. At least she was not yet encased in gold.

In the Campo dei Fiori, the flower market, there is a further example of how the officials of a church can act in a way directly contrary to their own teachings. There, in 1600, the Church, which proclaims love of enemies, tied the naked, gagged Dominican monk Giordano Bruno to a stake and burned him alive in God's name. His crime was to be a heretic: to have doubts about Catholic doctrines such as the Eucharist and to accept the findings of Copernicus that the earth revolves around the sun. His dark brooding statue dominates the flower sellers' stalls.

I met up with Sister Regina again for a few days and helped her give out an evening meal to homeless, stateless people from a basement room near the Terminus Railway Station. Some men, mostly from Eastern Europe and Russia, were also given a bed in an adjoining building, a bit like the shelter we had worked in together in Melbourne. During the day Sister Regina showed me around San Gregorio, where the sisters looked after infirm indigent men in part of a monastery close to the Colosseum and the ruins of Diocletian's baths, that were completed in AD 306. The MCs had transformed the monks' chicken coops and storage sheds into a convent.

Ironically, the sisters in Rome used computers to work on Mother Teresa's canonization. I'm sure she wouldn't have approved, and I can just see her storming in and ripping out the cords. "Sisters, we choose not to have these things," she would say. "You should be ashamed to be richer than Christ and our people."

Around Rome, flyers advertised Fabrizio Costa's movie *Mother Teresa*, starring Olivia Hussey. When I saw the film later in Australia it didn't ring true. A priest was cast in a lead role as having a very close association with

Mother and the sisters, but I didn't know who he was meant to represent. In the film he regularly ate in the sisters' refectory, which didn't happen in real life. The movie depicted the trainees who left the order as spoiled women who were not made of the right stuff.

After I left the order I was like a sailor navigating without a compass. The ultimate question for me was whether love or chaos ruled the universe. Mother experienced the darkness and shadows of life, an emptiness and sense of futility that were real, not a manufactured spiritual trial. Unlike Mother, I concluded that there is no divine presence to set everything right. Only human love and natural beauty give us hope. We need to endure, as Mother said, "just this terrible pain of loss . . . of God not being God, of God not really existing." All that matters in the end is that we have tried to love one another.

Mother reminded me of the Maori chief in the New Zealand film *The Whale Rider*. He had been nobly formed in the rich tradition of his ancestors, but these ancient teachings also blinkered him. He failed to see his granddaughter's gifts because, to his mind, these qualities couldn't be found in a girl. The traditional Catholic beliefs and spirituality that Mother inherited were both her strength and her weakness. Although she was a visionary, tradition blinded her in some areas. Some women have been harmed by trying to follow her and have left the order confused and disillusioned. Others struggled to remain true to what they believed God was asking of them. For some this fidelity came at great personal cost.

The oppressive discipline of the order has harmed women. We tend to treat others as we have been treated, and a cluster of scandals has haunted the MCs. In one example a sister was prosecuted for allegedly burning four children's hands as punishment for a misdemeanor and on another occasion children were tied to beds, purportedly to keep them safe. These incidents illustrate a problem at the heart of the MC's *modis operandi*. A person does not suddenly use unacceptable forms of punishment on children. Other sisters may have noticed patterns of unacceptable behavior and been thwarted in their attempts to redress it by being told not to judge. The sister may have needed psychological care herself. Similarly, it is possible to implement safer ways of restraining children, but our minds have to be open to alternatives and new ways of doing things. It is a recipe for disaster if all initiative and suggestions are quashed, and a sister who questions the morality of an incident is condemned as proud. Until the human needs of the sisters are recognized and they are permitted to think and learn, these problems will continue.

Mother's successor, Sister Nirmala, has a reputation for being compassionate, and for having started out along a path of mutual respect and responsibility. But a deep paradox lies at the heart of Mother Teresa's order. Courageous compassion was a cover for an organization that demanded blind submission and suppression of the intellect. From my time with her I learned that I need to test all ideas, including the values inherited from the culture of my birth, and to question the prevailing mores and prejudices that pervade any society. Goodness is not served by acquiescence but by being courageously true to yourself.

My visit to the Holy City further loosened the faith on which I had based my life. My beliefs had protected me against despair, even though I feared they were not true. I had also thought that society would be poorer without the ideals, empathy, and ethics embodied in Christianity and the art, architecture, and music it has inspired. But if there is a God, that God is love and truth, and He or She wouldn't be fearful of questions from our tiny human intellects. The time is over for churches and other centers of religion to demand blind adherence and assent; people cannot continue to submit their minds to that which is irrational. For instance, how can wearing a condom be a greater evil than transmitting AIDS? The Church uses the weapons of censure and excommunication to silence dissent. This is unnecessary, as Truth is quite able to defend itself in an open debate.

Science teaches that, fourteen billion years ago, there was absolute nothingness. Inexplicably, an intensely hot, dense something—matter— emerged, exploded, and expanded to the almost infinite mass of the cosmos. About four billion years ago our small, insignificant planet began to cool. Atoms coalesced, molecules formed. By random chance and natural selection, life evolved, complex and beautiful, into myriad forms. It is hard to accept that this intricately structured world was a chance occurrence, that a human being is the product of inanimate, indifferent, evolutionary forces, a collection of molecules that has come to know "I am." I thought that perhaps God straddled the gap between nothingness and being.

The world is magnificent but also insensible. Innocents are hurt, starved, wracked by disease. The meek do not inherit the earth; they are dispossessed. A sparrow may not fall to the ground without the heavenly Father knowing, but millions of children seem to. The Christian response is that there is hope beyond life's pain in the promise and bliss of eternal life, that death and suffering are aberrations that came into the world because of sin. Yet, clearly, every living thing has its allotted life span; decay and disease have always been part of the world order. Destruction is an inescapable consequence of the forces inherent in nature. In the animal world, predatory behavior and suffering are part of the web of life. None of this is a consequence of sin, as Christianity proposes.

If the cornerstone of the Resurrection is knocked out, the whole edifice of hope crashes. Any belief I still had in some form of Divine Presence was finally washed away in the Boxing Day tsunami in 2004. Without faith, I felt as if I had been on an arduous journey following the wrong maps, lost. "You have led . . . me into darkness, not light. . . You have wrapped yourself in a cloud too thick for prayer to pierce" (Lamentations 3:2, 44).

Sifting through alternative belief systems in search of a credible place to stand, I found theism, atheism, hedonism, and consumerism all unsatisfactory, but, reluctantly, became an agnostic. There is so much that is unknown and unexplained that I couldn't call myself an atheist. Belief was at the core of my being; without it, I felt hollowed out.

Despite the jeering of those intellectuals who mock "God-botherers" and proclaim religion to be a virus and the "root of *all* evil," belief can be beautiful. I have experienced that beauty. Does Richard Dawkins sincerely believe that without religion, there would be no evil in the world? Do these zealous atheists discount the countless heroic and compassionate actions of religious people as worthless or diseased? The peace of the Hermitage of Assisi, the Gregorian chant, the great holy edifices of the world are expressions of beauty that well up from deep within the soul. They are harmonious, not pathological.

I don't share the cocky confidence of scientists who teach that, given time, science will answer all life's questions. There may be no answers to the questions of why we suffer and die, yet as the Auschwitz survivor Viktor Frankl taught, a person's mental health depends on finding a reason to live. Belief, in some form, is inherent in human cultures. The brain itself evolved to create beliefs if not in a deity then in theories or political systems. I fear that the overthrow of the despot of theism may unleash a chaotic, egocentric materialism. Buried in the mud of religious hypocrisy and intolerance are nuggets of gold, gleaned from thousands of years of reflection and experience. We dismiss these insights at our peril. Happiness cannot simply be grasped; it has to be given away in love, service, and compassion, before it can be truly acquired.

For twenty years I kept moving as I had done when I was in the order, never really belonging anywhere. The beliefs that had supported my life had crumbled away. I was stranded in a lonely place and continued to search for a way out. One thing of which I am still certain is that the chasm between the wealthy and the poor is a critical problem for our world. Extreme poverty is an enemy of peace. We waste more than we give. Our affluence fills the world with effluent, which, if unchecked, will destroy us.

Thousands of years ago, prophets exhorted the rich:

Share your bread with the hungry, and shelter the homeless poor.
    Clothe the man you see to be naked and do not turn away from your own kin.
    Then will your light shine like the dawn . . . and your shadows become like noon (Isaiah 58:6–8, 11).

Thousands of years later, we still haven't learned the lesson. It sounds simple—"I was hungry and you gave me food" (Matthew 25:31)—but compassion can also cause problems, such as aid-induced dependency, victimization, and paternalism. I know that my eleven years of effort were only a drop that quickly disappeared without a ripple on the ocean of need. Even after leaving the MCs I struggled to find a balance between giving and receiving, between the needs of others and my own. The Peace Prayer of St. Francis that I said thousands of times as an MC asked that we seek to love rather than be loved, to give rather than to receive. I felt guilty that I wanted my love reciprocated at least sometimes. I wondered about the ethics of enjoying myself on a holiday or overseas trip while others were hungry. If I suppressed these thoughts, I was in danger of swinging to the other extreme and turning away from the poor altogether.

Without belief in life after death, the search for a just world is more urgent. The tasks we once assigned to God become ours. Rather than praying for the hungry and for peace, each of us has to decide what we can do to address the issues of starvation and war. As Mahatma Gandhi said, "Be the change you want to see in the world." Heaven is an insidious idea that makes death more acceptable to the politicians and generals who command the world's armies and to the suicide bombers who kill themselves and others in the hope of entering paradise.

I revised my pacifism, which was based on the Gospel exhortation to love one's enemies, and decided that a people has to defend itself from genocidal rage. How could we be passive in the face of the Holocaust, Pol Pot, or Rwanda? How could the Timorese not respond to the deaths of tens of thousands during the Indonesian occupation? The dilemma was how to respond to evil without becoming evil ourselves.

I find meaning now in beauty and friendship, but I know these are as ephemeral as I am. To live truthfully and with compassion is my spirituality of agnosticism. Without hope based on an afterlife the only tools left to deal with the ultimate human mystery of suffering and death are stoicism, courage, and compassion. Our civilization is emerging as the first to deal with life and death without religious beliefs and ceremonies. Although religious faith still plays a role in our society, increasing numbers of people can no longer believe, and this will profoundly change our culture, the way we teach our children, and how we deal with life's milestones. My mother will have a Catholic funeral, but my faith has died.

One of my earliest memories is of Mum taking me around the garden in Leeton, showing me the flowers and saying, "Pretty." Since 2003 Alzheimer's disease has eroded her memory. Most days her face still lights up when she first glimpses me walking up the corridor toward her. She used to ask for her own mum and dad and wondered why they hadn't visited; it grieved her when I explained that they had died, so in the end I made some excuse to get us through the moment. I had never lied to her before. Mercifully her memory of them has also faded.

While she was still fit enough to get in and out of the car, she stayed with us on weekends, sharing a meal, patting the dog, playing with the grandkids, but as the day wore on she was distressed by phantoms and anxieties that couldn't be chased away. The old worries of our childhood tormented her. "Have we paid the bills?" "Where are the boys? Why haven't you picked them up?" On one occasion, in the twenty minutes it took us to return home from dropping her back at the hostel, she left eight messages on my answering machine. She spoke in a quavering voice of her abandonment: "I was wondering if you could get in touch with me here. I feel so alone. I don't know what's happening. I don't know what to do. . . . I'm sorry you're not here. I don't want to worry you but there is something wrong. I haven't heard from anyone since I left up there. . . . I feel as if I've been forgotten. I'm ringing to see how you are. . . . I was wondering what's happened and whether I'm going home. If you could ring me, I'd be real happy." The messages went on in a steady stream of pleading that made me feel helpless because I had been with her less than half an hour before. That was when she still knew what a phone was and how to push the automatic dialing button.

After two years she is no longer aware enough of her surroundings to be wracked with anxiety, and seems happy. Each time we see her the thread of recognition is more tenuous. Her speech has become a word salad of unrelated phrases: "Why are you staring at me because you've got no hair? It will grow again. It's better in pink. I want to be warmer; I want to be hungrier; I want to be asleep. Where is my mother? Do you know where she is? She must have a lot to read to do the right thing all the time. Colette! [Talking to her doll, Doris, that had belonged to my sister Judy.] Can you walk yet? You have to walk. There's a bed full of flowers, but they're not in water. You've got beautiful eyes. Your eyes are lovely, as if they can see the world. And what can I see? Twenty-six. He has no bananas. I've got to go to this picnic because I have to see my brilliant children." She is still warm, funny, and a great talker, even as her mind fails.

Sometimes she needs to be prompted to eat; sometimes she retreats into a blank, impenetrable stare and doesn't recognize us. Her world no longer makes sense, and her experience has made me fear old age. In this second childhood, the hope of youth is gone. Mum lacks control of her bodily functions, her sleep is disturbed, and she cannot walk safely. As in infancy, she is put through the cycle of bathing, feeding, and washing and also feels separation anxiety.

Faith used to give me a defense against despair. It provided a reward for a life well lived and the promise of ultimate justice. If faith were only true, it could provide answers to many questions. But there are no answers. All I can do is live with the silence, the unknown, with cruelty, death, and everything for which there is no explanation, and do what I can along the way. This is how I now try to live out my youthful ideal. It is often necessary to accept things that can't be changed rather than futilely railing against them.

I am no longer sure what makes a person good or holy. I am not sure of life, which seems so ephemeral, or of love because I feel alone. I battle with the constraints of another timetable, the medical appointment book, trying to be punctual without depriving people of the gift of time. The health system creaks under the weight of unmet need. As a young person I thought conditions would improve in my lifetime. I am in a lucky part of a lucky country, but still many people have to struggle to keep going.

I sit on the veranda at home, my hands wrapped around a hot cup of sweet tea, watching the explosion of bird life in the shimmering trees. On weekends I work in the garden trying to restore the diversity of natural vegetation to the monoculture of tenacious privet and lantana that had invaded our block. I know that in spring the red-and-green flash of the king parrots will be outside my window, and our pruned fruit trees will shoot again, more vigorous than before. The bare winter branches in the orchard will blossom and yield summer fruit. Hope endures.

The journey is all there is; the ones we love along the way are our deepest joy. The road is not easy, so I strive to learn courage and compassion.

I am a slow learner. Yet hope endures.

BIBLIOGRAPHY

Beatificazione di Madre Teresa Di Calcutta. Program. Tipografia Vaticana, October 19, 2003.

Doig, Desmond. *Mother Teresa: Her People and Her Work.* London: Nachiketa Publications, 1976.

Frankl, Viktor. *Man's Search for Meaning.* New York: Washington Square Press, 1984.

Hitchens, Christopher. *The Missionary Position: Mother Teresa in Theory and Practice.* London: Verso, 1995.

Huart, Albert. "Mother Teresa: Joy in the Night." *Review for Religious,* September–October 2001: 494–502.

Jerusalem Bible, Pocket edition, 1985, Sarton, Longman and Todd Ltd. 1985.

Kolodiejchuk, Brian. *Come Be My Light, Mother Teresa: The Private Writings of the "Saint of Calcutta."* New York: Doubleday, 2007. Pp. 186–188, 192, 199, 238.

Lapierre, Dominique. *The City of Joy.* London: Arrow Books, 1986.

Leonard, Tracey. *The Full Catastrophe.* Sydney: Hodder, 1999.

Missionaries of Charity. *Constitution of the Missionaries of Charity,* 1980.

Muggeridge, Malcolm. *Something Beautiful for God: Mother Teresa of Calcutta.* London: William Collins & Co, 1971.

Neuner, J. "Mother Teresa's Charisma." *Review for Religious,* September–October 2001: 479–493.

Sebba, Anne. *Mother Teresa: Beyond the Image.* London: Weidenfeld & Nicolson, 1997.

Tagore, Rabindranath. *Collected Poems and Plays of Rabindranath Tagore.* London: Macmillan, 1973. Tagore's poems reprinted with permission of Visva-Bharati Press, Kolkata.

Travers-Ball, Ian (Brother Andrew). "Letter." *The Messenger.* January–February 1988.

———. *The Song of a Wounded Healer.* Privately published, God's Farm, Gracewood, 2002.

Acknowledgments

I would like to thank:

My family, especially my mother, who died as I was working on the final edit of this book.

Mary Cunnane for her insight and faith in the manuscript, which made publication possible, and her assistant, Isobel Wightman, who assisted me in many ways.

My publishers, who took a risk with an inexperienced and unknown author.

The sisters of the Missionaries of Charity, who still recognize the sacred in the poor and marginalized and respond to them with love.

My friends, who with great patience have listened to the vicissitudes of the book's progress.

Professor Kumkum Bhattacharya and Visva-Bharati Publishing, the publisher of *Collected Poems and Plays of Rabindranath Tagore*.

Marella Hogan for her earnest record-keeping of our time at school and her trip to Papua New Guinea.

ABOUT THE AUTHOR

Colette Livermore was born in Sydney, Australia, in 1954. At eighteen, she joined Mother Teresa's Missionaries of Charity after seeing a film about Mother's work with the poor. As Sister Tobit she was with the order for eleven years, serving in Papua New Guinea, India, Hong Kong, and the Australian outback. After she left the order in 1984 at age thirty, Livermore earned her medical degree from the University of Queensland. Since then she has worked in Australia's Northern Territory; in Aileu, East Timor; and on the New South Wales Central Coast, where she currently lives.